Live & Work
— IN —
ITALY

SECOND
Completely
revised and
updated
EDITION

Victoria Pybus

Published by Vacation Work, 9 Park End Street, Oxford
Web site http: //www.vacationwork.co.uk

LIVE AND WORK IN ITALY

First Edition 1992, Victoria Pybus & Rachael Robinson
Second Edition 1998, Victoria Pybus

Copyright © Vacation Work 1998

ISBN 1-85458-182-1 (softback)
ISBN 1-85458-183-X (hardback)

Publicity: Roger Musker

Cover Design byMiller Craig & Cocking Design Partnership

Typeset by WorldView Publishing Services (01865-201562)

Printed by Unwin Bros Ltd.
The Gresham Press, Old Woking, Surrey, England

Live&Work
— IN —
ITALY

SECOND

Completely
revised and
updated

EDITION

Contents

SECTION 1 — LIVING IN ITALY

GENERAL INTRODUCTION

RESIDENCE AND ENTRY REGULATIONS

SETTING UP HOME

SECTION II — WORKING IN ITALY

EMPLOYMENT

STARTING A BUSINESS

MAPS AND CHARTS

APPENDICES

Acknowledgments

The author and publisher would like to thank the following, in no particular order, for their invaluable help in compiling this book: Alessandra Dolloy of Fondazione CENSIS Rome, Barry Walker of the Italian Chamber of Commerce in London, Francesca Piovano of FILEF, Linda Travella of Casa Travella, Morfa Downs of The British Chamber of Commerce in Milan, the Reverend Richard Major of St Mark's, Florence, Angelika Smith-Aichbichler of Piedmont Properties. Also, Maria Makepeace, Georgina Gordon-Ham, John Matta and Roger Warwick for providing us with case histories of their own experiences of living and working in Italy.

Telephone area code changes.
On April 22nd 2000 there are to be a number of changes to certain area telephone code prefixes in the UK. The most important of these is that the current 0171- and 0181- prefixes for London will be replaced by the prefix 020-, followed by 7 for current 0171 numbers and 8 for current 0181 numbers. Also affected will be Cardiff (numbers will begin 029 20), Portsmouth (023 92), Southampton (023 80) and Northern Ireland (028 90) for Belfast; contact directory enquiries for other numbers in Northern Ireland). In addition, as from the same date the numbers for various special services including freephone and lo-call numbers will begin with 08 and all mobile phone numbers will begin with 07. Telephone operators are planning to ease the transition by running the current 01 numbers in parallel with the new 02 numbers until spring 2001.

Foreword

Live and Work in Italy is part of a successful series of books which provide a guide to the opportunities for work, starting a business or retirement in different countries around the world. The aim of these publications is to provide an information base concerning the many and various regulations and practicalities still involved in moving abroad, even within the EU. There are complications inherent in buying a new home and starting a new job simultaneously in a country which has very different laws and procedures to those with which you are familiar. However, we hope that by using *Live and Work in Italy* as a reference manual you will be able to take this giant step briefed with the knowledge of what to expect, instead of the whole process turning into a nightmare. The book is divided into two sections, *Living in Italy* and *Working in Italy* respectively, which cover all aspects of such a venture from how and where to open an Italian bank account, how to arrange a mortgage in Italy, employment regulations and opportunities, advice and ideas for setting up a small business to the finer points of Italian etiquette, language and culture.

An estimated 91,000 Britons live in Italy, of whom around two thirds are home owners there. The remaining third divide their time between Italy and other countries. The majority of Brits have set up home in the rolling hills of Tuscany and Umbria, and increasingly, Le Marche and there are others to be found in less publicised regions like Liguria, Piedmont and Puglia. Their peaceful lives (earthquakes not withstanding) are in contrast to the frenetic ones led by expatriates who live in the big cities of the north, Milan, Turin etc. and in the capital Rome. It is not just the climate that attracts foreigners to Italy. Their reasons for moving there are as various as the regions of Italy itself. Some will be posted there by international companies, some have a deep-seated love of the country and wish to immerse themselves in Italian culture, and some will have spotted a gap in the commercial market and a way to make a living and who knows, even a fortune.

Despite its disorganized and corrupt state bureaucracy, Italy also has one of the most dynamic and efficient business areas of Europe – northern Italy, one of the most friendly peoples and a cultural heritage that is the cornerstone of Western civilization. Rewards, both financial and personal, await the diligent and the entrepreneurial in Italy.

Although the cost of property in northern Italy and the popular, idyllic regions of Tuscany and Umbria is higher than in the UK, there are still bargains to be found in Le Marche, Abruzzo, Puglia etc. The cost of living is higher in Italian cities eg. Rome, Milan, Bologna etc. than in the UK, but so is the quality of life.

Until 1990, Italy's economy was one of the most booming in Europe. This was followed by several years of recession, and political upheaval caused by the corruption scandals which swept away the Christian Democrat party, which had held the balance of power for nearly fifty years. By all accounts, particularly her own, Italy has put all past political and economic problems behind her and thanks to a Euro tax in 1997 and a 1998 budget designed to get her economy in shape, she will meet the convergence criteria for European monetary union in January 1999.

Although traditionally parochial in outlook, the relaxation of currency restrictions has woken Italians up to the potential of international investments and there is a huge market for international consultants. Other areas of particular demand include teachers of English language, medical and dental practitioners, estate agents and financial services, particularly insurance and pensions.

The European union has made significant progress towards its goal of a synchronised Europe and although there are still many big question marks over the single currency, there is no doubt that greater oppportunities exist for living and working abroad, while media and modern communications enable you to keep in touch more easily with friends and family in the UK. Italy is one of the keenest players in the European Union and offers a wide range of opportunities for those who are aware of them. This book will tell you how, where and why to go for the Italian experience.

Victoria Pybus
March 1998

CONVERSION CHART

LENGTH (N.B. 12 inches=1 foot, 10 mm=1 cm, 100 cm=1 metre)

inches	1	2	3	4	5	6	9	12		
cm	2.5	5	7.5	10	12.5	15.2	23	30		
cm	1	2	3	5	10	20	25	50	75	100
inches	0.4	0.8	1.2	2	4	8	10	20	30	39

WEIGHT (N.B. 14 lb=1 stone, 2240 lb=1 ton, 1,000 kg=1 metric tonne)

lb	1	2	3	5	10	14	44	100	2240
kg	0.45	0.9	1.4	2.3	4.5	6.4	20	45	1016
kg	1	2	3	5	10	25	50	100	1000
lb	2.2	4.4	6.6	11	22	55	110	220	2204

DISTANCE

mile	1	5	10	20	30	40	50	75	100	150
km	1.6	8	16	32	48	64	80	120	161	241
km	1	5	10	20	30	40	50	100	150	200
mile	0.6	3.1	6.2	12	19	25	31	62	93	124

VOLUME

gallon (UK)	1	2	3	4	5	10	12	15	20	25
litre	4.5	9	13.6	18	23	45	56	68	91	114
litre	1	2	3	5	10	20	40	50	75	100
gallon (UK)	0.2	0.4	0.7	1.1	2.2	4.4	8.8	11	16.5	22

CLOTHES

UK	8	10	12	14	16	18	20
Europe	36	38	40	42	44	46	48

SHOES

UK	3	4	5	6	7	8	9	10	11	12
Europe	36	37	38	39	40	41/42	43	44	45	46

SECTION I

Living in Italy

General Introduction
Residence and Entry Regulations
Setting Up Home
Daily Life
Retirement

General Introduction

Destination Italy

These days, those contemplating living and working abroad are increasingly likely to turn to Europe, and in particular to countries that make up the European Union. The dismantling of the economic and trade borders between member nations and the creation of a vast European market is all but complete at the time of press. The final phase will be economic and monetary union which Italy is on course to join. EMU will be sealed with the arrival of the single currency, the Euro, on 1 January 1999. After that it will be a question of extending the union to take in the countries of eastern Europe.

The prospect of being an expatriate worker is becoming a growing likelihood for many professionals and for qualified and unqualified workers alike. Practising your profession or skills anywhere in the European Union is possible through a comparison system for different national qualifications, which is becoming more familiar to employers. The EU directives concerning the recognition of most academic and professional qualifications gained within the EU have been in place since 1993 and. Likewise, prospects for setting up businesses abroad are expanding enormously as the governments of EU nations vie with each other to offer the most attractive incentive packages to foreign investors.

As a country in which to live and work, Italy is considerably more complex, and is probably less well understood than many of our other European colleagues. Italy as a unified country did not exist until 1861 and regional loyalties are still paramount to Italians. Unfortunately long-established stereotypical images have given rise to a number of misconceptions that have had a trivialising effect on the world's view of Italy and Italians. According to popular caricature Italians eat vast quantities of pasta, and (if they are male) worship their mothers, pinch bottoms and sing Verdi in the street. The reality is somewhat different, not least because there are many different kinds of Italians. One of the most enduring myths is of an Italy governed by the Mafia. Although the sinister brotherhood's influence is pervasive in politics and commerce, the mafia does not run Italy. Mafia influence is however distinctly powerful in its traditional fiefdoms of Calabria, Naples and much of the island of Sicily (while its tentacles reach much further).

There is however, considerable substance in the two nations perception of Italy which arises from the differences between the north of Italy whose inhabitants are generally, more serious, industrious and prosperous and the *Mezzogiorno*, the traditionally poor, violent and criminally-ruled south. However it would be an error to write off the *Mezzogiorno* as an area in which to live and work, since the Italian government is offering huge financial incentives for foreign business interests in certain areas like Puglia, Molise and Abruzzi where in consequence, prosperity is increasing.

Regions & Major Cities of Italy

Pros and Cons of Moving to Italy

Those seeking employment or business opportunities in Italy will find that the country has many advantages to recommend it: the presence of many major Italian and international companies offers a huge range of possibilities for employment. There is a dynamism about northern Italian business people which puts some of their fellow Europeans to shame. However, Italians do not like to be hustled and will observe all the social niceties before clinching a deal. Italians work late but quite often mix commerce with pleasure: a working supper or weekend meetings with business connections being customary occurences. Many British people like this *modus operandi* and once they have adapted to it find they prefer Italian working practices to those of other countries and enjoy working with Italians more than other nationalities.

Those who might be concerned that they are moving to a country where living standards and infrastructures leave a lot to be desired and where the government is inherently unstable will find only a few of their worst fears justified. Generally, Italy is a highly developed country where even the farmers have the latest model Lancia or Audi tucked away in a barn, and where workers know the exact market value of their skills in the work place. The Italian postal system, especially for internal services, is probably the most inefficient in Europe, but the telephone system which until recently was comparable with the post, has undergone complete modernization, and the Italians have embraced the mobile phone like no other nation. The road system which owes much to the Romans, Mussolini and the charging of staggeringly high tolls, is one of the best in Europe. The much publicized fifty plus changes of government since the end of the Second World War, amount to little more than reshuffles: Italy was dominated by the same political party, the Christian Democrats, for fifty years. Ironically, this made Italy one of the more politically stable countries in Europe. Italy has made well advertised efforts to clean up politics in recent years by weeding out the corruptors and corrupted and prosecuting them where necessary. Similarly, there has been a concerted move to bring the big Mafia bosses to trial and bang them up for long jail sentences. It remains to be seen how effective this will prove: apparently in some cases, Mafia women have been running things while the menfolk are in jail.

One of the disadvantages for foreigners wishing to set up businesses, especially in northern Italy is that costs are extremely high: office space and service costs etc. seem disproportionate to other factors including official salary levels (which are lower than in the UK). Actual individual income is however virtually impossible to assess, as nowhere in Europe is the pastime of tax evasion practised with such verve as in Italy where a recent check by the Italian Inland Revenue showed that nine out of ten tax payers were dodging at least some of their dues. In part, such large-scale evasion derives from the fact that many Italians have second or even third jobs. Thus whilst the level of salaries does not correspond to the otherwise obvious prosperity of many Italians, the fact is, that they manage to contrive to have more spending money than their counterparts in France and the UK. Admittedly some aspects of life in Italy are cheaper than in the UK, notably public transport and housing.

Italy has a marvellous climate which is a distinct advantage in the eyes of Britons contemplating setting up home there. However the glorious cities which are a main attraction for tourists and foreign residents alike, often seem to be cared for indifferently by their denizens: traffic problems, pollution and a shortage of funds have all conspired to make many cities, even the historic ones, look dilapidated. With such an enormous heritage of art and architecture it is perhaps hardly surprising that there is insufficient money to cover the maintenance of all such treasures.

Moving from the UK to Italy inevitably involves some language problems. Unless you are already proficient in Italian it is essential to take an Italian course as otherwise you will be at a disadvantage in a country where business and social life are virtually intertwined. Furthermore, unlike some Europeans, notably the Scandinavians and Germans, Italians are not noted for their fluent grasp of English. While this situation has been remedied by the inclusion of English in the school curriculum it should nevertheless be unthinkable for foreigners to live in Italy without learning Italian.

Pros:

There are favourable employment prospects for skilled workers and professionals.
Industry is very advanced and successful, particularly in the north of Italy.
The Italians have a strong economy that is paying dividends to foreign investors: the 100 most profitable companies in Italy are foreign owned.
Housing and public transport are considerably cheaper than in the UK.
Managerial salaries are around 30-35% higher in Italy than in the UK.
The climate in most regions is marvellous and Italy has some of the most beautiful landscapes in Europe.
Italy has by far the greatest art and architectural heritage of any European country.
Italy has much to offer by way of lifestyle and living standards.
Italians are extremely receptive to foreigners.

Cons:

A knowledge of Italian is essential to conduct business in Italy as state bureaucrats and most Italian business people speak virtually no English.
Large parts of southern Italy are unsuitable for business ventures thanks to the vicelike grip of the Mafia.
There are enormous differences in business practices between northern and southern Italy.
Italy has a Byzantine bureaucracy that is notorious for being oiled by the proferring of *bustarelle* (little envelopes), ie. bribes (a.k.a. *costi aggiunti* – added costs).
Start up costs for businesses in northern Italy can be horrendously high and employers pay very high employee social security contributions.
Italian social behaviour and customs can seem totally at odds with the British way of doing things.

Political and Economic Structure

History

There is not space here to do justice to Italian history which is in effect the history of the former kingdoms, states and duchies that make up Italy. However, it is necessary to have a basic knowledge of the country's recent past including Il Risorgimento (the Unification), in order to understand Italy and Italians today. It could be argued that the first proponent of a unified Italy was Napoleon I, who managed during the fifteen years of French occupation from 1796 to 1814 to set up a modern, meritocratic civil service regulated by the Code Napoleón. Unification proper took place in stages beginning with the annexation by Count

Camillo Cavour (Italy's answer to Bismarck), of most of northern and central Italy during 1859 and 1860. Meanwhile the popular hero and guerilla fighter, Giuseppe Garibaldi (1807-82) joined Cavour's Piedmontese northern alliance and conquered the entire south of Italy which was then united with the north under the Piedmontese king, Vittorio Emanuele II. The remaining pieces of the Italian jigsaw, Veneto (the region around Venice) and Lazio (the region around Rome) were added in 1866 and 1870 respectively. During the process of Risorgimento the seat of government moved three times: until 1865 it was in Turin, followed by a six-year sojourn in Florence before finally settling in Rome in 1871.

In the aftermath of the First World War Italy was in a demoralized and confused state beset by crippling strikes accompanied by a breakdown of law and order. There was a very real possibility that the country would succumb to a communist revolution. Enter Benito Mussolini, a former journalist who managed to exploit fear of the communists on the part of the wealthy and the middle-classes sufficiently to win himself and his Fascist Party 35 seats in the 1921 Parliament. Later the same year there occurred a complete collapse of government and Mussolini staged his famous 'March on Rome' when, accompanied by 30,000 *camicie nere* (his black shirted supporters) he entered Parliament and convinced the government and the king that in the absence of any other competent powers he should be awarded outright dictatorship. The King and parliament agreed, initially for a one year period, which in the event extended to 21 years of Fascist rule. Under Mussolini the Italians were probably more organized than they have ever been since the Romans, (an era constantly evoked in Mussolini's military iconography). At home, Mussolini drained the Pontine Marshes, made the trains run on time, and instigated the Lateran Pact with the Vatican, thus creating a workable relationship between Church and State for the first time in Italian history. Abroad, the Italian Empire of East Africa was created following the shockingly brutal take over of Abyssinia in 1935. Mussolini contributed greatly to the restoration of national pride at the expense of almost all civil liberties, but he managed to avoid most of the unspeakable excesses of the parallel regime in Germany. Italy was allied to Germany by the Pact of Steel signed with Hitler in 1939.

Following the collapse of his regime towards the end of the Second World War, Mussolini and the diehard remnant of his supporters fled Rome which had fallen to the Allies in 1943, and set up the Independent Republic of Salò in the north east corner of Italy. The Mussolini era was bought to an ignominious end in 1945 with the capture and execution of 'Il Duce' by partisans in 1945. As a final post mortem indignity, the bodies of (Mussolini) and his mistress, Claretta Petacci were hung by their heels in Milan's busiest square, the Piazza Loreto.

In May 1946 Italy held a national referendum to decide whether to retain the monarchy or institute a republic. The republic won, and the last king of Italy, Umberto II, went submissively into exile. Elections followed for the Constituent Assembly whose function was to decide what kind of constitution Italy would have and to draw it up. Two years later in 1948 the first parliamentry elections of the new republic saw the Christian Democrats romp home to victory and begin their lengthy domination of parliament until their demise, mainly through corruption scandals, in 1994.

At the pinnacle of the state is the President of the Republic who also controls the armed forces and the Judiciary and is elected for a seven-year term by both chambers plus regional representatives. Next in the hierarchy is the President of the Senate and third comes the President of the Chamber of Deputies. The powers of the President correspond approximately to those of the British monarch, i.e. they are mainly ceremonial and include dissolving parliaments, approving or vetoing the appointing of prime minsters and the signing or vetoing of new laws. The seat of government is in Rome. Parliament is made up of two chambers, the *Camera dei Deputati* (Chamber of Deputies) and the *Senato* (Senate). Since neither of these chambers takes precedence over the other, frequent conflicts over parliamentary bills are the norm. The Camera dei Deputati comprises 630 members (fewer than 10% of them women) housed in the Palazzo Montecitorio. The Senato meanwhile occupies another establishment, the Palazzo Madama, and has around 320 members some of whom are elected for life. Proceedings in both chambers are generally conducted less boisterously than in the British House of Commons.

The Italian voting system is immensely complicated involving hundreds of candidates per electoral region. Since most of the candidates are unknown to the voters, a system has evolved whereby major political figures put forward their names for several constituencies simultaneously and then stand down in favour of lesser-known candidates allowing them to sail home on their votes. This is perfectly legal and readily employed.

The proportional representation system has been gradually reduced so that nowadays, two thirds of candidates are chosen on a first past the post system and the rest by proportional representation. In the past proportional representation has meant an average of around twenty-five parties being represented in Parliament so Italy can only be ruled by a coalition of parties who are broadly banded into centre-left or centre-right groupings.

The Italian fashion of adopting celebrity candidates is, like many things Italian, done more flamboyantly than elsewhere; take the outrageous election of the porno-actress Ilona Staller ('La Cicciolina'); somehow Glenda Jackson does not have quite the same ring! More durably, Alessandra Mussolini, granddaughter of Benito (and former glamour girl and actress) was elected as a MP for Naples and Ischia in 1992. She now a force in the Alleanza Nationale which was part of the briefly lived Berlusconi administration in 1994. The AN is a rightist party led by Gianfranco Fini and is itself part of an alliance of right wing parties known as the 'Polo' which hopes to gain power at the next election.

Italy changes prime minister almost every year. At the time of writing it is Romano Prodi.

Political Parties

Foreign observers of Italian politics may find themselves hard pressed to spot any discernible differences between many of the political parties. In common with many First World countries, Italy has experienced the increasing prosperity of the once poorer classes which has resulted in a corresponding decrease in extremism that once characterised the leftist parties, so that even the *Partito Comunista Italiano* (Italian Communist Party) is broadly comparable to New Labour in Britain. Italian political parties tend to splinter into *correnti* (factions) which gravitate around the more powerful political leaders. Thus to achieve any kind of political power, tactical manoeuvring of the most machiavellian kind is required. Strategic alliances are formed and broken on purely opportunistic grounds. The imperspicuity of Italian politics is deepened by the lengths to which party leaders will go to win the loyalty of the local electorate. Italian political parties are funded to a staggering extent by the state. In 1990 they were awarded a total of 150 billion lire between them. With such funds the political support of whole villages and communities can be bought on the promise of extra jobs through the creation of an entirely useless state office or wing of a hospital for which ficticious wages and even false pensions will be paid. The main parties are:

Democrazia Cristiana: The Christian Democrats held the balance of power in Italy for nearly fifty years after the Second World War before being brought down by the *Mani Puliti* (clean hands) campaign of former magistrate Antonio Di Pietro which weeded out the corruption and criminality behind the respectable facade. Nominally a Catholic party, the CD took a hard line on abortion and divorce but a liberal line on most other issues including the treatment of terrorists. The CD occasionally coalesced with the small Socialist Party (see below) in order to achieve a ruling majority. Early in 1994 the CD party changed their name to the Italian Popular Party (PPI), but a large section split away to form the Centre Christian Democrats. The rump disintegrated in 1995.

Partito Socialista Italiano: The Socialist Party is no such thing, being vehemently right wing and incorrigibly corrupt. Its leader, Bettino Craxi was Prime Minister for four years. The SPI has about 14% of the national vote but a disproportionate share (30%) of the administration. Furthermore it was able to manipulate the CD which needed the cooperation of the PSI to stay in power.

Partito Democratico della Sinistra (PDS): The Democratic Party of the Left was the former Partito Comunista Italiano (Italian Communist Party). The PDS is the traditional main opposition party but during the years of Italian prosperity has become the virtual equivalent of the CD except that it portrays itself as the (only) party free from corruption. Its main base and spiritual home is the supremely wealthy city of Bologna. The PDS won 34% of the votes in 1976 and in 1997 was the single biggest party in the 'Ulivo' (olive branch) government of Romano Prodi.

Alleanza Nazionale was formed when the *Movimento Sociale Italiano (MSI)* was dismantled in 1994. the MSI was a Neo-Fascist party founded just after the Second World War. There has always been a certain amount of nostalgia for Il Duce (Mussolini) and the recruitment of Alessandra Mussolini, his granddaughter to party ranks, helped turn the fortunes of the MSI around as did the renaming of it as the AN. The old MSI-DS also included sympathizers of the deposed Bourbon royal dynasty and some right-wing thuggery in the form of extremist youth movements. They now have a credible leader in the smooth-talking Gianfranco Fini (a kind of Italian John Redwood). The AN is trying to drop its neo-fascist image – difficult when you have a Mussolini on board who is determined to wow the neo-fascist voters.

Partito Republicano Italiano: Founded in the 19th century by Mazzini, the PRI is the patricians' party whose members are well-heeled, progressive in outlook and fervent internationalists. They command a mere 2.3% of the electorate.

Partito Socialdemocratico Italiano: Notoriously adept at buying votes to the tune of 3% of the electorate, they have little going for them politically and with any luck will sink under the weight of their own corruption.

Partito Liberale Italiano: One of the major historical ie. nineteenth century parties, which may have to merge with the PRI to survive.

Partito Radicale: Created in the 1950s, the PR is chiefly renowned for getting the pro divorce and abortion laws through Parliament in the face of determined opposition from the DC. During the 1980's their policy of putting forward controversial figures as candidates, notably Cicciolina, and the convicted terrorist, Tony Negri rivetted the attention of the media guaranteeing the PR a high profile.

Rifondazione Communista: a hard line leftist party which formed part of the centre-left coalition of Romano Prodi's 'Ulivo' government elected in the early summer of 1996.

I Verdi and *Verdi-Arcobaleno:* The Greens and the Rainbow Greens scored well in the Euro-Elections thanks to increased awareness of Italy's various ecological disasters. They may merge to form Italy's fourth largest party.

Lega Nord: In the May 1990 local elections, a new political party of the right, the Lega Lombarda was voted in. Other similar regional parties in northern Italy, notably the Lega Veneta did not do as well but these two have now combined into the Lega Nord. This is a worrying trend as the force unifying them is anti-southern feeling, and their success reflects the growing division of north and south.

It is possible that in the future political parties may have to achieve electoral support of a minimum of 5% to be eligible for parliamentary representation.

Economy

Italy's post-war economic aims are to a large extent responsible for today's massive division between north and south. The powers of the time decided to open up Italy's economy and go for an international export market rather than concentrate on restructuring production for self-sufficiency at home. This was about the extent to which the Italians went to plan a postwar economy and up until the last couple of years policy in this area can best be summed up as *laissez-faire*. In other words, production was allowed to rally to the demands of the open market with virtually no controls or restraints. Such an economic 'policy' was to a great extent dictated by circumstance, namely that Italy possessed few of the resources ie. iron, coal, oil etc. essential for most industrial processes. Italy's main markets were Western Europe and America. Thus rather than pour money into modernizing agriculture which would have resulted in mass unemployment in the south, resources were directed at expanding the industries of the north while using the south as a cheap source of labour to offset the cost of importing the resources necessary to maintain manufacturing processes. The years between 1958 and 1962 were years of thriving economic growth for Italy. However with their economy so closely linked with America's the lira, which was pegged at 625 per dollar until 1971, collapsed along with the whole system of fixed exchange rates when America devalued the dollar. Italy's next period of the doldrums lasted up to the beginning of the 1980s as was clearly reflected in its poor man of Europe image. In the 1980s the economy then took off again at breakneck speed. However as always there is a downside: as a result of having had no clear discernible economic policy for years the national debt has now grown to the extent that it exceeds Gross Domestic Product at 123%. The good news is that the budget deficit which was running at 6% has been reduced to 2.8% (partly by raising VAT rates in October 1997) where it has to be kept in order to maintain European Union targets for entry into European Monetary Union.

If stringent budgets are the solution to one of Italy's economic problems the other one still remains. The workforce of the north is highly motivated (some say by runaway hedonism) which makes it an excellent area of Europe for those thinking of living and working abroad. In economic terms, Italy claims to have done better at reducing its budget deficit than either France or Germany. If this is true then it means that Italy is in a better state to join the single currency than either of those nations. In which case, it is probably more serious for monetary union than for Italy. However, such a claim is belied by the enormous national debt, 12%+ unemployment (22%+ in the south and down to 6.6% in some north-east regions) and the drain on government resources caused by the enormous welfare needs of the south.

One good bit of news is that inflation is down from double figures of a few years ago to around 2%. According to the OECD's annual economic outlook growth rates of 2.1% and 2.6% are forecast for Italy in 1998 and 1999.

One factor that is not usually taken into account when assessing the state of the Italian economy is the mind-boggling amount of revenue lost through tax evasion. There are signs that the government is at last making some catches in these teeming waters to the extent that tax revenues have shown progressive increases since 1988. The current target is Italians living abroad who are suspected fiddling the residence criteria to avoid paying their motherland's taxes.

The home of the Italian stock market, and therefore Italy's financial capital is Milan. The Milan stock market (*la borsa*) is small (only 215 companies are listed compared with 2,500 and 3,000 in London and New York respectively) and it has been run for decades by the same families and insider dealing was legal until quite recently. Italian stockbrokers are doubtful that recent legislation against insider dealing will be effective against a practice which is so engrained and difficult to prove.

The 'borsa' has been privatised under Italy's big sell off of state assets and from 1998 the government is hoping to entice small companies to be quoted by offering generous tax incentives, as well as encouraging larger companies to reinvest profits in the market by cutting tax on them by nearly 50%.

Securities trading companies are known as *Societa di Intermediadiazone Mobiliare* (SIM) and are the sole stock market intermediaries.

Italy in the Future

Despite certain drawbacks already mentioned above, Italy is optimistic about the future and continues to attract large amounts of foreign investment. Italian economists used to be largely pessimistic; in their view the economy was like the Titanic – heading full steam toward disaster which is probably why the Italians are so keen on European Monetary Union and the stabilsiing effect of the European Union generally. There is no doubt that government faces economic problems including debts and the fact that one mainstay of the economy, the Italian fashion industry has been greatly undermined by the upsurge of designers in countries which have traditionally bought Italian clothes (ie. Germany), and the undercutting of the market by designers who have clothes made up in the Far East. But some of the old problems are being tackled: there is at least a government policy behind the economy which is being stewarded towards meeting the criteria for EMU. However, Italy still imports 80% of its oil while having voted in a national referendum in 1987 to phase out the entire Italian nuclear power programme. Meanwhile the separation between highly developed north and poor south is being exacerbated by the continuing economic success of the north at the expense of the south and a continuing threat by the Lega Nord movement to partition Italy into northern and southern states.

Geographical Information

Mainland and Offshore Italy

Italy occupies an area of 116,000 square miles (301,278 sq km). As well as the long peninsula which, as most schoolchildren learn, is shaped like a boot, Italy's offshore elements include the island of Sicily situated off the toe of the boot across the Strait of Messina, the islands of Pantelleria, Linosa and Lampedusa which lie between Sicily and Tunisia, the island of Elba located off Tuscany, and the rocky, barren island of Sardinia which lies west of Rome and south of Corsica.

The Tyrrhenian Sea bounds the south west of the peninsula, with the Ionian Sea under the sole of the boot. The Adriatic Sea lies on the eastern side between Italy and former-Yugoslavia. Italy shares borders with France, Switzerland, Austria and Croatia.

Main physical features include the Alps which form the border in the north. Also in the north are Italy's main lakes: Guarda, Maggiore and Como. An offshoot of the Alps curves round the Gulf of Genoa and runs spine-like down the peninsula to form the Appenines. The longest river, the Po, lies in the north and flows from west to east across the plain of Lombardy and into the Adriatic. On Sicily, the still active volcano, Mount Etna rises to 10,741 feet (3,274 m).

Earthquakes & Volcanoes

The European fault line runs right through Italy from north to south. The main risk areas for quakes are central and southern Italy where about 70% of the terrain is susceptible. Tremors are quite common in Umbria and the Appenines. Seismologists claim that the number, strength and frequency of quakes hitting central Italy is increasing. Italy's last big disastrous earthquake flattened Messina in 1908, killing 84,000 people and causing the shoreline to sink by a half metre overnight. Other serious ones were Friuli (1976), Irpinia (1980), and Umbria (1997).

As if this were not excitment enough, Italy has three active volcanoes the most infamous of which is Vesuvius near Naples which buried 2,000 inhabitants in their hedonistic city of Pompeii in AD79. These days the volcano's rumblings are under continuous monitoring so there should be plenty of warning before it pops again. The other volcanoes are comfortingly off shore (unless you live there): Etna on Sicily and Stromboli on a small island off the west coast of southern Italy.

Regional Divisions

For administrative purposes Italy is divided into twenty regions and ninety-six provinces which are as follows:

ABRUZZO – Chieti, L'Aquila, Pescara, Teramo.
BASILICATA (LUCANIA) – Matera, Potenza
CALABRIA – Cantazaro, Cosenza, Reggio di Calabria
CAMPANIA – Avellino, Benevento, Caserta, Napoli (Naples), Salerno.
EMILIA ROMAGNA – Bologna, Ferrara, Forli, Modena, Piacenza, Parma, Ravenna, Regio Emilia.
FRIULI-VENEZIA-GIULIA – Gorizia, Pordenone, Trieste, Udine.
LAZIO – Frosinone, Latina, Rieti, Roma, Viterbo.
LIGURIA – Genova, Imperia, La Spezia, Savona.
LOMBARDIA (LOMBARDY) – Bergamo, Brescia, Como, Cremona, Mantova (Mantua), Milano, Pavia, Sondrio, Varese.
MARCHE – Ancona, Ascoli Piceno, Macerata, Pesaro.
MOLISE – Campobasso, Isernia.
PIEMONTE (PIEDMONT) – Alessandria, Asti, Cuneo, Novara, Torino (Turin), Vercelli.
PUGLIA (APULIA) – Bari, Brindisi, Foggia, Lecce, Taranto.
SARDEGNA (SARDINIA) – Cagliari, Nuoro, Oristano, Sassari.
SICILIA (SICILY) – Agrigento, Caltanissetta, Catania, Enna, Messina, Palermo, Ragusa, Siracusa (Syracuse), Trapini.
TOSCANA (TUSCANY) – Arezzo, Firenze (Florence), Grosseto, Livorno (Leghorn), Lucca, Massa Carrara, Pisa, Pistoia, Siena.

TRENTINO-ALTO-ADIGE – Bolzano, Trento.
UMBRIA – Perugia, Terni.
VAL D'AOSTA – Aosta.
VENETO – Belluno, Padova (Padua), Rovigno, Treviso, Venezia (Venice), Verona, Vicenza.

Population

Italy's population numbers approximately 58 million; a million more than the UK which has nearly fifty-seven million. However the Italians have more elbow room than Britons with 190 persons per square km compared with 232 in the UK. Surprisingly for country associated with large families, Italy has the lowest birth rate in Europe with many couples choosing not to have children and those that do having a single child. The population includes a large number of immigrants from ex-colonies: Somalia, Libya and Eritrea. Most of the immigrants have arrived within the last fifteen years as a result of Italy's liberal entry regulations. These have however been tightened up under the Schengen Agreement. There are also significant numbers of Eastern Europeans, Filipinos and Brazilians. There is no official census of the number of immigrants; around half a million have arrived through official channels but the majority remain illegal (aided by Italy's 8000 km long and difficult to patrol coastline), and the total number is believed to exceed two million. Naples now has a large African population while Rome has become home to a wide variety of ethnological backgrounds amongst its population of nearly four million. The most recent influx of immigrants and refugees to Italy has come from the stricken country of Albania. An estimated 80,000 Albanians have entered Italy (both legally and illegally), amongst them a ruthless criminal element who are rumoured to be more deadly than the Mafia whom they are replacing in some areas, particularly Milan.

The populations of the other largest Italian cities are:
Bologna – 493,282; Palermo – 996,000; Firenze (Florence) – 441,654; Torino (Turin) – 1,181,698; Genova (Genoa) – 787,011; Venice – 305,000; Milano – 1,724,557; Verona – 255,000; Napoli (Naples) – 1,214,775.

States within the State

Within its borders Italy contains three micro, sovereign states the most famous of which is the Vatican City. No less arcane, but wielding considerably less temporal power are San Marino and the Knights of Malta. Each of these three states has its own goverment, head of state and car licence plates:

The Vatican City: The Vatican City (area: 116 acres; population: 730), became a sovereign state in 1929 and is located within the boundaries of Rome. Its high walls enclose all the apparatus of a mini-state: the secret archives, Radio Vatican, Vatican Television, the Vatican bank, the Vatican Museums, the Vatican Newspaper (*L'Osservatore Romano*) and a legion of staff including accountants, Swiss Guards, Vatican Police, the Palatine Guard and even its own football league made up of teams from each of these. Small wonder it is that the Vatican is considered to be less of a spiritual entity than a political one, the Catholic Church being as faction ridden as any Italian political party. During a period of liberalization in the sixties and seventies under popes John XXIII and Paul VI, many intellectuals of a progressive outlook were elected to positions of power in the Church and its associated lay organizations such as the Azione Cattolica. The retrogressive tendencies of the present incumbent 'Papa Wojtyla' and his 'presage-of-doom view' of mankind's future need no further elaboration here. For the effect of Wojtyla's conservatism on the Italian church see page 100, Chapter Four, *Daily Life*.

Saint Peter's Church and parts of the Papal Palace designated as The Vatican Museums are open to the public.

San Marino: The largest of the micro states, San Marino covers an area of 24 square miles (61 square kilometres) and has a population of 22,000. Best known for its large and colourful postage stamps, San Marino lies between the regions of Emilia Romagna and Marche about fifteen miles inland from Rimini and has been in existence since the Middle Ages.

The Knights of Malta: The Knights have several enclaves which, like the Vatican City, are located within the boundaries of Rome. The venerable Knights are an international brotherhood led by a Grand Master who is seventy-eighth in a line dating back to the Middle Ages.

Climatic Zones

The climate of Italy shows the kind of regional variation one would expect from a country with its head in the Alps and its toe in the Mediterranean. At the foot of the Alps in the north is the flat and fertile Plain of Lombardy which is also one of the main industrial areas. Cold and wet in winter, those who find themselves living and working in the north can escape to the cold, dry Alps further northwards for winter sports, or to the Italian Riviera (Liguria) which is mild in winter or go to the south or Sicily, where the winters are even milder and typically mediterranean. In summer and winter, the middle regions of Tuscany and Umbria, which are home to many expatriates, have the best of both worlds: neither too cold in winter nor too parched in summer. However the higher areas of even these favoured regions can be cold and snowbound in winter. The far south and Sicily are generally considered too hot for comfort in summer.

Average Temperatures

City & Province	Jan	Apr	July	Nov
Ancona (Marche)	42°f/6oc	56°f/14°c	77°f/25°c	55°f/13°c
Bari(Puglia)	46°f/8°c	57°f/14°f	77°f/25°f°	59°f/15°c
Bologna (Emilia Romagna)	37°f/3°c	56°f/15°c	78°f/26°c	50°f/10°c
Florence (Tuscany)	42°f/6°c	55°f/13°c	77°f/25°c	52°f/11°c
Genova (Liguria)	46°f/8°c	56°f/14°c	77°f/25°c	55°f/13°c
Milan (Lombardy)	36°f/2°c	55°f/13°c	77°f/25°c	48°f/9°c
Naples (Campania)	48°f/9°c	56°f/14°c	77°f/25°c	59°f/15°c
Palermo(Sicily)	50°f/10°c	61°f/16°c	77°f/25°c	50°f/16°c
Rome (Latium)	45°f/7°c	57°f/14°c	78°f/26°c	55°f/13°c
Trieste (Friuli-Venezia)	41°f/5°c	55°f/13°c	75°f/25°c	52°f/11°c
Venice (Venetia)	39°f/4°c	55°c/13°c	75°f/24°c	52°f/10°c

Regional Guide

Historically, Italy as a unified country has existed for little more than a hundred and thirty-seven years. Before the *Risorgimento* (unification) the whole region was a collection of city-states, kingdoms, duchies and the republics of Venice, Naples, Lombardy, Florence, Piedmont and Sicily. The result of such a relatively recent union is that Italians have not really had time to adjust to the concept of national identity and instead consider themselves Neapolitan, Piedmontese etc., and only Italian as an afterthought. This regionalism is expressed by the word *campanilismo*, from the word for a bell-tower, (ie. a village) and thus, in a slightly derogatory way, expresses the Italian obsession with discussing the finer points of the differences in character and culture of the inhabitants of the many different regions that make up the country.

In view of the separate historical development of the Italian regions it comes as little surprise that not only do customs and outlook vary considerably amongst them, but also the language spoken. Dialects abound in every province and are a source of pride to Italians as a way of defining their identity. Italians from almost every area are able to speak their local dialect and make themselves incomprehensible not only to those struggling to get by with evening-class Italian, but also other Italians.

In France and Spain there are areas favoured by expatriates for setting up home for a long-term stay, or a permanent one if they are retired. This is no less true of Italy where hilltop dwellings in Tuscany and more recently Umbria, have been selling steadily to the Brits, the Dutch and the Germans, among others. High-powered executives on the other hand are more likely to find themselves based in the prosperous cities of the north: Milan, Genoa or Turin or in the capital, Rome. While anyone who is teaching English as a foreign language, or practising their skills as a nurse or a car mechanic, could find themselves in almost any city from Como to Cagliari.

Information Facilities

An excellent starting point for information is the Italian State Tourist Board (ENIT), which supplies free maps and brochures as well as the invaluable, annually updated *Travellers Handbook* packed with useful information on everything from how to get an audience with the Pope to where to go for Italian courses. In Italy itself every regional capital city has its own tourist board called either: Ente Provincial Turismo or Azienda Promozione Turistica. For specialist maps like the large-scale road maps or maps for hiking, contact Stanfords of London.

Useful Addresses

Italian State Tourist Board: 1 Princes Street, London W1R 8AY; tel 0171-408 1254; fax 0171-493 6695.
Stanfords: 12 Long Acre, London WC2; tel 0171-836 1321. Perhaps the best known map shop in London. Large Italian section including regional Italian driving maps and town plans of all major towns and cities of Italy.

THE NORTH WEST

Regions: Piedmont, Lombardy, Liguria, Val d'Aosta.
Main cities: Turin, Genoa, Aosta, Milan.
At the north west extremity of Italy the two regions of Piedmont (Piemonte) and Val d'Aosta are probably the two least Italianate regions of Italy. Tiny Val d'Aosta is wedged between France and Switzerland and is a mountainous, bilingual (in French and Italian) area. The regional capital, Aosta is picturesquely ringed by

peaks and as you would expect ski resorts are plentiful.

Until the end of the nineteenth century the Piedmontese were also French speaking. In the eleventh century the kingdom of Savoy-Piedmont which included the Val d'Aosta was founded by Umberto Bianca-mano. Unfortunately situated on the invasion route from France, the kingdom suffered its fair share of intrusions. However, a successful swipe at the French on their way to Lombardy to fight the War of the Spanish succession enhanced the prestige of Duke Vittorio Amadeo II of Savoy-Piedmont, who not only gained Sicily but was also elevated to kingship at the Treaty of Utrecht (1714). Turin (Torino), the main regional city has the distinction of being at the centre of the drive for Italian unity and was home to the first Italian Parliament in 1861 when unificaton of the greater part of Italy had been achieved. The giant corporation FIAT (*Fabbrica Italiana di Automobili Torino*) and Olivetti have their headquarters in Turin; the former company since its founding in 1899. The Turin area is also famous for its good quality wines particularly Barolo and Barbera, and the internationally-known aperitifs Cinzano and Martini, which are produced there. Wealthy Turin is not everyone's choice of a place to live and work but it is handy for the Alps, France and the Italian Riviera and is less atmospherically polluted than Milan.

Throughout history Lombardy has dominated northern Italy and continues to do so. Not only is it the most commercially and industrially successful area but it is also the country's financial powerhouse. It is the most heavily populated region of the country with an estimated eight million inhabitants, many of them workers from the south. The heavily industrialized area around Milan produces around 40% of Italy's GNP and Milan is easily the most expensive and luxurious city in the country. Historically, Lombardy is one of the great battlefields of Europe; most noticeably perhaps during the Thirty Years War (1618-48), when the French, Spanish and Austrians were simultaneously rampaging over the landscape in a dispute over Valtellina. The resulting privations led to a long period of economic decline in Lombardy which was reversed in the more constructive period of the eighteenth century. This welcome respite from war lasted until the return of the French under Bonaparte in 1796, which culminated in his coronation as King of Italy in Milan (1805). Following Napoleon's defeat, the Kingdom of Lombardy-Venetia was absorbed into the Austrian Empire until the unification of the greater part of Italy with Piedmont was achieved in 1861.

The Liguria region, also called the Italian Riviera is a coastal strip that follows on eastwards from the French Riviera and is centred on the ancient trading port of Genova (Genoa) which was one of the five great maritime republics of Italy in the thirteenth century. Successively invaded by the French and the Austrians during the seventeenth and eighteenth centuries, the port of Genoa suffered progressive economic decline. During the period leading up to the Unification, the area became a haven for political refugees and the popular hero of the Italian liberation movement, Garibaldi (1807-82), came from the region. In the nineteenth and twentieth centuries an economic resurgence in the form of heavy industry made Genoa Italy's third most important industrial centre. Its fortunes have since taken a nosedive with the decline of heavy industries like steel production, thus forcing many of the region's one million, seven hundred thousand inhabitants to move to other areas of Italy in search of work.

The majority of the foreign business community are based in the north, particularly Milan, rather than Rome as one might expect. Those who can afford it have a city flat and a weekend house at one of the nearby lakes.

THE NORTH EAST

Regions: Trentino Alto-Adige, Veneto, Friuli-Veneto-Giulia, Emilia Romagna.
Main Towns: Bolzano, Trent, Udine, Trieste, Cortina, Verona, Venice, Parma, Ferrara, Bologna, Ravenna.
The first three of these regions contains the scenically beautiful Dolomite mountains which run along the north-eastern edge of Italy forming a natural border with Austria. Justly famed for its wine producing qualities this landscape is usually only visited by foreigners in search of mountain holidays, notably winter sports. Trentino-Alto Adige was part of the Austrian Empire until 1918 and German is still spoken there. In fact linguistic squabbling between German and Italian speakers in the region is an on-going source of tension there. Ethnic Germans claim they were 'italianised' by Mussolini and want to revert place names to German versions, while rival factions like the Ladins, who claim their origins and language go back to the Romans, want their Italian language rights protected. The region's population is around 800,000 and is a semi-autonomous section of the Veneto region.

Like Trentino-Alto Adige, Friuli-Veneto Giulia which has a population of just over a million, also came within the ambit of the Hapsburgs in the nineteenth century. Later,in the chaotic aftermath of the Second World War it was partitioned between Italy and Yugoslavia. Their last dispute over the area was not settled until the 1970s. As a legacy of its history it is ethnically mixed and more eastern European than typically Italian. Trieste, the regional capital which projects into Slovenia is being revitalised by a more open Europe.

The Veneto region is one of the undisputed treasure houses of Europe. In addition to Venice, the cities of Verona, Vicenza and Padua are also of great cultural interest. By the year 1000, Venice had become powerful in the region through commerce and maritime prowess which enabled her to be the main conduit for trade between Europe and the Orient. This supremacy lasted until the mid-thirteenth century when the Black Death swept across Europe. In the twelfth century when the German Kings were making their unrealisitic claims to the Veneto, the first Hohenstaufen Emperor Barbarossa (red beard) had already conquered Milan, before the Trevisan League of cities, with Venice at their head, routed his army and then negotiated with Barbarossa to be the sole supplier of the imperial armies on their future sorties in Italy. During the fifteenth century, the existence of Venice was threatened by the rival state of Genoa. These being two great maritime republics, the contest naturally took place on the seas and resulted in victory for the Venetians. Venice reached its *terra firma* limits with the conquests of Brescia and Bergamo in the first half of the fifteenth century. The long decline of Venetian greatness was heralded by fall of Constantinople (1453) with whose fortunes those of Venice were inextricably linked. During the sixteenth century the policy of the Venetian Republic proceded along defensive lines treading a delicate path of diplomacy amongst the expansionist powers of the time, the Hapsburg Empire and France. There was also the added irritant of political interference by the Pope. However, by far the main threat to the Venetians were the Turks who were in the process of usurping the supremacy of Venetian trading interests. It was this struggle, principally a maritime one, that gradually enfeebled Venice and left a vacuum for the ascendancy of the old arch-rival, Genoa. In 1797 Venice took up Bonaparte's unrefusable offer to become part of the Austrian Empire. After crowning himself Emperor of France in 1804, Bonaparte returned to Italy to organize its reconstruction. The result was a kingdom of Italy which included Lombardy and Venice. Having more pressing matters to attend to, Napoleon left his stepson, Eugéne Beauharnais, in charge of the Kingdom as its Viceroy. After Napoleon's defeat, Venice returned to independent status which lasted until 1849.

For all its incomparable glories, Venice is notoriously foggy in winter and smelly in summer which may be one reason, along with the high prices and excess of tourists, why its native population has shrunk by two thirds in the last 20 years. Within the same period the prosperity of the Venetian hinterland has been considerably revived with the creation of many new companies producing small, high-quality goods including shoes, medical equipment, spectacle frames and machine components. Treviso is the headquarters of the Benetton group. If it were not for the dismal winters many more foreigners would probably choose to settle in this commercially upbeat region.

Emilia Romagna takes its name from the ancient Roman road to Rome, the Via Emilia, and Romagna, the name of the former Papal State which covered the area which now contains the provinces of Forli and Ravenna. The northern part of the region is characterized by a flat and featureless wheat prairie while the south takes in the foothills of the Appenines. An extremely prosperous region, its main town, Bologna experienced an economic boom in the eighties largely through the development of high-tech industries. As a place in which to live and work, Emilia Romagna has obvious attractions: above all it has beautiful towns and a rich gastronomic heritage; Bologna is the seat of Europe's oldest university. However the main problem for foreign residents would be the expense: the cost of daily living in Bologna matches, if not exceeds, that of Milan or Florence. Properties in the region are however reasonably priced but are not much sought after by either foreigners or Italians and so you might feel isolated unless you were near enough to Bologna to make use of the social life there. There is a small community of foreigners in Bologna who speak highly of their adopted home and find it lively, congenial, cultivated and relatively tourist free. There are also possibilities for teaching English as a foreign language there (see the chapter *Employment*).

THE UPPER CENTRE

Regions: Toscana (Tuscany), Umbria, Marche.
Main cities: Pisa, Florence, Siena, Orvieto, Perugia, Urbino.
Of all the regions of Italy, Tuscany, and increasingly Umbria, continue to attract the most foreign residents and superlatives: best climate, best scenery, best cultural heritage, etc. Parts of the western, central region of Tuscany are now 'colonized' by foreigners including Britons, Northern Europeans, and Irish. While the Brits continue to flock to Tuscany (there are currently around 8,000 permanent residents and many more holiday home owners), the Italians are streaming out. The two trends are not necessarily connected. The departure of the Italians has more to do with the economic depression of the area than a wish to flee from the delights of 'Chianti-shire'. Even this beloved region of hilltop villages, vineyards and files of cypress trees is not without its drawbacks: water and electricity supplies are a problem in the remoter regions and tourists overrun the principal attractions, Florence, Siena, Pisa and the coast, for six months of the year. Originally a marquisate under Matilda of Tuscany, the area became prosperous through the woollen and cloth industries in the fourteenth centuries. The history of the region is essentially centred on Florence which was the focus of the Renaissance and existed as a republic under the Medicis in the fifteenth and sixteenth centuries, until Cosimo Medici made himself the first Grand-Duke of Tuscany in 1570. During the eighteenth century Tuscany became part of Austria until 1859 when the Risorgimento was in process. There was however a brief fifteen year interlude under the French during the Napoleonic era.

Despite its propensity for earthquakes, the landlocked region of Umbria has become the other 'in-place' for foreign residents to set up home. With a smaller population than Tuscany, and somewhat overshadowed by the spectacular glories of that region, Umbria nevertheless has some lures for the prospective foreign resident, not the least of which are property prices which are about half those of Tuscany. However, the rapidly growing popularity of the region with both foreigners and Romans means that this financial advantage may quite soon evaporate. The main problem for foreign residents appears to be that communications are not brilliant. Rome airport is reasonably convenient for those living in the southern part of Umbria: Rome to Perugia takes about three hours by road. For those in the north coming from Pisa airport, it takes considerably longer. The region's attractions include Assisi, a mecca for pilgrimages dedicated to St Francis, the patron saint of Italy, and the walled town of Spoleto. Sadly, the earthquake which hit the region in 1997 destroyed much of the renowned frescoes in Assisi's Basilica of St Francis and highlighted the fact that Europe's fault line runs down almost throught the centre of Italy. The Umbrian city of Foligno was also badly hit by the quake which bought down the cathedral's bell tower. Umbria also has a Foreigners' University (*Universita italiana per gli stranieri*) based in Perugia, to which students from all over the world come to take courses on Italian art and culture and language, which would be extremely useful for the foreign resident determined to absorb Italian culture in order to integrate.

Marche, situated between Umbria and the Adriatic is a mountainous but varied region almost unknown to foreigners. Italians flock to its coastal strip where resorts such as Rimini and Riccione are the playgrounds of northern Italians throughout the summer. As a result property prices on the coast are pushed high by the demand for summer flats. The hinterland is just beginning to attract foreign buyers but the remoteness of the region is regarded as something of a drawback. Communications with the north are excellent from the coast and once the region opens up, are likely to improve in the hinterland. The southern part of Marche used to be regarded as part of the Mezzogiorno but owing to increasing prosperity it has now had its financial benefits withdrawn by the government. Historically, Marche made a major contribution to civilization through Frederico da Montefeltro, whose patronage of some of the greatest artists and architects to build and embellish his palace at Urbino, made it one of the most aristocratic and civilized courts of the Renaissance period. Ascoli Piceno is another large town which flourished in the same period.

THE LOWER CENTRE AND SARDINIA

Regions Lazio (Latium), Abruzzo, Molise.
Main cities: Rome, L'Aquila, Isernia.
The region of Lazio encompasses the Italian capital Rome, which, as the centre of the former Roman empire shaped Western civilisation. However it seems more through geography than suitability that Rome found itself capital of modern Italy. Following full unification in 1871, Rome appeared ideally situated between northern and southern Italy. She was however far from being the largest or most important city of the time: the claims of Milan, Turin and Naples were greater since they had been administrative centres or capitals for centuries. In contrast Rome had nothing to offer but glorious and symbolic antiquity and the Vatican. The ruinous expense of building her up into a capital city of appropriate grandeur lasted well into Mussolini's time. Nowadays Rome is notorious amongst other things for being the headquarters of the state apparatus whose thousands of functionaries drive anyone who has dealings with them to distraction with the

legendary innefficicency and corruption that characterizes the national administration. Many of these state employees are from the south of Italy which aggravates the northerners' contempt for Rome and the south. The perception is of Rome squandering the hard-earned wealth of the north on the lazy and unproductive south. Since the 1980s Rome's slightly backward reputation has diminished thanks to industrial expansion particularly in the high technology field. However it still lags behind Milan and Turin in the league table of industrial cities. However exciting the prospect of living and working in the city and its environs may seem, there are considerable drawbacks including the difficulty of finding accommodation and traffic congestion which has reached unendurable limits while it fills the narrow, high-sided streets with noxious fumes that cannot disperse. However, for all its faults and frustrations Rome has a deep fascination, not the least of which is the civilized atmosphere engendered by two thousand years of occupation.

After Milan, Rome has the second largest community of foreigners living and working in the city and its environs.

Formerly the Abruzzi, the region east and south of Rome has been partitioned into the two regions of Abruzzo and Molise since 1963. Both areas are mountainous and sparsely populated and to many foreigners they seem wild and forbidding. Folk traditions which have faded out in the more developed areas of Italy survive here among the hilltop villages along with witches and wolves. The latter can be found in the Parco Nazionale dell'Abruzzo along with brown bears and chamois. Over recent years Abruzzo has overtaken poverty-stricken Molise, by taking full advantage of government incentive schemes for businesses and proving that factories in Abruzzo can operate as efficiently and productively as anywhere in the north of Italy. The Abruzzese have also been quick to develop the potential of their Adriatic seaboard and in particular Pescara, which has become a popular holiday spot for Italians. The main town of Abruzzo, L'Aquila (meaning eagle) has a 99-spout fountain (one for every village from which the city's original population is reputed to have been formed), and a brooding sixteenth century castle built by the Spaniards during their period of influence in Italy which spanned about 150 years.

Poor and backward Molise, which is about half the area of Abruzzo, is where the south begins. The entire Abruzzi area is an earthquake zone which constitutes a damper on the real estate market there. The main town of Molise, Isernia, is still propped up by scaffolding from the quake of 1984. It is a shortish distance from the coast across the Adriatic to Albania and Croatia and the connections between the regions are evident in the customs and dialect of the region. There is an incipient coastal resort at Termoli.

Sardegna (Sardinia): Sardinia, the Mediterranean's second largest island after Sicily, has long been on the periphery of Italian affairs. At one time in the possession of the Spanish it was taken over in 1718 by the Dukes of Savoy. The barren and harsh landscape of the island is capable only of subsistence agriculture. The islanders speak Sardo (see *The Italian Language, Daily Life*). A small community which speaks undiluted fifteenth century Catalan is an even more curious linguistic anachronism. As a place in which to live and work Sardinia is not a very serious option. Prospects for business and jobs are limited to holiday developments, and English language teaching. The island's main town is Cagliari and millionaires' row is the Costa Smerelda in the north east.

THE SOUTH AND SICILY

Regions: Campania, Apulia (Puglia), Basilicata, Calabria.
Main cities: Naples, Amalfi, Lecce (Lucca), Bari, Brindisi, Reggio.
It is a widely-held belief that the South of Italy is penurious throughout and crawling with gun-toting mafiosi who will knee-cap or assasinate anyone who seems to threaten their interests. If this were the case, the possibility of any normal business activity would be nil. In fact there are pockets of wealth and industry in the south, eg. in Puglia and Sicily which rival anything in the north. Such development has been greatly encouraged by enormous financial incentives offered by the Italian government (see the Chapter, *Starting a Business*). However there are areas where the risk of Mafia interference should be taken extremely seriously: these include virtually the whole of Campania, the toe of Calabria and much of Sicily. As the homeground of the various brotherhoods: the *camorra*, 'ndrangheta (the Calabrian Mafia), and the Sicilian Mafia, these are regarded as virtual no go areas, particularly for small businesses which are less resilient to threats than the large corporations which can hope to shrug them off.

Campania

Campania is dominated by the city of Naples which represents the south in much the same way that Milan represents the north. The region was called *Campania Felix* by the Romans, whose elite built their palatial villas along the riviera of the bay of Naples. The Roman idyll is in stark contrast to the Naples coastline of today, which is blotted with the smokestacks and industrial installations of the city's more recent heritage. Naples is largely neglected by foreigners who perhaps fear the reputation of its pickpockets, its *bassi* (slums), and its notorious rubbish disposal problem – the result of the chronic innefficiency of the local council. Naples' touristic heyday was probably the eighteenth century when it was an obligatory stop on the English gentleman's Grand Tour of Europe. Influenced by the Spanish for 300 years, it passed to the Bourbon French in 1734. Famed for its Roman ruins, in particular nearby Pompeii and Herculaneum in the shadow of Vesuvius. Naples acquired under the French a reputation for its courtesans. The city remained a hit with the British until the kill-joy Victorians denounced it as latter day Sodom. After the end of the Kingdom of Naples in 1860 the city became rapidly provincialized, a process which was accelerated when Rome was made the capital of united Italy.

Foreigners are unlikely to choose Naples as a place to live unless they are offered employment there. The endemic problems include extreme poverty, and the petty crime and organized criminal activity that go with it. Naples comes under the domain of the *camorra* (the Neapolitan version of the Mafia). In addition, the anarchic driving habits of the Neapolitans (who are oblivious to all roadsigns and traffic signals) give a new slant to the dictum 'see Naples and die'. Property on the three islands in the Bay of Naples – Ischia, Capri and Procida – rarely comes on the market and is reputed to be fabulously expensive. On the mainland the most attractive coastal areas are Sorrento, Amalfi, Positano and Ravello but one has to run the gauntlet of Neapolitan motorists (see above) on the precipitous cliff road, to get to them. Inland, property prices fall dramatically. However there is an inherent danger in the area from earthquakes. The 1980 one devastated the area behind Salerno. It is an acknowledgement of the poverty of the extreme south that all the *autostrade* south of Salerno are toll free.

Apulia (Puglia)

The olive and wine-producing area of Puglia is a long strip that stretches for over 250 miles (400 km) along the heel of Italy. Southern Italy, including Puglia was invaded by the Normans in the eleventh century (thus ousting the Moslems). The Normans left behind many fine cathedrals including those at Trani, Barletta, Bitonto, Ruvo di Puglia and Bari. The main city, Bari, is situated about halfway down the Adriatic coast of Puglia, and is one of the showcases of the south owing to a economic boom from high tech and service industries. The other main industrial area is located around the ancient port of Taranto which has long been given over to steel production. The upper part of the region, 'il Promontario del Gargano' (the Gargano Promontory), which juts into the Adriatic is considered one of the most attractive parts of Puglia with its wooded hills and stunning views of the sea. The area was once rich with religious sanctuaries and Monte Sant'Angelo, where the archangel Michael put in an 'appearance' in AD490 has long been a point of pilgrimage. Between Taranto and Bari are numerous *trulli* (circular, dry-stone built houses with conical roofs). You can see a whole town of them at Alberobello. While you may hear that they were prehistoric dwellings, it is generally accepted that they represent an early form of tax evasion from the Spanish invaders' tax on bricks and mortar in the 16th century. Lecce, in the far corner of Puglia is usually regarded as the architectural gem of southern Italy built in a particularly refined baroque style. Galatina is the home of the dance tarantella which is celebrated annually in a medieval festival. The dance, named from the tarantula spider, is supposed to reflect the writhings of those bitten by the deadly arachnid. The Isole Tremiti (Tremiti islands) 25 miles off Gargano, were once the Devil's Islands of Italy. The presence of prisoners has long since been replaced by that of tourists (an estimated 100,000 in August).

A number of foreigners have found the charms of Gargano irresistible and made their homes in these pleasant surroundings. Anyone thinking of retiring there could probably rent a holiday villa in the area while they carry out a reconnaissance. Unlike Campania, there is little organized crime in Puglia. From the ports of Otranto and Brindisi there are ferries to former Yugoslavia, and Greece.

Baslicata (Lucania) and Calabria

The two most southerly regions of Baslicata and Calabria are the poorest and most underdeveloped in Italy and best epitomize the plight of the Mezzogiorno. The traditional migration of southerners from these regions to the north in search of jobs continues apace, despite government efforts to bring industrial development to the south. In an effort to deal with the prosperity imbalance between north and south the Italian government set up a development fund, *La Cassa del Mezzogiorno* in the 1950s, which has since been superseded by various other bodies with specialized responsibilities. Massive government resources have been poured into the south to fund: irrigation projects, an improved infrastructure, modern communications, and industrial and touristic development. However the area has suffered from corruption on an unprecedented scale and gross inefficiency (there is no overall investment plan) with the result that most of the money has been squandered on political patronage (see the section *Politics* and has ended up in private bank accounts and the coffers of the 'Ndrangheta. From 1992, the EU Regional Investment Fund took over the organising of funding the Mezzogiorno. Despite this inpouring of financial help there are ominous signs that the north/south wealth gap is again widening and there are fears that these two regions will fall increasingly into the hands of the *malavita* (organized criminals).

The decimation of the populations of Basilicata and Calabria is the result of the constant migration of those desperate to escape poverty and the futility that goes with it. Add to this the mountainous and inhospitable landscape and the undercurrent of criminality, and there does not seem to be much here to appeal to the foreign resident. Basilicata's main city is Matera. A landscape feature are the *Sassi* cave dwellings where until very recently peasants slept with their animals.

Calabria, which forms the 'toe' of Italy has the attraction of its beautiful Tyrrenhian coastline which draws a regular summer tourist trade. In the sixth century the Greeks flourished in Calabria. This was probably the high point of its history. Malarial mosquitoes were a problem in the area up to the twentieth century. Towns like Crotone and Reggio Calabria have a pretty evil reputation. From the promontory of Tropea in the south west of Calabria you can see the Lipari islands and even Stromboli (whose last reported bout of volcanic eruption was in 1971). The main problem for anyone thinking of living in Calabria is the risk of kidnapping. Calabria is notorious for the practice and it is estimated that only one in ten victims are ever located by the *carabinieri* owing, it is said, to a combination of their incompetence and the difficulty of searching the terrain. It is reported that local shepherds have to be sent into the mountains to locate carabinieri who have become lost while attempting to perform their duties. Owing to a dearth of Calabrian industrialists, the kidnappers prey on the professional classes and their offspring. The kidnappings tend to be family affairs and well organized. Ransoms are likely to end up in the pockets of the local drug barons or the construction industry, which is known to be rife with *malavita* throughout most of southern Italy. There is even a rather macabre custom in Calabria of nicknaming hotels and apartment blocks after those whose ransom money has paid for them. As far as foreigners are concerned it is widely assumed that they are not regarded as prime targets since the ensuing publicity in the foreign media would put the Italian government in a position of ridicule and expose their incompetence at combatting the problem. Furthermore, such goings on would have a devastating effect on much-needed tourism in Calabria. Even so, hillwalking and child-rearing are not recommended pursuits for the area.

Sicily (Sicilia)

Main towns: Palermo, Messina, Catania, Syracuse.
Population: five million.
The island of Sicily which lies off the toe of Italy is a *regioni a statuto speciale* meaning that it has a greater degree of autonomy than most of the other twenty regions. This status has less to do with the fact that Sicily is the home of the Cosa Nostra (Mafia) who are a law unto themselves, but more to do with historical and ethnic differences. Nonetheless, to many people the name of Sicily is synonymous with the dark force of the Mafia. The origins of this brutal brotherhood are obscure; some claim that the Mafia have existed for two thousand years on a kind of freemasonary basis. It is however evident that the end of the nineteenth century marked the onset of their notoriety. During the 1920s the fascists under Mussolini lost no time in stamping out such an undesirable phenonenon. The responsibility for their revival in Sicily can be laid at the door of the American military, who having successfully invaded Italy during the Second World War, implanted several veteran mafiosi from New York to counteract the spread of Communism which they feared would take over Italy – a case of the cure being more deadly than the disease. There is no way of estimating the Mafia's clandestine wealth

worldwide, however in Italy their turnover is calculated at 12% of the GNP. Until the 1960s the Mafia area of operations was largely confined to Sicily, since then there are few areas of Italian commercial life which it has not penetrated and its multinational operations have made it probably the richest and most powerful criminal organization in the world. Palermo, Sicily's main city has the infamous distinction of being the world centre of the illegal drugs and armaments trades. With this awesome power over life, death and the economy it comes as little surprise that there are few who will stand up to the Mafia though there are some notable exceptions among the judicial profession. The young Sicilian judge Giovanni Falcone who conducted the much publicized *maxi-processi* (mega-trials) of Mafia luminaries, which put several, including Michele Greco the leader, behind bars. The price Falcone paid for his courage was to be the Salman Rushdie of Sicily, guarded round the clock by twenty-five armed bodyguards who were not sufficient protection from the (some say inevitable) assination that ended his life in 1992. The Mafia, like the Mounties it seems, always get their man.

Sicily is slowly modernising itself; there is even a Europe Office in Palermo offering information in English. It is perfectly possible to buy a house in Sicily, and many foreigners do have holiday homes there. Whether anyoneone would want to live in Sicily permanently is another matter and for the same reasons as Calabria it is probably not a suitable place to bring up children. Despite unemployment of 23% amongst the local population, it is possible to work on the island: there are opportunities for English teaching in Messina and Siracuse and there are Brits working for the oil companies at Gela. The island has many attractions including beautiful scenery and Greek ruins (Siracuse was the second largest city of ancient Greece). Trampled by others, including Romans, Moslems, Normans, French and Spaniards, Sicily is a fascinating mixture of styles as in the capital Palermo where Arab architecture meets Baroque. Another of the island's famous sights is Mount Etna (last eruption 1983), which lies in the north east between Messina and Catania.

While the railway from Palermo to the other major town Catania, remains single track and work on the motorway from Messina to Palermo is still unfinished it seems that work is about to begin on the grandiose and symbolic bridge across the Straights of Messina between Villa San Giovanni and Messina, more than a quarter of a century after the government began to plan it. The road and rail Bridge will be two miles long, 195 feet wide and building is expected to start in 1999 and last until 2006. The designers Stretto di Messina SpA claim it will withstand winds of over 200 m.p.h and more importantly it will be earthquake proof. The straights are one of Italy's seismic hotspots, most notably when the town of Messina was flattened by the big quake of 1908. The bridge will be funded internationally and it is expected to pay for itself in tolls after ten years. Obviously, the Italians have not heard about the Channel Tunnel investors' problems.

Getting to Italy

High Street travel agents and the travel pages of most national newspapers are obvious sources of discounted fares to Italy and there is plenty of choice. Non-stop flights are available from the UK to about 20 Italian cities. If you change to a domestic flight at Milan or Rome, you can reach still more.

Airlines offering flights from the UK:
Air UK: 0345-666777; Alitalia: 0171602 7111; Azur Air: 0181-785 3171; British Airways: 0345-222111; British Midland: 0345-554554; Debonair: 0541-500300;

Meridiana: 0171-839 2222;
   In addition to the above, Ethiopian Airways and Air Kenya fly London to Rome.
   Italy Sky Shuttle (0181-748 1333) operates the widest range of charters to Italy (to Bologna, Brindisi, Cagliari, Catania, Milan (Malpensa), Naples, Olbia, Palermo, Pisa, Rimini, Rome (Ciampino), Venice and Verona.
   There are also a number of travel agents in the UK that specialise in offering discount fares, to Rome and other airports in Italy.

Lupus Travel: 0171-306 3000.
Adelpi: 0171-620-4455.
Citalia: (0891-715151 – 50p per minute) also sells tickets for trains to Italy and for travel within Italy.
Dawson & Sanderson: 0171-735 6170, extension 33.
Destinations: 0171-490 8800.
The Italian Connection: tel 0171-486 6890 or 07071 30 30 30. An Italy specialist that can handle all types of travel arrangements to Italy and all types of self-catering accommodation.
The Magic of Italy:
Major Travel: 0171-485 7071.
Toro: 0171-834 0567.

Residence and Entry Regulations

The Current Position

Anyone who thinks the creation of a European Union means less red-tape for those who wish to move around within it for longer than just a holiday, might be disappointed when it comes to getting a residence permit to stay in another member state. Although British nationals have a similar entitlement to Italians to live and work in Italy, there is still a bureaucratic rigmarole involved with taking up residence there. The regulations concerning residence permits are dealt with below. In theory the procedure for obtaining them should be the same anywhere in the country. In practice there may well be differences depending on the comune in which you are living and your particular circumstances. The main thing to bear in mind is that Italy is excessively bureaucratic and the bureaucracy is as much a bugbear for the Italians themselves as it is to foreigners.

The Permesso di Soggiorno

If you are from another EU country and you arrive in Italy with the intention of working there you must apply at the police station (*questura*) for a *Ricevuta di Segnalazione di Soggiorno* which entitles you to stay for up to three months looking for a job. In order to obtain a *Permesso di Soggiorno* you must take the *Ricevuta* together with a letter from your employer confirming your employment back to the police station. Reports vary as to how long it takes for the stay permit to be issued, but three months is the offical delay. The only document required to obtain this permit is your passport.

If you have prearranged a job in Italy, or you are arriving with the intention of practising your profession, the first step is still to apply directly to the Questura for a *permesso di soggiorno*.

Other requirements for the *permesso di soggiorno* may vary: for instance, in many cases you will be required to produce proof of financial solvency, of having some kind of income and be able to name your intended profession while in Italy if this is relevant. The soggiorno is free of charge and issued initially for three months and then either every two or five years. Note that failure to renew the document can result in a a substantial fine. Renewals are made through the *comune*, or the *questura* in large towns and cities. The *Permesso di Soggiorno* has to be renewed every five years, no matter how long you live in Italy. All renewals must be made on special document paper, *carta bollata*, which can be purchased from most tobacconists (*tabaccherie*).

Libretto di Lavoro

Even if you are from an EU country, you may also be asked to apply for a work registration card (*libretto di lavoro*) even though this is not strictly necessary for EU nationals. You need to obtain the Permesso di Soggiorno first and then apply for the *libretto* at the town hall (*municipio*). The *libretto di lavoro* once obtained, should be held by the employer. During any periods of unemployment it will be kept by the equivalent of the job centre (*Ufficio di Collocamento*).

Certificato di Residenza

Once you have obtained a *permesso di soggiorno* and moved into your new Italian home, you will find it to your advantage to apply for residence certificate, *certificato di residenza*. This document entitles the holder to many vital privileges. The residenza is also proof that you are no longer resident or domiciled in the UK for tax purposes. This can be important in the event of a death, where the estate left is liable for tax if the British tax authorities regard the deceased as having being domiciled in the UK, in spite of having lived abroad for years. The residenza also enables the holder to numerous other benefits eg. to apply for a driving licence, open a bank account, claim health care and to send children to local schools. The number of certificates which you are required to obtain once in Italy for other, more obscure reasons, will vary greatly depending largely on the commune in question and on the nature of the local *maresciallo* (head of the commune).

Entering to Start a Business

EU nationals who wish to enter Italy to start up a business are free to do so and no prior authorization is required (further information is given on this in Chapter Seven, *Starting a Business*). Anyone in this category should apply for a *permesso di soggiorno* in just the way described above and the main difference is that when applying for the *libretto di lavoro*, evidence of having registered with the local Chamber of Commerce (*Camera di Commercio*) will be required instead of a contract of employment. This is usually a fairly simple matter and can be done once in Italy.

Entering with Retirement Status

Anyone intending to retire to Italy must be able to show proof of a pension with which to support themselves in order to obtain the *permesso di soggiorno*. As with all other groups of expatriates, the residence permit must be renewed annually and with this further proof of funds each year. Further information regarding residence regulations for those retiring to Italy is given in the *Retirement* chapter.

The Carta d'Identità

All residents, native and foreign, are required to carry an identity card (*Carta d'Identità*) with them at all times. This is a regulation which the majority of Italians comply with, without feeling that it is any kind of infringement of their personal liberty, and British expats should try to adopt a similarly positive attitude. Permanent residents are issued with the identity card, which includes the holder's nationality and passport number, for a cost of a few thousand lire from the *comune*. However, this card is not valid as a passport outside Italy except for Italian nationals.

Registering with the British Consulate

Expatriates should also register with the British Embassy or Consulate in Italy – a full list of which is provided below. This registration enables the UK authorities to keep emigrants up to date with any information they need to be aware of as British citizens resident overseas and also enables them to trace individuals in the event of an emergency. The Consulates can also help with information regarding an emigrant's status overseas and advise with any diplomatic or passport problems. They may also be able to help in an emergency eg. in the unfortunate event of the death of a relative overseas. However, the Consulates do not function as a source of general help and advice, nor act as an employment bureau and they make this quite obvious in response to any such appeals.

Italian Citizenship

Residency is not synonymous with citizenship and those who wish to be adopted as a citizen of their host country may find that they have some difficulty in doing so. Anyone who is married to an Italian national definitely has the balance tipped in their favour; they can apply for citizenship after a minimum of six months of marriage. Those resident in Italy but without the tactical advantage of an Italian spouse will need to have lived there for a minimum of two years before applying. However, unless you are such an Italophile that you feel it essential to drop all links with your British past, then it should be no inconvenience to retain British nationality as you will have most of the rights, and also obligations, of an Italian national; expatriates can even vote in local elections. However, British males resident in Italy are not liable to perform military service (*il servizio militare*) – probably a privilege regretted by very few.

Non-EU Nationals

Citizens of Eire, Australia and New Zealand may enter Italy for a three month period, after which time they will need to apply for a visa through their nearest consulate. All other nationals should consult the relevant embassies regarding visa requirements. The visa and entry section at the Italian Consulate in London is open to the public from Monday to Friday from 9am to 12 noon. Applications for all visas must be made in person and the length of time which the visa takes to be processed ranges from twenty-four hours to five weeks; non-EU nationals will usually have to wait as long as five weeks during the busy summer months. The visa itself currently costs about £15.

Work permits for non-EU nationals will be issued only to people outside Italy, and only for jobs where the provincial Office of the Ministry of labour is satisfied that no Italian can do the job. The *Autorizzazione al Lavoro* must then be presented at the Italian Embassy in the applicant's home country. In other words, they are virtually impossible to obtain, except for elite jobs.

Immigration

Italy is currently tightening its immigration laws in an effort to restrict the flood of immigrants (legal and illegal) from Eastern Europe and in particular Albania, also North Africa and the sub-Sahara. These immigrants, form Italy's 'underclass' and are the main pillar of Italy's flourishing black economy. The *clandestini* as they are known, work without being registered, their employers save up to 50% of their usual labour costs as there are no social security or holiday benefit payments to be made. Although the official immigration figure for Italy currently stands at around a million, the true figure is probably double that. To combat this problem, immigration legislation has been introduced, visa controls are being imposed and large numbers of police and military units have been deployed across the country's massive land frontiers and coast lines in a concerted effort to repel the swelling ranks of Italy's illegal immigrants. Most recently there has been an influx of Kurdish refugees from Turkey and Iraq. Areas where vigilance has been especially concentrated are Sicily, Calabria and Puglia in the south and Friuli in the north.

The problems of illegal immigration are not limited to volume but include organised crime; either the illegal immigrants end up working for the mafia or, in the case of Albanians they turn out to be more deadly than the mafia whom they have managed to intimidate and supplant in northern cities like Milan. One of the new Immigration Laws enables the Italian state to deport any *clandestino* found guilty of committing a crime on Italian territory. The same applies if they are found to have a previous criminal record, or if they refuse to produce proper identification.

If a *clandestino* is unable to produce identification, he or she can be held at a detention centre for a maximum of 30 days while identification is being sought.

As a kind of amnesty (Italy has had a couple in the past), *clandestini* already living in Italy without valid documents will be allowed to appeal to have their situation regularised, if they can show good reason why they should be allowed to stay, they will almost certainly be allowed to do so.

The Schengen Accord

The introduction of new immigration laws and the extra vigilance at vulnerable border areas in Italy is not unrelated to the Schengen Accord which became effective in Italy in October 1997. There are now fourteen countries signed up to Schengen: the Benelux countries, France, Germany, Spain, Portugal, Scandinavia including Norway and Iceland, Greece and Austria). So far the United Kingdom and Ireland have declined to participate in the Accord.

The Schengen countries have agreed to eliminate passport and baggage controls in the airports of their countries. In some cases this has meant modification of existing airports like the Malpensa 2000 airport in Milan (opening October 1998) to accommodate the increased traffic. The next phase, due to be brought in over the next few years, will be the elimination of land border and main seaport formalities between France and Italy.

The main fear of other Schengen countries, particularly France and Germany, is that illegal immigrants will still find it easier to enter Italy which has 8000 miles of coastline, than other countries and will then pass through Italy to the other European countries.

The Schengen agreement will also allow nationals of countries from outside the the EU to enter a member country through the normal passport controls and then move around freely amongst the Schengen Accord countries. This seems a little like leaving the front door open for the burglar. To counteract possible abuse by the criminal fraternity, the so-called Schengen Information System (SIS) will connect 189 Consulates and Embassies worldwide to a centralised data bank in Strasbourg where the names and details of all known criminals will be stored and which can be accessed from various terminals including those at border controls for citizens external to the EU. Authorisation can then be requested, and granted or denied to let someone through. How the data bank can be checked by private citizens (as they are allowed to do under protection of personal data regulations, Law 675/96), or updated are matters not yet clarified.

Sources of Information

Enquiries regarding immigration to Italy from the general public can be dealt with between 3pm and 4.30pm Monday to Thursday by telephoning the Italian Consulate (tel 0171-235 9371). Be prepared for a long wait as there is always a waiting list of calls. Considering the unsettled nature of Italian immigration policies at the moment, it would be a good idea to give the Consulate a call before leaving the country to get an update on the current situation. People living in Scotland or Northern Ireland should contact the Consulate in Edinburgh, while those from Bedfordshire, Cambridgeshire, Norfolk, Northamptonshire or Suffolk should apply to the Vice Consulate in Bedford and anyone living north of Birmingham and Wolverhampton to the Manchester-based consulate.

Inhabitants of Rome, its province or region, who are floundering helplessly in a sea of incomprehensible bureaucracy can call the emergency telephone line (06-884 8484) which dispenses invaluable advice on where to go, what you will need to take with you and what the cost is of all of those *certificati* and *permessi* which you now find you need. This is a free public service known as Socialtel, provided by a local government, university, trade union and telephone company amalgamation, formed in response to the numerous calls incited by the Italian bureaucratic system. This helpline also provides helpful advice about finding work in Italy and information about medical treatment.

Useful Addresses

Italian Embassies and Consulates in the United Kingdom & North America:
Italian Embassy: 14 Three Kings Yard, Davies Street, London W1Y 2EH; tel 0171-312   220 ; fax 0171-629 8200.
Italian Consulate General: 38 Eaton Place, London SW1; tel 0171-235 9371.
Italian Consulate General: 111 Piccadilly, Manchester M1 2HY; tel 0161-236 9024. Easier to get through to than the London Consulate. For latest regulations send a request and stamped addressed envelope to the Visa Department.
Italian Consulate General: 32 Melville Street, Edinburgh EH3 7HA; tel 0131-226 3631; 0131-220 3695.
Italian Vice Consulate: 7-9 Greyfriars, Bedford MK40 1HJ; tel 01234-356647. Operates 9.30am-12.30pm Monday to Friday.
Italian Embassy: 1601 Fuller Street NW, Washington DC 20009; tel 202-328-5500.
Italian Embassy: 21st Floor, 275 Slater Street, Ottawa, Ontario, KIP 5H9; tel 613-232240; fax 613 233 1484.
British Embassies and Consulates: (note that to dial Italy from the UK is 00 39 + area code, deleting the first zero).
British Embassy: Via XX Settembre 80a, 00187 Rome; tel 06-6797479/06-4825551/06-4825441. 8am-1pm & 2pm-4pm.
British Consulate: Viale Colombo 160, 09045 Quartu SF, Cagliari, Sardinia; tel 070-828628; fax 070-862293.
British Consulate: Palazzo Castelbarco, Lungarno Corsini 2, 50123 Firenze; tel

055-248133;fax 055 219112.

British Consulate: Piazza della Vittoria 15/16, Third Floor, Genoa; tel 10-564833; fax 10-5531516.British Consulate-General: Via Francesco Crispi 122, 80122 Napoli; tel 081-663511; fax 081-7613720.

British Consulate: Vicolo delle Ville 16, 34124 Trieste; tel (040) 764752.

British Consulate: Accademia, Dorsoduro 1051, 30123 Venezia; tel (041) 5227207.

Setting up Home

At the time of press it is evident the UK will not enter European Monetary Union 'in the first wave' of countries (which will include Italy, France, and Germany) in 1999. This is a further indication of Eurodoubt amongst an influential part of the British establishment which does not appear to have lessened since the last edition of this book. While the British government wrestles with the delicate subject of how European Britain should be, thousands of British citizens, have already voted with their feet to be fully integrated Europeans by setting up home in another EU country with France, Italy, Spain, Greece and Portugal being the most popular destinations. Over the past three decades, Italy has been the dream destination of thousands of European immigrants, particularly those who wish to escape the northern European winters and who also have a passion for Italian landscape and culture. They can be found in assorted properties including converted convents, shepherds' cottages, farmhouses, seaside flats, Renaissance villas and 18th century palazzi. For many foreign residents, the favoured regions are the picturesque provinces of Tuscany and Umbria and increasingly Le Marche. The number of British expatriates resident in Italy is estimated at around 40,000, with a further 20,000 owning holiday homes there. This is a small number compared with France and Spain which each has over twice as many British foreign residents as Italy does. Some might say this shows the exclusivity of Italy while others would point to the potential risks to property that may be subject to whims of the European fault line which runs through Italy. This causes reasonably frequent tremors to occur in Umbria, Tuscany etc. or serious damage, as shown by the 1997 earthquake in Umbria. On the plus side, at the time of press the strong pound meant that Italian property prices are again looking attractive to the British buyer. Also, for building work carried out during 1998 and 1999, including restructuring of private houses, the Italian government will allow 41% of costs incurred to be tax-deductible over a period of five years following completion of the work.

There is no disputing that Italy has glorious scenery, a nonpareil cultural heritage, and a relaxed lifestyle. In theory it is of course possible to buy property anywhere in the country, but in reality, it will depend on where you are working in Italy or where English-speaking estate agents are operating. The above-mentioned areas have been popular with overseas housebuyers for decades and so it is probably easier to find an English-speaking estate agent to look for suitable property there. Which is not to say that if you have set your heart on Liguria or the Italian Alps that you will not be able to find an agent for these areas as you undoubtedly will, but there will be fewer agents and it will take a bit longer to track them down.

There are other parts of Italy where attractions equal those of Tuscany and Umbria, these include Le Marche (pronounced markay) and north-eastern Puglia (pronounced poolia), Piedmont and Calabria. British-based estate agents barely cover these other regions, with the exception of Brian A. French and Associates (see below), Liguria specialist, Casa Travella or for Piedmont, Piedmont Properties. If you cannot find a property you want in the area of your choice, you will probably have no option but to make several trips to the region to find an agent in the locality or to deal directly with the vendor. Unless you have a thorough knowledge of the region in which you are interested, and have Italian friends and contacts, and/or you speak fluent Italian, the latter option would be like jumping overboard at shark feeding time. In other words getting through the buying procedure in one piece would be *un miracolo* so, unless you have very special connections, it is definitely not the recommended way to buy Italian property.

Property buying procedures in Italy are bound to be unfamiliar to the majority of expatriates and although this chapter explains the main processes involved, it is essential that professional advice both in the UK and locally is taken before any financial commitments are made. Such advice is easily obtainable from property agents and lawyers in the UK and Italy, and personal recommendations can be obtained from those who have already set up home in Italy.

At the time of going to press the property market in Britain has emerged from the recessionary paralysis of the initial 1990s. This means that selling your UK home should be easier and the likelihood of your making at least a modest profit greater, which is useful if you are intending to move to Italy permanently or intend to do a lot of restoration.

One of the advantages of the EU is the abolition of financial barriers between member states. One possibility arising from this is that if you are already an expatriate in France, Spain or Portugal and are trying to sell your property there in order to move to Italy and are having problems offloading it on the British market, you could try to sell to Italians. Until 1990 Italians were unable to buy property abroad because of government currency restrictions. Now that these have been completely abolished, Italians are snapping up properties in the above countries. Some Italian property agents may be able to help you with this and/or provide Italian contacts.

The Price of Property

Properties are advertised for sale in all the main Italian newspapers, but they tend to be city properties which are of interest only to a minority of foreigners. In ever popular Tuscany, price-tags can start at around £19,000 for a derelict farm house requiring three times that amount to restore it. However, more typical prices are £175,000+ for a farmhouse ready for occupation with 30 acres of land, and up to 1.3 million pounds for a dilapidated eighteenth century villa with twenty-five bedrooms and 350 hectares of land. Properties in need of restoration and those located far from the telephone, gas and electricity mains are always cheaper.

Umbria is slightly cheaper than Tuscany and some say, just as beautiful. Properties in Le Marche are cheaper all round: a habitable, three-bedroomed house would cost about £38,000 and a typical farm house with a little land and in need of restoration would be in the region of £70,000 to £80,000 (though as little as £19,000 is possible). In Abruzzo, further south, properties are even cheaper: a modern, furnished, two-bedroomed seaside apartment in Pescara would cost about £34,000 (unfurnished about £27,000). In Calabria which is generally overpriced and full of illegal developments it is still possible to find a a completely restored large house on three floors with a sea view for around £54,000.

How do the Italians Live

The Italian concept of home is virtually inseparable from the family. A high proportion of Italians therefore tend to live in a large family *appartamento* in a *palazzo*, which can mean a palace but is more likely (depending on the circles you move in) to refer to a fairly modest block of flats. Even when children do move out of the parental apartment, usually to get married, like as not they will voluntarily take a flat in the same block as their parents, thus keeping the umbilical cord intact. Despite families living on top of each other in this fashion, there are surprisingly few social problems, which may come as a surprise to Anglo-Saxons with their cherished belief that everyone needs a personal space in which to develop. However, in some areas this family proximity reaches undesirable extremes: in Naples for instance, overcrowding resulting from poverty and an acute housing shortage, means that sprawling families live in large single-room apartments, the notorious slums (*i bassi*) of that city. As a result of the way Italians live, irremediably bonded in tight family units, bachelor apartments or single accommodation (ie. small flats) are extremely difficult to find.

Another aspect of Italian life that is liable to come as a shock to an unsuspecting foreigner is the noise level in and around apartment blocks and other residences. Italians do seem to have an abnormally high decibel tolerance.

As in France, Spain etc. socializing with those outside the family circle does not usually take place around the family hearth, but in restaurants etc. Amongst younger Italians however, the custom of inviting friends home casually is catching on. Should you be invited into an Italian home, you will invariably find that, as with their persons, Italians keep their homes immaculately.

Owing to the ever-worsening traffic and public transport problems, there is a trend towards city-centre dwelling, usually in the old part *centro storico* which most Italian cities of any note possess. The area just outside the centre is known as *il semicentro* where most of the purpose-built palazzi are located. The suburbs, (*periferia*) are where the least well off generally live.

Council accommodation (*le case popolari*) does exist in Italy but it is an administrative disaster area and is nowhere near as widespread as in the UK or other EU countries. Council tenants are charged *equo canone* (fair rents) which is an understatement, since many have not been increased since the 1960s. In any case the question of council rents is an academic one since an estimated 80% of tenants have not paid any rent at all for the last decade. Around 78% of Italian families are owner occupiers; the rest live in rented accommodation (*un appartamento in affitto*).

Rich Italians looking for a second or holiday home in their own country rarely go for the type of quaint, rustic property favoured by foreign residents. They are more likely to buy or rent a luxury seaside flat or a house in the mountains.

Estate Agents

Whenever there is a boom in demand for Italian property, estate agents seem to leap out of nowhere, hit the ground running and then disappear or switch to another area of Europe when things go quiet. The real Italy specialists are likely to manage the leaner years by letting out Italian property, and improving their contacts ready for when the next boomlet occurs. They may be based in Italy or have long standing contacts based there. The Federation of Overseas Property Developers and Consultants (FOPDAC) represents a handful of British Agents dealing with Italy who meet their very strict criteria for membership. Italian estate agents (*agenzie immobiliari*) are not as numerous as you might expect as Italian buyers tend to buy privately from the vendor. The profession has however developed in Italy to the extent that all estate agents whether Italian or foreign, must be registered and have a document from the *comunale* (borough) attesting to their legality. The Italian association of real estate consultants is the AICI (Via Nerino 5, 20123 Milan; tel 02-725291; fax 02-86452597).

UK-based estate agents usually operate in conjunction with local associates in Italy who may be either English or Italian. A list of estate agents in the UK and Italy who deal in Italian property is given below.

Useful Addresses

Estate Agents in the UK & FOPDAC:

Brian A. French and Associates: tel 0171-735 8244. Offers the widest range of areas of any of the British agents including Tuscany, Umbria, Le Marche, Abruzzo and Calabria.

Babet Ltd: 6 North Street Farm Workshops, Stoke-sub-Hamdon, Somerset TA14 6QR; 01935-825772. Specializes in central and northern Tuscany and Umbria including the popular area of Lake Trasimeno; also Le Marche.

Chalcross: 18 Market Place, Chalfont St. Peter, Bucks SL9 9EA; tel 01753-886335; fax 01753-886336. Deals in property, for both renting and buying, particularly in Tuscany but also Umbria. Contact: Ken Arton.

Eurovillas: 36 East Street, Coggeshall, Essex CO6 1SH; tel 01376-561156. In business for 30-40 years. A letting agent for the Lake Garda area and Tuscany around Lucca. But can also provide purchasing contacts in these areas and can rent you a place from which to carry out a reconnaissance of likely properties.

Federation of Overseas Property Developers & Consultants (FOPDAC): P.O.Box 3534, London NW5; tel 0181-941 5588. Can supply a up-to-date list of a handful of members dealing with Italy.

Hello Italy: Woodstock, Forest Road, East Horsley, Surrey KT24 5ES; 901483-285002. Letting agent for northern Tuscany (about 30 minutes from the Ligurian coast). Can provide introductions to purchasing contacts in the area, help with restoration and building, and sales after care. Many clients who buy, have then used Hello Italy as a letting agent.

Piedmont Properties: 4 Beechcroft Close, Ascot, Berks SL5 7DB; tel 01344-624096; e-mail:(pp@smithgcb.demon.co.uk). Contact Angelika Smith-Aichbichler. Specialises in marketing villas and vineyards in the Monferrato and Langhe regions of Piedmont (south and west of Asti).

Undiscovered Tuscany: Woodstock, Forest Road, East Horsley, Surrey KT24 5ES; tel 01483 284011; fax 01483 285264. Started in 1987. Deals with property mainly in the Lake Como area (other lakes as well) and Liguria and Tuscany. Can arrange long and short term rentals and provide full property purchasing service. Contact: Linda Travella.

Estate Agents in Italy:
Concept Italia: via Vittorio Emmanuelle II 54, 55100 Lucca; tel +39 338 7127122; fax +39 583 32740939. Contact: Sally Adams.
La Rocca: Louise Rocca di Vecchi, via Torino 51, 20123 Milan; tel +39 2 7252141; fax +39 2 89010909. Covers all regions of Italy.
Michael Goodall: tel +39 577 941703. Property agent.
Giorgio Vigano: +39 003914. Milan estate agent deals with property all over Italy.
Villaman: Via di Cecina 610, 55029 Ponte a Moriano, Lucca; tel/fax +39 583 404066.

Useful Publications

Ville & Casali: Edizioni Living International (ELI) SpA, Via Anton Giulio Bragaglia, 33-00123 Rome; tel +39 6 30884122; fax +39 6 30889944. Ville & Casali is a national property and decoration magazine in Italian, the classified property advertisements are listed in both Italian and English.
Porta Portese: comes out in Rome on Tuesdays and Fridays and contains a useful accommodation section.

Home Swaps and Letting your UK Home

If you are not sure which region you would like to buy a property in, or you would like to 'try the region out', or if you would like to have a base from which to look around for a property, you might like to consider a home swap as a way to do this. There are branches of the main home swap organisations in Italy:

Useful Home Link Addresses

Home Link: Via Brescia 34, Rome; tel 06-8535424; fax 06-85354524.
Green Theme International: Euroculture, Via A Rossi 7, 36100 Vicenza. Home swaps for those who care about the impact of tourism on the environment and the culture of the country they are visiting who want to swap homes with like-minded travellers.
Homelink International: Casa Vacanze, Via San Francesco 170, 35121 Padua. Worldwide organisation with branches in 32 countries. Founded in 1952.
Intervac International Home Exchange: Via Oreglia 18, 40047 Riola (BO). Private organisation started in 1953 to give people the change of affordable holidays and to enable them to have a true experience of other ways of living.

There are various reasons why someone might not wish or need to sell their UK home but would prefer to let it in their absence. You should bear in mind that being an absentee landlord is not always a good idea, particularly if your visits to the UK are infrequent. There are companies that will act as your agents including TWG Estates Ltd (36/37 Maiden Lane, Covent Garden, London WC2E 7LJ; tel 0171-240 0300/e-mail twg.estates@virgin.net/fax 0171-836 1500. Relocation agent who provide a comprehensive service for those wishing to sell or rent out property located in London and the Home Counties while they are abroad.

Finance

Mortgages with Italian Banks

One of the easiest ways to finance buying an Italian home is from the proceeds of the sale of a UK property because this enables you to buy a house the way Italians usually do, by outright purchase in one go; though in Italy all the family will probably chip in. Mortgages (*ipoteche*) can be arranged with Italian banks in Italy, but bear in mind that they can be expensive. Also, financial sector services verge on the moribund (see *Banking* in *Daily Life*) and arranging a mortgage with an Italian bank can easily take one to three months – and that's just for the paperwork approving the loan!

Very few Italian banks will grant more than a 75% mortgage on a property ready for habitation. Abbey National in Milan might go up to 85% on some types of mortgage. A few banks offer a *mutuo per ristrutturazione* (a mortgage for properties requiring restoration) of 90%. Most Italian banks offer a choice of fixed or variable interest mortgages, *tasso fisso* and *tasso variabile* respectively. Some banks in the Mezzogiorno and Sardinia offer reduced interest rates (*abbattimento tasso*) in order to attract buyers to certain areas. Such banks include Banco Sardegna and the Cassa Risparmio Calabria. Most banks do not have an upper limit (*importo massimo*) on the amount of the mortgage; the few that do including Monte Paschi, Ambro Veneto and Banca di Sicilia vary from 100 to 200 million lire maximum.

Recent years have witnessed an increase in specialist mortgage departments of financial institutions in Italy, including Benetton and the Banca Nationale Agricultura (BNA) which can provide up to 80% mortgages over a fifteen year period. This could be a possibility for anyone earning an Italian salary.

Useful Addresses

Banca Nazione di Lavoro: Direzione Generale, Via Vittorio Veneto 119, 00187 Rome.

Banca Nazionale dell'Agricultura (BNA): Direzione Centrale, Via Salaria 231, 00199 Rome.

Banca Woolwich SpA: Milan Regional Office: Piazza della Repubblica 8, 20121 Milan; tel +39 2 290401; fax +39 2 290 40619.

Conti Financial Services: 204 Church Road, Hove, E Sussex BN3 2DJ; tel 0800 018 2811; fax 01273-321269. Conti have many years of experience arranging finance for clients (both UK and non-UK nationals) purchasing properties overseas and is an independent mortgage broker.

*Credito Romagnola:*Via Zamboni 20, 40126 Bologna.

Istituto Monte dei Paschi di Siena: U.S.I.E. Sett. Serv. V.le Toselli 60, 53100 Siena; tel 0577-294589.

Mortgages With UK Institutions in Italy

Banca Woolwich which operates in Italy provides banking services geared to Italians and expatriates living and working in Italy. At the time of press the Woolwich Bank was considering re-introducing their mortgage service for British residents buying holiday homes in Italy. For an up-date on this telephone the Woolwich Bank on 0181-298 4400 or try Banca Woolwich SpA in Milan (+39-2 584881. Abbey National have a branch in Florence (+39 55 500 1514) which could be useful for those already living in Tuscany and who speak Italian. If you are arranging a mortgage for an Italian property from outside Italy, you should deal with the Milan branch of Abbey National (Mr. Pietro Bertollo or John Dodds tel +39-2 66 72 910; fax +39-2 66988955).

Italian banks and financial institutions tend to process mortgage applications more slowly than British ones. For instance it takes a minimum of five days to get a mortgage approved with a UK building society or bank, compared with a minimum of one month with an Italian bank or financial institution. The main reason for this difference is that the client vetting procedures of the Italian banks are extremely cumbersome. However, increased competition from foreign organizations will undoubtedly compel Italian banks and finance institutions to streamline their procedures.

Useful Addresses

Abbey National Mutui S.p.A: Via G.Fara 27, 20124 Milan; tel 02-66729.1; fax 02-66988955.

Abbey National Mutui S.p.A. Via Dante 16. Milan; tel 02-72022881.

Abbey National Mutui S.p.A: Via Cicerone 58, 00198 Rome; tel 06-3214910; fax 06-3221536.

Abbey National Mutui S.p.A: Via San Tommaso 24, 10121 Torino; tel 011-542000; fax 011-546110.

Abbey National Mutui S.p.A: Via Nicolo Putignani, 137, 70122 Bari; tel 080-5237030.

Banca Woolwich SpA: Via Pantano 13, 20122 Milano; 20122 Milano; tel 02-584881; fax 02-58488511.

Woolwich Europe Ltd: 30 Erith Road, Bexley Heath, Kent DA7 6BP; tel 0181-298 4771; fax 0181-298 5315.

ECU/Euro Mortgages

When Britain joined the European Rate Mechanism (ERM) in October 1990, interest grew in ECU mortgages. The ECU, or European Currency Unit is a compilation of EU currencies, dominated by the Deutschmark, the Community's strongest currency at present. The ECU is a currency in its own right and can be lent or borrowed like any other currency. Interest rates for ECU loans have been generally lower than in other currencies like the lire and sterling. However the ECU rate is by no means exempt from fluctuations which are dictated by the movements of the currencies of which it is comprised. From 1990 to 1991 the ECU remained remarkably stable; however, since its greatest component is the Deutschmark, a sharp decline in the German economy has the greatest adverse effect on the ECU.

In January 1999 when countries participating in EMU (European Monetary Union) jointly switch to Euros, ECUs will be transformed into Euros at the rate of one for one.

UK Mortgages

It is extremely unusual for a British building society or bank to lend money for the purchase of a property abroad. However a number of people have managed to buy homes abroad by remortgaging or taking out a second mortgage on their UK property in order to pay in cash in Italy. The property owner should be aware that he or she is liable to lose some UK tax relief if a UK property is remortgaged and if part of the original loan was used for home improvement or capital raising. It is worth noting that if you currently have relief on loans available prior to 1988, then you could lose this.

Offshore Mortgages

Another option open to expatriates is to take out an offshore mortgage. Expatriates with substantial assets usually deposit them in one of the world's tax havens where their investments attract tax-free interest. For those with less impressive portfolios, such as first time buyers with their sights set on a modest Umbrian farmhouse in need of renovation, there are no particular advantages in offshore mortgaging, as the administration fees would almost certainly outweigh any tax gains.

The way an offshore mortgage works is that initially the house purchaser sets up a trust fund with one of the many offshore companies, the addresses of many of which can be found in expatriate magazines (eg. *Resident Abroad*). In order to purchase property, the trust is then used to form a limited company which purchases the property on behalf of its shareholders. An independent mortgage broker such as Simon Conn (01273-772811) should be able to advise you on this.

The Purchasing and Conveyancing Procedure

Professional Assistance

The official usually appointed to handle a property sale is a *notaio* (public notary) who in Italy acts for both the vendor and the purchaser. There are also some lawyers (*avvocati*) who are qualified to handle property transactions. Foreigners, who are generally not versed in Italian property buying procedures may wish to appoint both a notaio and an avvocato. There are a few Italian lawyers based in the UK who will protect your interests (see addresses below) when you are buying Italian property. The notaio's responsibility is to gather together all the necessary documents, check that the title deeds are in order and that the property is legally registered and has no illegal buildings on it. Having ascertained that this is the case, the next step is for the purchaser and vendor to sign a preliminary contract of sale.

You may also want to call on the services of a surveyor (*geometra*) to check the soundness of the building, point out any structural defects and estimate the cost of putting them right. Unlike in Britain however, surveys are not compulsory and many Italians do not bother with them. For foreigners buying older buildings, especially those in need of restoration, a survey is almost certainly essential.

A *geometra* can draw up contracts, carry out land searches, monitor building work and make orders to suppliers.

Italian lawyers based in the UK

Giovanni Lombardo Dobson & Sinisi, 1 Throgmorton Avenue, London EC2N
  2JJ; tel 0171-731 8304 or 0171-628 8163.

Claudio del Giudice: 5-7 Folgate Street, London E1 6BX; tel 0171-377 1138.

For Italian lawyers in Italy who are members of the British Chamber of
Commerce in Milans, see list of *Major Employers* in the *Employment* chapter.

The Compromesso

The *compromesso* or preliminary sale agreement outlines the conditions of
purchase and any get-out clauses for the prospective purchaser, which may be
applicable in some circumstances. These may include planning permission not
being granted or failure of the purchaser's mortgage application. The
compromesso also sets a date by which the transfer of property will be completed.
Alternatives to the Compromesso: *Promessa d'Acquisto* (purchase proposal) or
Promesso di Vendita (promise of sale) are sometimes used.

Once either of the above documents has been authenticated the purchaser then
pays a deposit (*caparra*) which is usually about 10% but can be up to 30% of the
purchase price and is deductible from it. The *caparra* is forfeited if the purchaser
backs out of the agreement for a reason not covered by the compromesso.
Likewise, if the vendor backs out of the sale, or does not hand over the property
by the date given in the compromesso, then he or she is legally obliged to
reimburse the vendor with double the amount of the *caparra*.

The Rogito and Under-Declaration of Value

The *rogito* is a legally binding deed that transfers ownership of the property to the
purchaser. Once the conditions of the promesso have been fulfilled and the
balance has been handed over, the rogito can be drawn up by the *notaio*. The
rogito includes a declaration of the price at which the property changed hands.
The price on the rogito and the actual price paid can be vastly different. The
purpose of this typically Italian wheeze is to avoid paying capital gains tax. By
under-declaring the property's price considerable savings can be made on Capital
Gains Tax which is charged at between ten and forty per cent. In some areas,
property values are well known and to under-declare excessively would be to
arouse the suspicion of the tax authorities who are then liable to make their own
snap judgement on the property's worth and tax accordingly. In the vicinity of
Rome, or big cities in the north, under-declaration is usually a modest 10% to
20%. In less well-documented rural areas like Umbria, Abruzzo, Calabria etc.
under-declarations of up to 60% are commonplace. When negotiating the price to
be entered on the *rogito* the purchaser should be aware that the Italian
government, in its pursuit of lost revenue, is tightening up its controls, by
encouraging local authorities to revise their estimates of local property values to a
more realistic level. However, this will almost certainly not result in stamping out
the practice. Moreover, if you are perverse enough to insist on declaring the actual
price, the Italians are liable to consider you intellectually challenged.

Charges for Property Purchase

There are a number of charges payable by new purchasers of property. These
include the notary's fees which are usually 2-3% of the amount shown on the
rogito, the estate agent's commission (usually 3% of the actual purchase price)
and the fees of any other professionals (eg. lawyer, accountant surveyor etc.)

whose services have been engaged by the purchaser. In addition, new owners pay land registration fees (stamp duties), which vary according to the type of property involved. The highest fees are for agricultural land (17%) and the lowest for new properties purchased from the developer (4%); on other houses and apartments the rate is 11%. If you are buying new property, IVA (Italian VAT) is payable at 10% of the value. All rates are calculated on the price declared on the rogito. Typically, total charges come to around 12% of the purchase price compared with about 2% in the UK, 10% in Spain and Portugal and as much as 15% in France.

Ownership of Property and Land

Normally sane foreigners looking for land or property abroad can sometimes develop a light-headedness in the Tuscan or Umbrian air, that apparently causes them to abandon any caution that they would normally exercise when buying a house or land in their home country. Having appointed a representative to handle a property transaction it is essential that the buyer ensures that the title deeds to the property are in order. It is also a good idea to find out whether any major developments are imminent in the immediate vicinity. This can best be done by making local enquiries, particularly amongst the inhabitants of the region. It also gives you a chance to make contact with prospective neighbours. You should also check on the likelihood of a *coltivatore diretto* being exercised (see below).

Coltivatore Diretto

One of the potential hazards lying in wait for the unsuspecting foreigner who is considering buying land and property in Italy is the *coltivatore diretto* (farmer's right). This Italian law enables smallholders to increase the size of their farms by giving them the right to buy land or buildings adjacent to their property for up to two years after it has been sold. The *coltivatore diretto* is dependent upon the farmer being able to pay the price on the rogito. If the figure on the *rogito* is a gross under-declaration of the property's value (see details above) the foreign purchaser is liable to find a chortling peasant gloating over his former luxury villa and swimming pool which he can obtain at a knock-down price, unless that is, steps are taken to preclude the possibility of such an occurence. The best way to do this is for the prospective purchaser's legal representative to furnish the farmer with a Special Delivery document, asking the farmer to confirm within 30 days whether he or she intends to exercise a coltivatore diretto. If, when thirty days have elapsed the farmer has not expressed his intention to claim the land, he then waives any future right to do so.

The coltivatore diretto is only applicable to rural property registered as a *casa rurale*. Houses designated *case urbane* carry no such risk.

The coltivatore diretto can also work in favour of the foreign resident who wishes to preserve his or her privacy. In order to qualify for a *coltivatore diretto* you have to earn at least 70% of your income from agriculture or agro-tourism (bed and breakfast, riding holidays etc.). Not only will foreigners registered as coltivatore diretto be able to stop anyone building in uncomfortable proximity, but they may also be eligible for government grants and soft loans (see Chapter Seven, *Starting a Business*).

Obtaining Planning Permission

As with many things in Italy, it can be difficult to perceive any consistency in official procedures, and planning permission is no exception. In some areas, it is obvious by the way monstrous blocks of flats have been built without any regard for their surroundings that they are illegal constructions. However, such is the lack of resources for dealing with the legislation and enforcing it, that the perpetrator usually pays a fine and the building remains. Areas where planning regulations are pretty rigorously enforced include Tuscany and Le Marche. Many see this is a blessing as it has meant that the landscapes have never been spoiled by unsightly buildings. If you put up a building in the Tuscan countryside, it has to be made from local materials. In Le Marche, you are not allowed to build new property in the countryside, (except farm buildings). However, you can restore existing buildings.

Estate agents who deal in land, normally do so only for terrain for which planning permission *permessi communali* has been granted. If for some reason you find yourself interested in a piece of land for which permission has not been granted then you should allow about three months to complete this process. You can find out if planning permission has already been granted by checking with the *comunale* (town hall). You should do this in any case rather than just accept the word of the vendor. One of the main problems for illegal buildings is that they cannot be connected to gas, water, telephone etc.

Renting Property

Those who are employed by British or other foreign companies in Italy will most probably have their accommodation arranged for them as part of an overseas job package. Those who arrange their own jobs in Italy will have to make their own accommodation arrangements. It is no less difficult finding property to rent in most of the big Italian cities than it is in a British or French one, and cost can be a problem. Although not high by British standards, rents in Italy when measured against Italian salaries can be expensive. If you decide to do as the Italians do and have three jobs and not pay any, or minimal tax, then you will probably not find this a undue hardship. As already mentioned, Italians tend to live in large family apartments and so the main difficulty for foreigners is to find single accommodation, which is comparatively scarce. You can get round this by staying as a lodger with an Italian family. However, Italians tend to be very welcoming and this can be claustrophobic for those who are used to having a place of their own.

Those intending to buy property in Italy in order to become resident on a long-term or permanent basis will probably want to rent a villa, farmhouse. apartment etc. to use as a base from which to look for a property to buy or in order to decide in which area to settle. There are a number of firms offering holiday rentals and a full list may be obtained from the Italian State Tourist Office (see below).

Useful Addresses

Eurovillas Italy: 36 East Street, Coggeshall, Essex CO6 1SH; tel 01376-561156. Rents property in Tuscany; can also arrange sales.
Hello Italy: Woodstock, Forest Road, East Horsley, Surrey KT24 5ES; 901483-285002. Letting agent for Lunigiana, northern Tuscany (about 30 minutes

from the Ligurian coast). Can provide introductions to purchasing contacts in the area, help with restoration and building, and sales after care. Many clients who buy, have then used Hello Italy as a letting agent.

Italian State Tourist Office: 1 Princes Street, London W1R 8AY; tel 0171-408 1254.

Tailormade-Tours: 22 Church Rise, Forest Hill, London SE23 2UD; tel 0181-291 1450. Holiday properties in Tuscany and Umbria for rent. Does not help arrange sales/purchase.

Vacanze in Italia, The Courtyard, Bignor, Pulborough, West Sussex RH20 1QD (01798 869426) has several hundred properties covering most areas of Italy, but concentrated in Tuscany and Umbria.

Where to Look for Accommodation

Apart from following up *affitasi* (to let) signs outside palazzi, the other obvious place to look for accommodation is in the classified sections headed *appartamenti da affittare* (flats to let), of main local papers such as *Il Messaggero* a Roman daily and in the free newspapers which are published in most major cities. In the Milan area there are often accommodation advertisements in the bi-weekly publication *Seconda Mano* published on Mondays and Thursdays and available from news-stands. For other papers see the section, *Media and Communications* in Chapter Four, *Daily Life*. You may also wish to consult one of the relocation specialists (see page 174) that offer accommodation services to individuals. The MORE agency, based in Milan with representatives in major cities, has in the past been able to find rooms for foreigners with employment, but no accommodation. Another possible alternative would be to consult university noticeboards and even the noticeboards of large international companies and organizations where adverts for accommodation are displayed, primarily for the benefit of staff, but potentially useful to outsiders brazen enough to use them *in extremis*.

Useful Terms:

un apartamento ammobiliato: a furnished apartment. Naturally, more expensive than an unfurnished (*da ammobiliare*) one.

attico: it may be an attic in the country, but in the city it means a penthouse.

il bagno: bathroom.

il balcone: self explanatory; also called la terazza.

la cucina: kitchen.

la salla da pranzo: dining room.

un giardino: garden. Not many flats or palazzi have these, even on the ground floor.

monolocale con servizi: one-room with kitchen and bathroom. Average price around £350 a month but difficult to find.

piano: floor. *primo/secondo/terzo piano* (first/second/third floor).

il portiere: doorman/janitor in charge of a block of flats.

il salotto: (sitting-room). For many Italian families this doubles as an extra bedroom.

i servizi: kitchen and bathroom. Advertisements do not include these when giving the number of rooms.

stanze: room. *un appartamento di due/tre/ quattro stanze* a two/three/four-roomed flat.

stanze da letto: bedroom.

terra: ground floor.

un villino: cottage.

Tenancy Laws

Obtaining a tenancy agreement is undoubtedly easier if you are a non-resident since anyone with *residenza* status is protected by state laws from being evicted (*sfrattato*). The length of rental contracts varies but is normally for four years. When the landlord or lady (*padrone/padrona*) wishes to have the property back the tenant (*inquilino*) will be sent a notice to quit.

Communal Apartment Blocks

In Italy, a communal apartment block is known as a *condominio*. As virtually all Italian property is sold freehold, it is not necessary to pay ground rents to a landlord who is reponsible for the upkeep of the building, as is usual in London. The Italian arrangement (becoming more common in UK) is that the residents have to make all the decisions regarding the upkeep and repair of the communal parts of the building; the roof, lifts, hallways, central plumbing and heating, etc. and are jointly responsible for the cost. If you are renting a flat in a condo, you will presumably have an agreement with the owner, about who is going to pay the communal charges set out in the building's convenant. Important decisions concerning the future running of the building are made by the residents at the residents' meetings (*riunione di condominio*) which are held at not less than one year intervals.

In blocks of flats containing five or more apartments it is obligatory for the owners to appoint an agent *amministratore del condominio* to manage the property on behalf of the owners.

Letting Out Property

Once your Italian property is furnished, letting it out can be a useful way of helping to pay off the cost, particularly if it is a second home. It is worth remembering that if your property is in a rural area of Tuscany, Umbria etc. the main letting period will be from spring to autumn. The income you can expect will vary according to the degree of luxury offered and whether the let is in high season (July and August), mid-season (June and September) or low (April, May and October). Rentals range from about £200 for a studio apartment to £1,700 a week for a seaside villa. Rentals are usually a week or longer. In the main season two weeks is usual while out-of-season lets tend to be shorter. It is possible to let to Italians or foreigners; including the British. Of course not everyone relishes the idea of a constant stream of strangers marching through their property inflicting additional wear and tear but you can always stipulate no animals, small children or pop stars if you are particularly fastidious about your furnishings. For those who decide to go ahead and hire out their villa, farmhouse or seaside apartment, there is no shortage of holiday villa rental companies which can be approached and the Italian State Tourist Office can provide a list. Such companies include Eurovillas (tel 01376-561156).

Insurance and Wills

Italy has a bad reputation for burglary and theft, though this is much worse in the cities than in country areas where villagers often leave their homes unlocked. The rates of crime detection are appalling – less than 10% of burglaries are solved. As a result, premiums are high and because it it is expensive to ensure house contents, most Italians do not bother. Foreign residents from Britain will find that insurance quotes from Italian firms are at least double what they would expect to pay in the UK. Turin and Milan have some of the highest premiums in Italy. Italian insurance companies are also notoriously slow about settling claims.

Estate agents sometimes offer their clients house and contents insurance at competitive rates and it is worth asking them about this. British company, Holiday Homes Insurance, will insure rural properties in Italy. Annual rates vary depending on the extent of the cover but are roughly £3.50 per £1,000 of the house value and £6 per £1,000 of the contents value. On a typical property valued at £50,000 with contents worth £10,000 the annual premium would be around £277 for the first year. Although the company specializes in holiday home insurance they will continue to insure property after Italian residency has been granted, providing that the premiums are settled in sterling. It is important to note that if you are moving to the earthquake zone, most insurance policies exclude earthquake damage.

Owing to the difficulty of insuring city apartments, it is prudent to take anti-burglar precautions: multiple locks and bars on ground floor windows are two of the absolute basic requirements.

Useful Addresses:

Andrew Copeland: contact Roy Thomas (0181-656 8435).
Holiday Homes Insurance: Scottish Mutual House, 27-29 North Street, Hornchurch, Essex RM11 1RS; tel 01708-458222; fax 01708-453555.
John Holman: 01277-633345. Has overseas house-insurance designed for owners of property in Europe (expatriate and holiday homes).
Barlow Redford & Co: 71a High Street, Harpenden, Herts. AL5 2SL; tel 01582-761129; fax 01582-462380.
O'Halloran and Co: 01522-537491. Will arrange cover for holiday homes in Europe.
Property Insurance Abroad: P O Box 150, Rugby CV22 5BR; tel 01788-550294; fax 01788 562579. Will provide a free quote.
Jon Wason: 72 South Street, Reading, RG1 4RA: 01734-568800. Does basic expatriate homes cover. Will also insure holiday homes abroad.
Woodham Group Ltd.: 1 Goldsworth Road, Woking, Surrey GU21 1JX; tel: 01483-770787. Insurance Consultants linked to Holmans (above).

Wills

It is unlikely that anyone who has accumulated assets in the form of property in Italy will not have made a will leaving it to their heirs or directing it to be sold and the proceeds distributed amongst the heirs. Under Italian law a foreigner's will, drawn up outside Italy is deemed to be governed by the laws of the foreigner's nationality. Therefore a British subject can make a will in the Anglo-Saxon form or Scottish form and it may be executed in Italy. If the will is straightforward, ie. the property goes directly to the remaining spouse or the children there will be no problem. However, theoretically, problems could occur when Anglo-Saxon Common Law clashes with Roman Law as practised in Italy. In Anglo-Saxon law, executors are appointed by the deceased to administer the will according to his or her wishes. Under Italian law, the death duties paid on the estate are minimal on bequests to next of kin and swingeing on distant or non-relatives; the concept of an intermediary ownership as practised by English executors does not exist and it therefore poses a problem for Italian lawyers who must reach some kind of compromise. In order to keep complications to a minimum it is advisable to have a will drawn up by a lawyer with experience of both the Italian and the British legal systems.

Utilities

It is important for anyone contemplating a move to Italy to be aware that if their property is not already connected to the gas or water mains, or is without electricity, they may have a long wait in store before their arrival. Also the further away the property is from the nearest telephone line, or mains, the greater the cost of linkage. Such costs can add considerably to the price of an Italian property and you should therefore expect to pay a lower price for property without utilities than would be asked for a property with them.

In Italy it is unwise to delay paying your bills: whereas in the UK it is customary to be sent a politely-worded reminder from BT, British Gas etc. that you have seven days left to settle the bill, in Italy there is no such finesse and services are liable to be cut off peremptorily from subscribers whose payments are overdue. Conversely, getting reconnected can take an inordinate length of time.

Electricity

The national electricity company is *Ente Nazionale per l'Energia Elettrica* (ENEL). Before you can be plugged into it, an ENEL inspector will have to ascertain that the wiring and earthing that you have had installed meets ENEL specifications. It is important that if your property is being wired for the first time, the electrician is aware that you wish to be connected to the national supply, as some householders prefer to run a private generator; in such cases the wiring may be done to a lower standard. Once the ENEL inspector is satisfied, you will be allowed to take out a contract with the electricity company on a non-resident or a resident basis. The latter is preferable as non-residents pay a premium rate. In order to obtain a resident's contract one needs to produce a residence certificate (see *Residence and Entry Regulations* chapter.

In very rural areas where the lines are strung out for miles, the power can be feeble or subject to wild fluctuations which can be damaging to sensitive electronic equipment including television.

The easiest way to pay bills is by direct debit from your bank. The electricity company bases its bills on estimated consumption and biannually adjusts them to the exact amount. The adjusted bills are invariably a bit of a shock.

At the time of press ENEL is about to be privatised and its monopoly on importing electrical power (which currently comes from Switzerland or France) will expire at the end of 1998.

Gas

Gas is widely used in northern Italy for central heating and cooking. Most cities and large towns are supplied by the *Societe Italiana per il Gas* (SIG). Unfortunately the SIG network does not penetrate rural areas or any of the south including Tuscany and Umbria where many foreign residents buy homes. For inhabitants of these areas who wish to have central heating, the solution is a gas tank, known rather alarmingly in Italian as a *bombolone*. Gas tanks can be loaned from the larger gas companies and installation is governed by strict regulations. The property owner must provide a concreted site for the tank and it must be surrounded by a padlocked, metal fence. The site must also be equipped with a fire extinguisher-scarcely effective, one would imagine, in the event of a bombolone igniting. For obvious reasons, the tank should not be immediately adjacent to the house or road, which means that pipes have to be laid to connect the supply to the house. The contract with the gas company supplying the liquid gas will stipulate a minumum annual purchase usually in the region of £800, and additionally, that the gas will only be used for heating and hot water. The size of the tank depends on your needs and the number of deliveries etc. Your gas company should advise.

Potentially less nerve-racking than living with a bombolone is the ubiquitous gas bottle (*bombola*), which is used in rural areas for cooking. It can also be used for heating: in Italy as in other Continental countries, special heating appliances for use with bottled gas are available. For those who do not wish to go to the bother or expense of arranging connection with mains gas, particularly if their Italian home is only used for holidays, the bombola is a useful alternative to mains gas. Unlike mains gas there is no difference in the rate for residents and non-residents and it can usually be delivered.

Water

Italy's notorious water shortage may not be acute by Saharan standards, but it can still be a possible inconvenience some people thinking of setting up home in Italy (apart from in the north). In summer, the water supply is liable to be cut off during the day and resumed at night. For this reason it is essential for those in rural areas and in the south to have a storage tank (*cassone*) which can be topped up when the water supply is on. For those living in flats in the main cities a 500 litre tank may be sufficient. In isolated dwellings in the rural south it may be necessary to store several months' supply of water in huge underground tanks. If the water in your area is metered (most of northern Italy already is) water is rationed to a fixed number of litres per house, regardless of the number of occupants.

The water supply is under the control of the local *comune* and there are conditions governing the various uses of this often precious commodity. For instance if you wish to water a garden, a separate contract from that which deals with household water becomes necessary. With such rigid controls it is perhaps no surprise that swimming pools are out of the question in some areas, which can come as a shock to the sybaritic foreign resident. However, for the clued-up and those with a little ingenuity, there are solutions for both gardeners and swimmers. It is possible to recycle water used for washing and bathing for the garden by draining it into a separate tank. Water thus recycled should not however contain bleach or detergent or the results will be disastrous. Pure soap suds on the other hand are harmless to plants. The way round the swimming pool ban is to build what is a called a *vasca*. A vasca is an artificial water basin common in rural areas and ostensibly for domestic use when the mains water is cut off. The idea is that it fills up during the winter when rain is plentiful; it may also be fed by a spring or well. With a proper lining and some kind of filtering system to keep the water pure, a vasca could be used as a swimming pool, the less obviously, the better.

Nothing beats having mains water for convenience, and for peace of mind a contingency plan (ie. storage tank) for when the supply is cut off. If you are lucky enough to have a well (*pozzo*) on your land, so much the better as this will make life a great deal easier. When looking for property to buy, it is advisable to take into account the water situation in the locality. You may even wish to call in the services of a water-diviner (*rabdomante*). Probably the most inconvenient position for anyone living in Italy is to be marooned in an isolated house in the dry south, with no mains water and no well. In such cases it is possible to have water delivered by tanker as happens in Portugal and Spain. However this service does not come cheaply and is far from being convenient.

Telephones

A decade or so of modernisation has transformed the Italian telephone service from one that inflicted daily outrages on its subscribers and made new ones liable to scandalous delays for a telephone installation, to a thoroughly modern telecommunications system. In October 1997, Telecom Italia was privatised and in January 1998 deregulation meant competition was introduced. This is not to say that there may not be problems for those living in rustic isolation who want to be connected – the cost of erecting a line of telegraph poles as well as the installation charges may still be prohibitive.

With the opening up of Italy's telecommunications to international consortia comes the end of the monopoly of Telecom Italia (the state telephone company). STET the Italian state telecommunications giant was merged with its subsidiary Telecom Italia which became the overall name in 1997). No longer are subscribers told which gadgets they may or may not plug their line into. Cordless telephones, fax and answering machines are offered in a profusion of choice which brings its own irritations in terms of having to change provider frequently as better and better deals come along.

Bills, though they may be coming down if you choose wisely, may still inflict some nasty surprises as wild inaccuracies in the company's favour; a problem for which there is very little remedy. You could try installing a metering device (*indicatore di conteggio*) . Should you convince the company of your right to a rebate, it is doubtful whether you could ever manage to obtain it. Bills are usually paid by banker's order. You should note that as in the UK, directory enquiries are chargeable to your account.

The Italians have taken to mobiles (*telefonini*) in a big way. The main providers are TIM and OMNITEL. For more information see *Telecommunications* in *Daily Life*.

Yellow Pages (pagine gialle) directories are issued on a regional basis, free of charge.

Regional Taxes

The main regional tax in Italy *Imposta Locale sui Redditi* (ILOR) was replaced in January 1998 by a new tax IRAP for which companies and organisations, individual entrepreneurs, professionals, artists will all be liable. IRAP also covers health contributions (*tasse sulla salute*) and is a tax on goods produced and services supplied. The basic rate is 4.25% with a lower rate for agriculture (3%) and a higher one for financial services including banking and insurance. There is also an additional regional tax attached to IRAP which will start off at between 0.5% and 1.1% to compensate the regions for other taxes like ICIAP which has also been abolished. It is planned that IRAP will be paid in the same way as income tax (i.e. two estimated tranches due in May and November).

Householders in Italy pay rates for rubbish disposal (*nettezza urbana*) and water rates (*acquedotto comunale*, both of which are calculated on the square meterage of the floor area of the property. House owners with their own water

supply (ie. well or spring) are exempt from water rates.
For more information on paying taxes see *Daily Life, Taxation.*

Removals

The amount of moveable possessions that a prospective foreign resident will take with them to Italy is likely to vary considerably. Generally speaking however, anyone setting up home in Italy will want to export a large enough quantity of bulky possessions to require the service of a professional removal company with international expertise. Before calling in the removers, there are naturally a number of bureaucratic formalities to be dealt with. The first step is to submit a list of the items you wish to import into Italy to the nearest Italian Consulate (see Chapter Two, *Residence and Entry Regulations* for addresses) who will officially stamp it. You must also apply for a *permesso di soggiorno* from the *questura* (police station).

Having obtained both documents you are ready to approach the removal firm who will require both the list stamped by the Consulate, the *permesso* and copies of documents relating to your ownership of property in Italy. If you have not been resident in Italy long enough to have obtained the *permesso* you should obtain an attestation from the commune to the effect that you have purchased or leased accommodation in the area.

Removal Firms

There are a number of large firms which specialize in removals abroad and it makes sense to consult one of these. A list of such companies will be sent by The British Association of Removers (3 Churchill Court, 58 Stations Road, North Harrow, Middlesex HA2 7SA) in return for a stamped addressed envelope. Be sure to ask for a list of international removers as these are a subgroup of the association's members. The BAR also publishes a free leaflet of handy hints for those contemplating removals overseas, available from the same address.

Useful Addresses
Baxter's International Removers: Brunel Road, off Rabans Lane, Aylesbury HP19 3SS; tel 01296-393335. Specializes in removals to Italy and Germany.
American Services Srl: Via Giacosa 3, 20050 Taccona di Muggio, Milano; tel 039/746181; fax 039-746429. National and Internation removals.
Bolliger Srl: Via N Palmieri 46; 20154 Milano; tel 02-844721; fax 02-89501233. International removals.
Franzosini SPA, International Removers: In business since 1845. Milan: 02-2640320; Rome: 06-6554824.
Interdean: European wide removals. Contact Mr. Benedetto tel 0181-961 4141; also has an office in Milan.
I.T.G. Srl: Via Edison 116; 20019 Settimo Milanese, Milano; tel 02-48910176. National and international removals and transport.
R.C. I B Group Srl-UTS: Via Vittadini 3, 20136 Milano; tel 02-58315516; fax 02-58318554. Domestic and international removals. Air sea freight forwarders.
Vinelli & Scotto: Move Plus International, Via A.M. Ampere 97, Milan; tel 02-26140557; fax 02-26140341; also at Venaria (Torino), Viale delle Industrie 22. Venaria; tel 011-736408; fax 011-736512.

General Import Conditions

The good news for those importing household goods into Italy is that there are no regulations about how long they must have been in your possession. However, a large selection of expensive, pristine equipment would undoubtedly arouse the avaricious instincts of the customs so it is advisable that such items show a few obvious signs of wear and tear in order not to attract import duty and VAT. The only regulation is that items must be imported within six months of taking up residence in Italy.

If you decide to take a loaded van of furniture and other items for your home from the UK to Italy, you should have no problems. If you are driving through Switzerland to get to Italy and you are stopped by Swiss customs, you should inform the Swiss customs that you are in transit to another EU country.

Importing a Car

Whereas non-residents may freely drive back and forth between the UK and their Italian holiday home with British car registration documents and an EU or International Driving Licence, residents are obliged to either officially import their British registered vehicle or buy one in Italy. In order to import a British-registered vehicle, it must have been in the importer's possession outside Italy for at least a year. On arrival at customs, the owner must present the registration documents, proof of insurance and a certificate of residence. After checking the vehicle against the documents the customs will issue a customs receipt (*bolleta doganale*). The owner may then drive the car with foreign plates for up to a year before the car has to be registered in Italy. There is no duty or VAT levied on cars imported in this manner, but it is a once in a lifetime concession.

To register a foreign vehicle in Italy it must first pass a *collaudo*, the Italian equivalent of an MOT. From then on the process becomes the usual Italian, time-consuming rigmarole. No wonder most people are happy enough to call on the services of one of the specialist agencies (*agenzie pratiche auto*) that wade through the necessary procedures on your behalf. Once the collaudo has been obtained it must be taken with all the car documents and a residence certificate, to a notaio who will apply for the car registration at the local (*Uffizio della Motorizzazione Civile e dei Trasporti in Concessione*) and register the vehicle with the local *Pubblico Registro Automobilistico*. The car will then be issued with a registration certificate (*carta di circolazione*). Licence plates (*foglio di circolazione*) are issued by the *Pubblico Registro Automobilistico*. Registration costs vary according to car size but in any case will not be less than £100.

Following registration you become liable for car tax. Note that from 1998 it will no longer be necessary to display a car tax disk (*bollo*) on the windscreen. You will also need an insurance badge (*contrassegno*). There are additional taxes for diesel driven cars and radios (but not cassette players).

For further information about driving in Italy, the rules of the road, buying or selling a car and insurance see *Daily Life, Cars & Motoring*.

Useful Addresses

Automobile Association (AA): Import Section, Fanum House, Basingstoke Hants RG21 2EA; tel 01256-20123. Information is supplied only to members of the AA. Ask for information on the permanent importation of a vehicle into Italy. For membership details contact your nearest AA office.

Automobile Club d'Italia (ACI): Via Marsala 8, 00185 Rome; tel 06-49981.

Importing Pets

The British are renowned for being inseparable from their pets, especially dogs and cats, affection for which often seems greater than for fellow human beings. To the Italians who reserve all doting pride for their children, a dog tends to be more of a fashion accessory than a faithful companion. It is a reasonably straightforward process taking man's best friend with you to your new home in Italy providing you take care to follow the regulations.

The animal must have a certificate of health issued by a British veterinarian who is registered as an inspector of the Ministry of Agriculture, Fisheries and Foods. A list of vets who have this designation is available from the Ministry of Agriculture. The certificate must be translated into Italian and accompanied by an additional certificate attesting to the animal having received a rabies innoculation not less than twenty days and not more than eleven months prior to crossing the Italian border.

Regulations now in force in most areas compel owners to have their dogs tatooed on the body as a means of registration. A more recent alternative to the tatoo, is for the dog to have a tiny microchip inserted under the skin of the neck. Any loose dog without either a tatoo or microchip is liable to be destroyed. The tatoo/microchip insertion can be done by a vet, or in some areas by the Unita Sanitaria Locale. Dog insurance against claims for damages is advisable for those with unpredictable animals and those whose canines have no traffic sense.

Rabies vaccinations have to be given yearly and a log-book will be provided by the vet for the purpose of recording these. Apart from rabies which is reputedly prevalent in the far north of Italy, hazards further south are more likely to include encounters with porcupines and snakes. For animals (and human beings) it is advisable to keep a supply of venom antidote in the fridge but make sure that it is regularly renewed before the expiry date has been reached.

Useful Addresses:

D.J. Williams: Animal Transport, Littleacre Quarantine Centre, 50 Dunscombes Road, Turves, Nr Whittlesey Cambs PE7 2DS; tel 01733-840291; fax 01733 840348. Pet collection and overland delivery service. Will collect from your home, arrange all the necessary documentation. Also return home service from Europe provided.

Ministry of Agriculture, Animal Export: Hook Rise South, Tolworth, Surbiton, Surrey KT6 7NF; tel 0181-330 8184. Details and an application form for a Ministry of Agriculture export certificate can be obtained from the above address.

Daily Life

The mostly uncomplicated and mundane rituals of daily existence in the UK are liable to assume a completely bewildering aspect when encountered in the context of a new home and a foreign, non-English-speaking country. Buying a car, using public transport, opening a bank account – such seemingly straightforward tasks can cause rising panic when you realize that you don't know whether your British driving licence is valid in Italy, you have forgotten the word for season ticket and what on earth is a banker's draft in Italian? This chapter deals with all of these, and many more everyday concerns and will help to familiarise you with Italian ways and lessen the headaches which arise with each new and intially daunting task. However, it cannot be over stressed that the key to coping successfully with life in Italy, whether domestically, socially or professionally, lies in the ability to speak and understand the language with some degree of fluency. Thus the first section deals with ways of brushing up, or initiating, your knowledge of Italian, either before leaving the UK or on arrival in Italy.

Please note that all information provided here is subject to regional variation and that the difference in procedures between city and country areas of Italy may be particularly striking.

The Italian Language

Italian is one of the easier European languages to learn. A romance language, Italian shares many features with French and Spanish and anyone who has a knowledge of either of these will find it all the easier to acquire mastery of Italian. Moreover, in the majority of cases, tortured attempts at pronouncing the most simple of Italian words and sounds will be met with a good humoured and largely enthusiastic response. Remember that when speaking to strangers, the third person is the polite form and using the second person is a mark of disrespect. An inevitable consequence of Italy's fragmented and internally strife-ridden history (unification, *Risorgimento*, wasn't achieved until as late as 1861) is that variations in dialect are strong throughout the country. Neapolitan, in particular, can be difficult to understand and the Sicilian dialect is different enough from conventional Italian as to be almost a separate language and to confuse native Italians and struggling foreigners alike. However, people will slip into more orthodox Italian with foreigners. Some of the inhabitants of the northern border regions don't, in fact, use Italian at all, speaking various forms of French and German (eg. the Val d'Aosta has a large French-speaking population while the Trentino-Alto-Adige harbours a very strong German-speaking minority). The majority of the island population of Sardinia speaks a mixture of Italian, Latin, Punic and Spanish while in Calabria and Sicily, entire villages still speak Albanian and Greek.

Anyone who moves to Italy assuming that all Italians can speak English is in for an unpleasant shock. Italians tend to be only mildly less untalented in speaking foreign languages than the British, and in some of the more remote southern areas you may well find that no English is spoken at all. Not all that much English is used at business levels either, and as Italian business is inextricably mixed with pleasure, Italian is a must, both professionally and socially, unless you decide to restrict your social and business life to a purely anglophone circle of expatriates. In order to avoid feeling inarticulate and alienated it is as well to begin learning Italian as soon as possible, ideally before leaving the UK. Many types of courses are offered by language schools and organizations both in the UK and in Italy and some of the most popular forms of language learning and the organizations which offer these are listed below.

Self-Study Courses

For those who prefer to combine reciting verb endings with cooking the dinner or repeating sentence formations while walking the dog, then self study is the most suitable option. The BBC produces an excellent series of work books and audio cassettes for a whole range of foreign languages. These cassettes are intended to complement radio and television programmes for which they are designed: for instance *Get by in Italian* is a basic business person's course consisting of a video, book and cassettes which can be bought separately, or at £29 for the package. The other beginners' course is *Buongiorno Italia!* (book £9.99 + three cassettes £19.99). This combination of texts and recordings focuses heavily on such aspects of everyday, conversational Italian as finding the way, shopping and understanding numbers and prices. The book contains texts of conversations recorded in Italy, language notes, information about the Italian way of life, exercises and a glossary. The conversations and interviews are on the cassettes. The text book, teacher's notes and cassettes can all be purchased individually. The BBC's other series called *Italianissimo* has a beginners' level (£12.99) and an intermediate level (£14.99) comprising book and cassettes, and is 'very modern'. There is also a homework book (£4.95). Further details on all BBB courses can be obtained from the BBC Mail Order/Shop in Newcastle (tel 0191-222 0381).

Linguaphone (Carlton Plaza, 111 Upper Richmond Street, London SW15 2TJ ; 0181-333 4898; fax 0181-333 4897) have courses which range from beginner courses that aim to teach a new language in twelve weeks to to very advanced level with prices from £49.99 for a video course to £399.90 for a minilab executive course (add £4.90 for postage and packing). You can also call in at the Linguaphone Language Centre (which is their shop) at 124-126 Brompton Road, London SW3 (tel 0171-589 2422).

For those who want to maintain or improve their fluency in Italian *Acquerello Italiano* audio magazine is ideal for anyone interested in Italian language and culture. *Acquerello Italiano* is a, hour-long programme on audio-cassette with news, features and interviews from Italy. Rather than teaching you to order meals or book a hotel room, the programme is aimed at helping you expand and update your vocabulary. The cassette comes with a magazine that has transcripts, glossary and copious background explanatory notes. There are optional study supplements also available. For six editions annually the subscription is £69 (study supplements an additional £18) from Aquerello Italiano (UK tel +44 171 738 9324; fax for orders 0171-738 0707; USA tel 1-800 824 0829; homepage: http://www.acquerello-italiano.com).

Intensive Language Courses

The Berlitz School of Languages: 9-13 Grosvenor Street, London W1A 3BZ; tel 0171-915 0909. One real advanatage of the international organization, Berlitz is that it offers language courses which, begun in the UK, can be completed on arrival in Italy. Each course is specifically tailored to the individual's own requirements as far as the language level and course intensity is concerned and the cost of the courses varies enormously depending on these factors. Further information on Berlitz courses is available from the above address or from any of the other Berlitz branches, located in Birmingham, Manchester, Leeds and Edinburgh.

inlingua School of Languages: 28 Rotton Park Road, Edgbaston, Birmingham B16 9JL; tel 0121-4540204; fax 0121-4563264. inlingua is another organization which has a worldwide network of privately-owned language schools: there are approximately 280 schools in all, 240 of which are located in Europe. The schools only employ native Italian teachers and tuition is offered on both an individual and a group basis. The cost of a 45-minute session is approximately £26. The most intensive course (50 lessons) costs £1,670 for a week including board, lodging and activities. Italian courses can also be arranged at centres abroad. There are also inlingua branches in Cheltenham and Torquay.

Linguarama: Head Office: Queen's House, 8 Queen Street, London EC4N 1SP (tel 0171-236 1992; fax 0171 236 7206. Linguarama offers many different language courses catering for a wide range of standards and abilities. Tuition can be given on an individual basis if requested. Linguarama has branches in Manchester, Winchester, Birmingham and Stratford. Accommodation can be arranged.

Part-time Courses

Part-time courses are ideal for those with domestic or professional commitments and are cheap compared with the the language courses offered by commercial organizations such as Berlitz, inlingua, etc. Local colleges of education and community or adult studies centres are the best option as they often run day and evening courses in a wide and amazing variety of subjects. The courses cater for a variety of standards, ranging from beginners who want to learn Italian for next year's holiday or for general interest to those who wish to take a GCSE or A level examination at the end of the course. Classes usually begin in mid-September or the first week in October and run for between two and seven months with a two or three hour class once a week. The fees vary but GCSE and A level classes are usually cheaper than non-examination 'conversation classes'. Enquiries about all courses should be made direct to the relevant organization, see the section, *Useful Addresses* below for further addresses of schools, colleges and community centres which offer similar courses in Italian. Alternatively, there is always an abundance of Italian nationals keen to exploit their earning potential as private tutors and who swamp the local papers each week with advertisements. Alternatively, the Italian Insitute can provide a list of Italian tutors on receipt of an s.a.e. In all cases, however, it is just as well to check just how qualified the 'teacher' is, and to pay them an hourly fee which reflects their level of expertise and experience. For unqualified 'teachers', you could suggest a conversation exchange, i.e. you take turns at teaching each other your own language.

Useful Addresses

The Italian Cultural Institute: 39 Belgrave Square, London SW1X 8NX; tel 0171-235 1461; fax 0171-235 4618. Runs courses at the Institute in London. Also, can advise on language courses throughout Italy. Helps undergraduates and postgraduates find out about courses at Italian universities.

Dante Alighieri Society: 4 Upper Tatchbrook Street, Victoria, London SW1V 1SH; tel 0171-828 9660. Worldwide organisation for the dissemination of Italian language and culture. Branches around England and Scotland and one in Cork. Organises year-round language courses. Contact the above address for details of your nearest Society.

Federazione Italiana Lavoratori Emigranti e Famiglie (FILEF): (96/98 Central Street, London EC1V 8AJ; tel 0171-608 0125; fax 0171-490 0938). Cultural organisation that runs Italian evening classes for all levels.

The Italian Community Centre: 96-98 Central Street, Islington, London EC1; tel 0171-608 0125. Organises language courses at the Centre.

Morley College: 61 Westminster Bridge Road, London SE1; tel 0171-928 8501. All levels of Italian from beginner to post A level. Day and evening classes.

Private schools which offer business Italian:

International House: 106 Piccadilly, London W1V 9FL; tel 0171-491 2598; fax 0171-409 0959.

Language Studies International: Woodstock House, 10-12 James Street, London W1M 5HN; tel 0171-499 9621.

St George's International: Language House, 76 Mortimer Street, London W1N 7DE; tel 0171-299 1700; fax 0171-299 1711.

Expatriate/Business Traveller Briefing Courses

The Centre for International Briefing: Farnham Castle, Farnham, Surrey GU9 OAG; tel 01252-721194; fax 01252-711283. Programmes aimed at expatriates and business travellers aimed at corporate clients so prices are high. Briefings last one to four days. Near-immersion language tuition also available.

Going Places: 84 Coombe Road, New Malden, Surrey KT3 4QS; tel; 0181-949-6237. Offers tailor-made expatriate briefing courses.

Courses in Italy

In almost all large Italian towns, there are facilities for foreigners to learn or improve their Italian; either at language schools or universities. These courses are aimed at a wide range of standards and abilities and usually run from early April until late August, each course lasting two to four weeks. The classes should be small and ideally no more than ten to a class. Accommodation is often available, either in dormitories and camp sites or university and hotel accommodation. Some schools also offer classes on Italian history, culture and art in conjunction with the language course. Various leisure time activities are organized for students, eg. film and slide shows and trips to museums, concerts and theatres. The fortnight-long courses are priced from approximately £300+ (including bed and breakfast) and mostly run throughout the year, although some are only open during the summer months. A list of Italian language schools etc. which offer a wide variety of such courses is listed in the *Useful Addresses* section below.

Useful Addresses

Centro Culturale Leonardo da Vinci: Via Brunelleschi 4, 50123 Firenze; tel 055/294420; fax 055-294820.

Centro di Lingua e Cultura Italiana: Vico S. Maria dell'Aiuto 17, 80134 Napoli; tel 081-5524331; fax 081-5523023; e-mail:l.italiano@ mbox.netway.it:

Centro Lingua Italiana Calvino: Viale Fratelli Rosselli 74, 50123 Firenze; tel 055-288081, fax 055-288125; e-mail: clic.plus@flashnet.it. School open all year. Residential summer courses are organised in Calabria. Example of tuition fees 1998 Florence: 2 week intensive course (6 hours per day) 680,000 lire; 4 week standard course (4 hours per day) 780.000 lire. Accommodation can be organised on request.

The Centro Linguistico Italiano Dante Alighieri: Via dei Bardi 12, Firenze; tel 055-2342984, telex 055-580072, fax 055-2342766; also Via B. Marliano 4, Rome; tel 06-8320184, fax 06-8604203.

Centro Linguistico Sperimentale (CLS), Florence: 1, Via del Corso Firenze; tel 055-210592/289817; fax 055-289817; internet: http://www.alba.fl.it /sperimentale. Courses run throughout the year.

CESA Languages Abroad: Western House, Malpas, Truro TR1 1SQ; tel 01872-225300; fax 01872-225400. Organises language courses in Florence Venice, Rome and Siena.

Istituto Europeo: Piazza dell Pallottole 1 (Duomo), 50122 Firenze; tel/fax 055-289145; e-mail : istituto.europeo@fi.flashnet.it. Language courses; also cultural, professional and music courses.

Istituto Italiano: Centro di Lingua e Cultura, Via Carlo Alberto 43, 00185 Rome; tel 06-4465798, fax 06-4465781.

Italiaidea: Piazza delle Cancelleria, 85, 00186 Rome; tel +39-6-68307620; fax +39-6-6892997. Internet: http://www.italiaidea.com

Politzer School: via Amendola 16, 40121 Bologna; tel/fax 051-249500. Language school, translations and interpreting. Formerly known as Learn and Travel.

Susan Howard Rees: Via Matteotti 45, Arese, Milan; tel 02-93 80 256; fax 02-93 58 13 00. Made-to-measure language courses especially for commerce.

Universita per Stranieri: Segretaria Studenti, Via Pantaneto 45, 53100 Siena, Italy; tel +39 577 240347/345/343; fax +39 577 283163. Courses for students engaged in European student mobility programmes, designed to enable them to reach a level adequate for attending university courses.

Italian Societies

It is essential to delve into Italian culture before leaving the UK if you want to avoid feeling culturally stranded on arrival in Italy. Various societies exist in the UK which organize social events and discussion groups of an endlessly diverse nature which will serve to soften the culture shock. The Italian Cultural Institute (see above) is the main Italian government agency whose function it is to promote cultural relations between the two countries. The Institute organizes lectures, exhibitions and promotes concerts and has a library facility of approximately 21,000 books (including subjects such as Italian literature, art, history, criticisms and essays). The library is open to the general public although only members are eligible to take the books out on loan. All scholarships for study and research in Italy are awarded by the Italian Ministry of Foreign Affairs and other Italian institutions through the Italian Institute. Membership of the Institute is on an annual basis and entitles members to receive information on all of the cultural events it arranges and free access to its facilities. The annual membership cost is £30 to those with London addresses, £15 for under 18's, full-time students, senior citizens and anyone with an address outside London.

Additionally, the Dante Alighieri Society (4 Upper Tatchbrook Street, Victoria, London SW1X 8NX; tel 0171-828 9660) founded in Rome in 1889, promotes Italian language and culture among Italophiles worldwide. The Society promotes lectures, conferences, films, concerts, theatre performances, cultural exchanges and scholarships for studies and research in Italy. The annual membership fee is £30 and £20 for full-time students and senior citizens.

Slightly different is the *Federazione Italiana Lavoratori Emigranti e Famiglie (FILEF)* based in London (96/98 Central Street, London EC1V 8AJ; tel 0171-608

0125; fax 0171-490 0938) the main aim of which is to keep Italians in Britain in touch with the cultural developments in their country and introduce Britons to Italian culture. FILEF provides advice, support and information to its members (subscription £4 annually). They also publish a newsletter and provide an interpreting and translating service. Could be great for making contacts.

Schools and Education

Although legislation to bring Italy in line with other EU countries is imminent, the legal requirement for school attendance in Italy is still only up to the age of fourteen. Consequently, many school children in the much poorer south leave school at fourteen to try to find a job which will contribute to the family's often inadequate income (although frequently only succeeding in joining the swelling ranks of the Mezzogiorno's unemployed). However, over the last ten or fifteen years, massive improvements have been implemented within the Italian state education system and Italy can now boast a system of education which equals most others in Europe. The system of education is administered centrally through the government, with the exception only of elementary schools which are usually run by the local commune. Unfortunately, a wide disparity exists between the state education available in the affluent north and that in the comparatively poor south of the country, and the standards of the schools in the large northern cities, Turin, Genoa, Rome and Milan, are much higher than those found in Molise, Calabria or Campania for example. Note that although state education is free in Italy, parents are responsible for buying their children's textbooks and stationery. Private schools also exist, of which nearly all are Roman Catholic (although pupils are not required to be) and day schools only. Although private schools do not carry the same kind of status with which they are often associated in Britain, they do form an attractive option to those who can afford them, especially in some of the large cities of the Mezzogiorno, particularly Naples, where some state schools are currently dealing with a serious and growing drug problem.

Obviously, the decision as to whether to educate children within the Italian or British system of education (see the section, *International Schools* below) is one which must include such considerations as the age of the child, the length of time for which you are planning to live in Italy and your financial situation. Remember also that the watershed age for learning a language with relative ease appears to be around eleven to twelve and after this it becomes more and more difficult to pick up the language quickly.

The Structure of the Education System

Pre-school. Obviously, pre-school education is not compulsory. However, children can go to privately or commune-run kindergartens, known as *scuola materna* or *asilo nido*, from the age of three.

Primary. Primary school (*scuola elementare*) begins at age six and continues to eleven. Lessons usually last for only four hours each day and this short time does not allow room for sports, music, drama, etc, which are largely regarded as extracurricular activities. The scuola elementare is the easiest stage at which to integrate foreign children into the school system; the younger the better as far as grasping some understanding of Italian itself is concerned. After passing some fairly straightforward exams, children pass on to the next stage, *scuola media*.

Scuola Media. This covers the ages of eleven or twelve to fourteen or fifteen. To successfully complete the scuola media, exams must be passed and an average of not less than sixty percent maintained throughout each school year. The *diploma di licenza media* is awarded to all those who get this far. At this point, the less academic tend to go on to one of the vocational *istituti tecnici* to study anything from accountancy to farming, while the rest stay at school for a further two years, taking either the *liceo classico* or *liceo scientifico*. This involves a certain amount of specialization although not to the same extent to which A levels in the UK dictate the course of all future study. At 18 or 19, the liceo students take the *maturità* (the equivalent of the French baccalaureat), while the tecnici students take a diploma which bestows the equivalent qualification of a British City and Guilds.

University. Since the reform of 1977, everyone who has obtained either the maturità or a tecnici diploma is entitled to go on to an Italian university. Consequently, universities are now flooded with students and Italy has one of the highest percentages of university students in Europe at 41.3 of the relevant age group, this is only just behind Denmark at 41.5% and more than France and Germany at 30.6% and 35.3% respectively. Italy, however has far fewer non-university higher education courses than the last two countries. However, this apparent merit is undermined by the fact that only one third of students enrolled for a university degree ever finish their courses.

Italian universities are the victim of under-investment and a lack of courses and venues and inevitably in many cases the degrees awarded are not particularly respected. Consequently, a degree is not necessarily a passport to a good job. Indeed a survey in 1995 found that graduates were only marginally better off in the job stakes than holders of a high-school diploma. One of the much needed reforms is to forge closer links between business and universities thus ensuring that academic products are competitive.

The picture is not however entirely bleak. Although not internationally renowned, some of Italy's universities have a very good reputation. For example, the private Bocconi university in Milan is excellent, particularly in the faculties of business studies and economics with fierce competition for the few available places each year. Rome's Libera Università degli Studi Sociali (LUISS) has a similarly high reputation. However, both of these universities are private and fees run into several thousand pounds each year, with only a few scholarships and other awards available. The state universities vary in quality but among the most prestigious are the Politecnico in Milan (famous for its engineering faculty), Bologna university which is the oldest in Europe and has a very high reputation in most subjects and the university at Pavia which excells particularly in medicine, while Naples boasts the Orientale, the oldest oriental language school in Italy.

The method of university teaching in Italy is similar to that in the UK; if anything it is even more remote and reliant on each individual's often faltering, self motivation. Lectures are frequently over-crowded, sometimes to the point that it's practically impossible to squeeze into the lecture halls. One peculiarity is that exams can be postponed indefinitely until the student chooses to take them, while no degree can be completed in less than four years. If exams are failed then they can simply be retaken the next time round; consequently most students graduate one or two years late. A large proportion of all courses rely on oral examinations. Italian universities are not residential and do not even organize accommodation for their students, so many live at home and go to a local university. One of the added problems of education in Italy is that every male should, in theory, do military service. All kinds of practices are resorted to in order to get out of it; this of course, does not affect foreign nationals.

International Schools

International schools tend to be regarded as the best alternative by expatriates who are considering the long-term education of their children. This, however, is primarily because they offer the qualifications better known to selection bodies for UK universities and this may be irrelevant if you intend your children to complete their education within the Italian system. Additonally, international schools can be seen to isolate children from the communities which they live in and accentuate cross-cultural divisions. There are under ten American schools in Italy which are a possible choice for British expatriates. However, the abundance of British schools combined with the high quality of education which they offer, usually tips the balance in favour of the British schools, if only because it is easier to switch back into the British education system from a British, rather than a US school abroad.

In the list below, the address and phone number of each school is followed by the age range of the pupils and the fees charged. A list of American schools is also included. This list, last compiled in November 1991, is available in full from the European Council of International Schools (21B Lavant Street, Petersfield, Hants GU32 3EL; tel 0730-68244).

International School of Milan: Via Bezzola 6, 20153 Milan (tel 02-4091 0067), ages three to 19, fees lire 750 000.

Sir James Henderson British School of Milan: Viale Lombardia 66, 20131 Milan (tel 02-261 3299; fax 2-261!0500), ages three to 18, lire 14.3 million annual fees.

Ambrit School: Via Filippo Tajani 50, 00149 Rome (tel 06-7182907), ages three to 14. Annual fees lire four to 18 million.

Castelli International School: 13 Via Degli Scozzesi, 00046 Grottaferrata, Rome; (tel/fax 06-94315779), 5-14 years annual tuition from lire 7,850,000 to 10,500,000.

International Academy of Rome: Via di Grottarossa 295, 00189 Rome (tel 06-3326 6071), ages three to 14, lire four to 18 million.

Kendale Primary International School: Via Gradoli 86, Tombe di Nerone, 00189 Rome (tel & fax 06-33267608), 3-10, lire 6,500,000-12,000,000.

Marymount International School: Via di Villa Lauchli 180, 00191 Rome (tel 06-3630 1742; fax 06 3630 1738. Roman Catholic school. Ages three to 19. Annual fees 7.5 to 18 million lire.

New School: Via della Camiluccia 669, 00135 Rome (tel 06-3294269; fax 06-3297546). Ages: three to 18 years.

Notre Dame International School: Via Aurelia 796, 00165 Rome (tel 06-6808801; fax 6806051), 10-18, lire 12,000,000.

Rome International School: Viale Romania 32, Parioli (off Piazza Ungheria, Rome; tel 06-84482650; fax 06-84482651.

Southlands English School: Via Teleclide 20, Casal Palocco, 00124 Rome (tel 06-5053922; fax 06-50917192). Three to 14 years.

St Francis International School: Via Massimi 164 (Balduina) Rome; tel 06-35341328; fax 06-35348719. Ages three to 14. American system.

St George's English School: Via Cassia KM 16, 00123 Rome (tel 06-3790141/23; fax 3792490), ages three to 18, 6 million to 18.3 million.

St Stephen's School: Via Aventina 3, 00153 Rome (tel 06-575 0605; fax 06-574 1941. Ages: 13-19, lire 19.5 million.

International School of Trieste: Via Conconello 16, Opicina, 34100 Trieste (tel 040-211452).

United World College of the Adriatic: Via Trieste 29, 34013 Duino (Trieste); tel 040-3739111; fax 040-3739225. Takes students aged 16 to 18 who spend the last two years before university at the college. Entry is exclusively by scholarship.*International School of Turin (A.C.A.T.):* Vicolo Tiziano 10, 10024 Moncalieri (tel 011-6407810/645967; fax 643298), 3-18, lire 7,000,000-12,500,000.

European School: Via Montello 118, 21100 Varese (tel 0332-286132; fax 332-283782. Ages four to 18. Annual fees 1.25 to 2.345 million. Waiting list of 2 years. 3285062), 4-18, BF5,200-18,000.

American Schools:

American International School of Florence: Via del Carota 23/35, 50012 Bagno a Ripoli, Florence (tel 055-640033; fax 55-644226), $2^1/_2$-19, lire 5,550,000-9,500,000.

American International School in Genoa: Via Quarto 13/C 16148 Genoa (tel 010-386528; fax 010 398700), 3-14, lire 5.5-12.6 million.

American School of Milan: 20090 Noverasco di Opera, Milano (tel 02-53 00 00 1; fax 02 57 60 62 74). Ages: 3-19, lire 7,350,000-12,100,000.

International School of Naples: Viale della Liberazione, 1H.Q. AFSouth Post, Bldg 'A', 80125 Bagnoli, Napoli; tel 81-721 20 37; fax 81-762 84 29; Annual fee 100,000 lire. Registration fee 150,000 and new students' admission fee 500,000 lire.

American Overseas School of Rome: Via Cassia 811, 00189 Rome (tel 06-33264841; fax 06-33262608. 8,000,000 to 21,500,000.

Kindergarten/Pre-school

Greenwood Garden School: Via Vito Sinisi 5, Rome 00189 (tel/fax +39 6 3326-6703); lire 6,750,000-7-7,650,000.

Media and Communications

Newspapers

In common with the Spaniards, the Italians are not avid newspaper readers, with only 60% of Italian families buying a daily newspaper. Perhaps this lack of literary enthusiasm stems from the almost exclusively serious nature of the publications on offer. There is no real equivalent of the well established British tabloids and only the downmarket papers, eg. *Il Messaggero* carry horoscopes, cartoons or fun features.

The most popular Italian dailies are *Il Corriere della Sera* (Milan, lire 1,500) and *La Repubblica* (Rome, lire 1,500) – both of which boast a daily circulation of between five and six hundred thousand. *La Stampa* (Turin, lire 1,500) follows with a dramatic circulation drop to just over four hundred thousand, and then *Il Giornale* (lire 1,500)at nearly two hundred thousand and *Il Messaggero* (lire 1,500).

Il Corriere della Sera and *La Repubblica* in particular are constantly vying for circulation supremacy mostly in the form of free supplements on computers, health, money matters etc. and compulsory paying inserts including a women's magazine and TV guide. Although the former is currently selling more copies, the latter, an unusually liberal publication, tends to create the most controversy and excitement, with its talent for political insight and cultural reporting. By contrast, the conservative *La Stampa* tends to back whichever government is in power at the time. In the five most widely read newspapers above, articles on social issues are comparatively rare (3.6% of space) compared with politics (19.6% and the economy (18.4%).

The two main financial dailies are *Il Sole/24 Ore* and *Italia Oggi*, both are fairly competent but not quite of the standard of *The Financial Times*. The three sports dailies are *Corriere dello Sport*, *Gazzetta dello Sport* and *Tuttosport*. The regional newspapers, which focus on national news but include several pages of local news and comment, are particularly popular and widely read in Italy. The most popular among these include:

La Nazione in Florence (Socialist)
Il Mattino in Naples (Christian Democrat)
Il Messaggero in Rome (Communist).
Il Resto del Carlino in Bologna.
L'Ora in Palermo; at the forefront of anti-Mafia movement in the media environs of Sicily.
Il Tempo (Rome)
La Gazzetta del Mezzogiorno (Bari)
La Nuova Sardegna (Cagliari)
Paese Sera (Rome)
Il Piccolo (Trieste)
La Nuova Venezia (Venice)

There are no Sunday papers as such in Italy; all of the national dailies print on Sunday and some of them have a day off on Monday. Colour sections are an innovation launched as recently as autumn 1987 in the *Corriere della Sera* and *La Repubblica*. All Italian newspapers can be confusing to the untrained eye as there is no front page list of contents conveniently indexing each section.

The English-language newspaper, *The International Herald Tribune* is available in Italy at newsagents or by subscription from the Paris office (181 Avenue Charles de Gaulle, 92521 Neuilly, Cedex Paris; tel 1-46 37 93 00). Those of you on the job hunt in Rome should try to get hold of a copy of the English-language newspapers, *Daily American* and *When in Rome*, both of which carry substantial job advertising.

Magazines

The Italian magazine market is swamped with publications which churn out the same themes, features and cover spreads week after week. Magazines rate far below the dailies as far as professionalism and quality are concerned. The main three publishing houses, Mondadori, Rizzoli and Rusconi are in constant competition to control a saturated market. The better-quality magazines include *Gente* and *Oggi*, both of which contain a good deal of serious and well-written news and arts coverage. At the other end of the spectrum, *Novella 2000*, *Eva Express* and the incredibly lurid *Stop* are pure gossip and scandal reading.

Italy boasts some of the classiest women and men's fashion and home furnishing magazines in the world. The most popular of which are *Moda*, *Marie Claire*, *King* and *Vogue Italia*.

English Language Publications

The English-language magazine, *Italy, Italy* (via M. Mercati 51, 00197 Rome; tel 06-3221441, fax 3223869) is full of useful articles on culture, politics, entertainment and general interest and is available by subscription from the above address. Another possibility is the expatriate magazine *The Informer* which is published monthly and contains a variety of both useful and interesting articles ranging from tax and money matters to general interest. Those interested in taking out a subscription should contact the Bureau Service, Via dei Tigli 2, 20020 Arese, Milan (tel 02-9358 1477 fax 02-9358 0280). The subscription rates are lire 70,000 (about £23) per year (ten issues) for delivery within Italy and 116,000 lire (about £38) for anyone living outside Italy. *The Informer* is also available from major international bookshops in Milan, Rome, Arese, Florence, Ispra and Varese. Also full of useful tips about how to survive daily life in Milan and northern Italy as a foreigner is *The Survival Guide to Milan* (32,000 lire incl. postage) from the same address as *The Informer* (see above). There are two other fortnightly English-language papers published in Rome: *Wanted in Rome* (http://www.wantedinrome.com) sold on newsstands and in some bookshops, and the *Metropolitan*. The *International Spectator* is a quarterly publication. A new arrival on the English-language scene is *Rome Elite*.

The *English Yellow Pages* (via Belisario 4/B, 00187 Rome; tel 06-4740861; fax 06-4744516) updated annually, will be invaluable to any new arrival in Italy. The directory contains listings for English-speaking professionals, businesses, organizations and services in Rome, Florence, Bologna and Milan and is available at international bookstores and from news-stands. For a free listing, contact the above address. Also from the same publisher is the English White Pages, an alphabetical directory of English-speakers living in Italy.

Books

The Italian publishing market tends to cater for the two extreme ends of the reading public; either the intellectual highbrow of contemporary literature or the downmarket, gossip and romance, Barbara Cartland-imitation junkies. The Italian best-seller list reflects the refined intellectual tastes of the literary minority. Surprisingly, foreign authors such as Milan Kundera and Gabriel García Marquez often sell better than Italy's homegrown talents such as Primo Levi, Leonardo Sciascia and Umberto Eco.

English-language bookshops
Anglo American Bookshop: Via della Vite 102, Rome; tel 06-6795222.
The Corner Bookshop: Via del Moro 48, Rome; tel 06-5836942.
Economy Book & Video Centre: Via Torino 136, Rome 00184; tel 06/4746877; fax 483661 (http://www.agora.stm.it/KEM.Bookcenter). New and used paperbacks, videos for sale and rent, mail order, special order, seminars and other events, greeting cards and gifts, discount cards, buys used paperbacks for cash/credit.
Lion Bookshop: Via Del Babuino 181, Rome.
Paperback Exchange Bookshop: Via Fiesolana 31r, Florence; tel 2478154; fax 2478856. All fields, hardbacks and paperbacks, new and secondhand, academic/library supplies, bibliographic service, special order and mail order.

Television

The Italians are telly-addicts; 99% of Italian homes own their own television. With literally hundreds of channels of programmes to choose from, they have ample fuel with which to feed their craving. This saturation of television space was the unsurprising response to the deregulation of the television board in 1976; before this time, there had only ever been one, black and white, state-run channel, heavily influenced and censored by church authorities. The great majority of these relatively new channels are crammed with rubbishy quiz shows and low quality sitcoms and soaps, while the three state-run channels, RAI 1, 2 and 3 manage to provide a higher quality programming and command higher viewing levels.

However, the standard is evidently not high enough and viewing figures are falling for the state-run channels. All of the state channels (RAI 1, RAI 2, RAI 3) are subject to political patronage and it is nearly impossible to succeed within the television career network without an influential and well-connected mentor. RAI3 tends to show more cultural programmes than the others.

The important independent television channels are Italia 1, Canale 5 and Rete 4 which collectively account for about 45% of Italian viewing. Although Rete 4 is thought to be more highbrow than the other two, none of them offer really serious news coverage although in 1998 Canale 5's new boss plans more emphasis on news and documentaries.

In 1996 there was something of a public crusade in Italy against the probable dangers of certain types of television on the psychophysical development of children and younger viewers. The result was a watershed of after 10.30pm for X-rated movies and other violent/sexually explicit programming. Italy was also a pioneer of the so-called 'violence chip' a piece of technology designed to filter out violent programmes on television when children are watching.

The RAI *canone* (television tax) for 1998 is 163,150 lire (about £57).

About 800,000 viewers subscribe to pay-TV.

For those unable to find enough substantial fare on Italian television there is always recourse to the the video. A video ordering scheme, Video Plus Direct (tel 01733-232800) has 17,000 titles to choose from including commercial movies and BBC television programmes. Send £5.99 (which includes postage abroad) for a complete catalogue, or telephone the above number to order items.

BBC World television (24-hours news and information) is available in Italy. Contact the agent Telepui (via Piranesi 46, 20137 Milan; tel +39 2 75 76 77).

Radio

The Italian radio network was deregulated in 1976, the same year as television, with the result that the airwaves are crammed with a diverse range of obscure stations; over two and a half thousand of them. However, the three main radio channels are Radio 1, 2, and 3. The first two feature light music and entertainment while Radio 3 is similar to the UK equivalent, broadcasting serious discussion programmes and classical music. Finally there are Radio 1 and 2 rock stations which, although technically part of RAI, are on separate wavelengths. The accumulated audience for rock stations is immense (12.5 million listeners). The total audience for radio nationwide is estimated at 35 million. However, there are so many stations that this audience is hopelessly fragmented and some local stations are estimated to have no more than a few dozen listeners.

As with television, the radio channels are all under the wing of a powerful sponsor who consequently has a substantial influence over the stations's output.

BBC World Service

A monthly publication *BBC On Air* which gives details of schedules, and advice and information about BBC World Service radio and BBC Prime and BBC World Television, is available on subscription (£24 annually) from the BBC, P.O. Box 76S, Bush House, London WC2B 4PH (tel +44 (0)171 557 2211 (answerphone); fax (0)171 240 4899).

Voice of America

For details of Voice of America programmes, contact VOA (Washington, D.C. 20547 (tel 1-202 619. 2358.

The Postal System

The Italian postal system, the Poste, Telegrafi e Telefoni (PTT), is one of the slowest and least efficient in Europe (hardly surprising considering the service has not been reorganized since the 19th century). Not even local letters are delivered the next day and the quickest service is three days door to door while cross-country letters can take up to two weeks. However, the overseas service works comparatively well, delivering mail within three of four days to Europe and overnight to New York.

Stamps can be bought from the post office (*ufficio postale*) and tobacconists (tabaccherie). Post offices are open Monday to Friday 8.15am to 2pm and until midday on Saturdays. The current tariff for internal letters is lire 750 (34p) for post up to 20g, lire 650 (30p) for postcards and postage plus a supplement of lire 3,200 (£1.45) for express letters (which won't necessarily arrive any faster than standard post).

For those who have no fixed address, the post restante (*fermoposta*) service is useful; just write the addressee's name, then *fermoposta* and the place name on the envelope; the addressee can then pick up his or her mail from the post office after providing a passport as identification.

The state-run ITALCABLE operates a telegraph service abroad by cable or radio; both internal and overseas messages can be sent over the phone.

Telephones

The Italian telephone giant is Telecom Italia which was privatised in October 1997 thus bringing Italy towards liberalisation of her telecommunications market in line with EU directives. Public telephones take either coins (lire 100 or lire 200 pieces) or tokens (*gettóni*) for lire 200 which are available from all post offices, tobacconists and some news-stands. There are also magnetic phonecards, purchased from machines at telephone offices, stations and airports for the value of lire 3000 or lire 10,000. Note that the sign you will see over a lot of public telephones, *guasto*, is Italian for 'out of order'.

At the time of press local calls are not flat rate but are still cheaper than in the UK. From March 1998, long-distance calls, which were some of the most expensive in Europe will come down. This is because the number of telephone zones into which lines are subdivided has been reduced from 1400 to 690 which means that calls which used to be long distance will now be in the enlarged local zone.

The cheap rate for evening calls in Italy doesn't come into effect until 10pm which means it is quite usual to make long distance calls late into the night. However a new price structure introduced in 1998 provides discounts on the numbers you call most often including your Internet connection number (known as *Numero Blu*).

With deregulation, user choice of provider within Italy is imminent. Contenders include domestic companies and international consortia made up of companies from Britain, France, Germany Italy and America. In order for users of one provider to communicate with users of a different one they will have to use an integrated network which will involve dialing all ten digits (i.e. including the area code) of the subscriber's number, even for local calls from midnight on June 19th 1998. Note that those dialing Italy from abroad (except to mobile phones) will have to add the zero after dialling the country code (39) for Italy. To further complicate matters, it is likely that some area codes (e.g. Rome 06), will be changed so as not to include a zero or a 1 which are reserved numbers. In recent years, telephone numbers have acquired a habit of changing with confusing frequency mainly as part of essential updating work on the archaic system. It seems this practise will carry on to accommodate the ever new technology.

Wily telephonic bargain hunters, particularly expatriates (*extracommunitari*) have already been able to get discounts, particularly on international calls by using alternative phone services that advertise in newspapers and magazines. This works by dialling the provider using Telecom Italia's line then renting a dedicated line from another company like AT&T, entering a PIN number and dialling the number. A typical comparison would be Telecom Italia to the USA for three minutes 4,362 lire; compared with 2,700 lire with the competition.

Extremists might even avoid Telcom Italia completely by making long distance calls through France Telecom, or Deutsche Telecom or Sprint etc. To do this you need a hardware gadget than allows you to connect direct with the provider. You need to contact a private telecommunications broker to do this (see below) or look in the telephone yellow pages of your city under *telefonia e telecommunicazioni*:

EcsTel: Via S. Simpliciano 1, Milano; tel 02 864283.

Trans World Telecommunications (TWT): Via Cassolo 6, Milano; tel 02 58300028.

Viatel: Viale Sabotino 19/2, Milano; tel 02 58314863.

Note that Italian telephone bills are liable for IVA (VAT) at the standard rate of 20%.

Internet

Out of fourteen European countries Italy has fewer Internet connections than all except Portugal and Greece. One reason for this has been the relatively expensive cost of dedicated telephone lines. At the time of press reductions on line costs were imminent.

Mobiles

Perhaps owing to the unreliability of Italy's telephones in the past, but more likely because the costs are falling, the mobile (*telefonino*) has become the vital accessory without which no self-respecting Italian would dare to be seen. Italy's two main mobile manufacturers are TIM and OMNITEL which between them offer a bewildering range of price structures depending on the type of service, the amount of time you spend on the phone per month and what time of day you phone.

TIM is Telecom Italia's mobile telephone subsidiary which has had tremendous success with its prepaid, rechargeable telephone card for inserting in the GSM handset. The card obviates the need for monthly fees and bills and comes with an integral microchip that contains the customer's data and telephone number. TIM did extraordinarily well with this in 1997 when 3.3 million subscribers signed up giving it a total customer base of nine million. Omnitel, TIM's competitor introduced their version called Valore which notched up 40,000 new clients in the first week of January 1998, but their total custom at 2.5 million subscribers shows they still have a long way to go to match TIM's. A third player is likely to enter the mobile market. Although at the time of press this was not confirmed it looked likely to be PCN.

In May 1997 TIM extended its short message and information service, SCRIPTIM using GSM cellphone display. This service is invaluable for anyone who wants sporting fixture results instantly and also more essentially, train and airplane timetables and news and weather forecasts.

Somewhere between the fixed phone and the mobile is the cordless telephone. The DECT cordless has a range of about three kilometres (1.8 miles).

To telephone the UK from Italy dial 00, wait for the continuous tone and then dial 44 and continue immediately with the UK number, omitting the first number of the UK code. For example, to ring Vacation Work Publications from Italy you would dial: 00-44-865-241978. To telephone Italy from the UK dial 00-39 and then the Italian number, again omitting the first zero (until mid-1998 – see details above) of the provincial code. For example to ring a Rome number of 06-000000 you would actually dial 00-39-6-000000. When dialling inside Italy, use the complete provincial code for the area you are calling (ie. include the zero). Obviously, if you are ringing a number in Rome from within the city you would not need to include the area code at all (but see notes about deregulation changes above), just the telephone number itself. The following is a list of some of the most popular provincial codes:

Alassio 0182	Naples 081
Aosta 0165	Palermo 091
Bologna 051	Pesaro 0731
Bolzano 0471	Pisa 050
Cagliari 070	Riccione 054
Cattolica 0541	Rimini 0541
Como 031	Rome 06
Cortina d'Ampezzo 0436	San Remo 0184
Diano Marina 0183	Sorrento 081
Florence 055	Taormina 0942
Genoa 010	Trento 0461
Grado 0431	Trieste 040
La Spezia 0187	Turin 011
Lido di Jesolo 0421	Venice 041
Lignano 0431	Verona 05
Milan 02	Viareggio 0584

Emergency & Useful Numbers

Ambulance	5510
Breakdown/Motorway Police	116
Carabinieri	113
International Directory Enquiries	170
Enquiries Europe & the Mediterranean	176
Telephone faults/engineers	182

Cars and Motoring

Roads

Driving in Italy can be a costly business. The tolls (*pedaggi*) on Italian motorways (*autostrade*) are expensive at about 1000 lire per ten kilometres. As you drive on to an autostrada you will pick up a toll ticket which you pay on exit. *Strade Statali* (SS) are the equivalent of British A roads. Both *autostrade* and *strade statali* are numbered, while smaller roads *strade provinciali* and *strade secondarie* are not. It is as well to realize as soon as possible that the law of the jungle applies to the Italian roads and only the fittest and most adept will survive without at least a couple of minor prangs as proof of having negotiated the Italian road system.

Fuel. Italian petrol (*Benzina*) is some of the most expensive in Europe – about lire 1,895 (65p/$1.07) a litre for *super*, compared to 50p per litre in the UK and lire 1,800 per litre for *benzina verde* (lead-free). The high price is why it is relatively common to see cars running on the cheaper LPG (Liquified Petroleum Gas) known as GPL in Italy. Petrol stations along the autostrade are open 24 hours while those on secondary roads usually open between 7am and 12.30pm and then 3.30pm and 6.30pm and close on Sundays.

Breakdowns and Accidents

Italy has one of the highest road accident rates in the whole of the EU. This is a result of lax enforcement by the Italian traffic police (*Vigili Urbani*), inadequate road laws (see below) and the frenetic style of driving which the Italians favour in the many built-up areas of Italy. However, although the accident rate is astronomical (approximately 250,000 injured each year), the death rate is mercifully lower (estimated at 7,000 deaths each year).

The Italian Automobile Club, Automobile Club d'Italia, is the Italian equivalent of the RAC and the AA. The head office of the ACI is at Via Marsala 8, 00185 Rome (tel 06-49981; fax 06-4457748 (General Secretariat), 49982426 (Presidency), 49982469 (Tourism Department).

The emergency 24-hour phone number is Rome 06-4477 with a multilingual staff provides round the clock assistance.

If your car comes to an unprompted and definitive halt, then dial 116 (ACI breakdown Service) from everywhere in Italy, both from telephone boxes and mobile phones.

On motorways, you can also use SOS boxes/phones placed every 2km, and connected with the motorways radio centres: road assistance can be provided either by the ACI 116 or by another operator. The service is permanently available on all roads throughout Italy. In all emergencies (personal injury and all kinds of accidents or mishaps) dial 113 (police), 112 (Carabinieri) or 115 (Fire Brigade).

Breakdown service comprises transportation of the car from the place of breakdown to the nearest ACI garage or, in major cities, the roadside repair of the vehicle if possible. Road Assistance provided by the ACI is free of charge only for tourists with an AIT or FIA Assistance booklet otherwise the service for all motor vehicles up to 2.5 tons is paid at normal tarif of about £50 (142,000 lire) on roads and 162,000 lire (about £55) on motorways. The cost of transporting a car (and all motor vehicles up to two and a half tons) beyond the nearest ACI garage is 65,000 lire for the first 20 km and 1,450 lire for each additional km. For caravans the fee is 81,000 lire for the first 20km and 1,500 lire for each additional km.

Driving Regulations

In theory, the Italian speed limits are as follows: 130 kph (80 mph) on the autostrada, 90 kph (55 mph) on highroads (*le strade statali*) and 50 kph (30 mph) in all built-up areas. Although the police have become a lot more enthusiastic over the last few years, they are notoriously slack at enforcing driving regulations. Nonetheless, be warned, if you are caught then charges are often made on the spot and fines always hefty.

It has only been compulsory for motorbike riders to wear helmets since 1986 (it is still legal to ride a moped without a helmet if you are over 18). Wearing seatbelts became law in 1986 and only as a result of EU directives and Italy planning to introduce drink drive legislation.

Italian road signs are standardized by European norms. Note that circular signs are used to announce restrictions (or the end of them), green ones are used on the autostradas and blue ones on the secondary roads.

Road Signs

Accendere i fari in galleria	Switch on headlights in tunnel
Attenzione	caution
Caduta massi	fallen rocks
Casello a ....metri	toll in ....metres
Curve	bends
Dare precedenza	give way
Deviazione	detour
Divieto di accesso	no entry
Divieto di sorpasso	no overtaking
Divieto di sosta	no stopping
Divieto di transito	no right of way
Lavori in corso	roadworks
Passagio a livello	level crossing
Pedoni	pedestrians
Rallentare	slow
Senso unico	one way
Sosta autorizzata	parking permitted
Strada ghiacciata	icy road
Tenere la destra	keep to the right
Transito Interrotto	no through road
Uscita camion	truck exit
Veicoli al passo	dead slow

Driving Licences

British citizens who hold the pink UK driving licence (which has now become the official EU licence) may drive in Italy with no alteration to their licence at all. However, holders of the old green driving licences must first obtain a translation, available free of charge from the Italian State Tourist Office (1 Princes Street, London; tel 0171-408 1254). However, owners of Italian-registered cars should theoretically have an Italian-registered licence; this involves converting your British driving licence, for which you will need a certificate confirming that you have never been convicted for a driving offence, available from the nearest British Consulate. In practice, however, many British residents avoid doing this and carry an international driving licence instead.

Finally, it is not essential, although definitely advisable to carry an international green card for your car and remember that it is a legal requirement to carry your driving licence (*patente*), all of your car documents (*libretto*) and passport with you while you are driving and you may be required to present them if stopped by the police.

An EU-approved driving test has recently been introduced to Italy, replacing the slightly ridiculous and typically Italian test which involved a mass of paperwork about mechanics and road saftey, but very little actual driving. Driving schools (*scuola guida*) are widely available, and listed in the *Yellow Pages*.

Buying a Car

British expats have the choice of importing their own cars to Italy (see page 62, *Setting Up Home*) or buying a new one when in Italy. All of the most popular makes, and spare parts for these, are available in Italy. The local ACI office can direct you to the nearest dealer of whatever make of car you are interested in. To buy a car with an Italian registration plate, you must be an Italian resident. If you do buy a car in Italy then you will be liable to pay ownership transfer fees (*passaggio di proprietà*), which cost about lire 200,000 (£100). When considering buying a car, it is worth bearing in mind that hiring a car in Italy is very expensive compared to UK rates. It currently costs around £200 a week to rent a medium-sized car with unlimited mileage.

Italy does not have an abundance of second-hand car dealers and once you have had a brush with the bureaucracy and expense involved, it becomes clear why this is not a booming market. First you have to pay ownership fees (*passagio di proprieta*) which come to about 300,000 lire (£100+). You then have to wait up to an incredible two years for the arrival of the car log-book (*libretto di circolazione*). As it is an offence to drive without having the log-book (commonly called the *libretto*) to hand, you must obtain interim documents (*foglio sostitutivo*) which have to be renewed every three months. Additional irritations are likely to include reminders to pay fines incurred by the previous owner – the inevitable consequence of the laggardly Italian bureaucracy.

When selling a car, the popular motor magazine, *Porta Portese* is invaluable. Alternatively, simply stick a 'for sale' sign (*vendesi*) in the car window. Alternatively, you may prefer to sell your car to a garage in part-exchange for a new one. A general proxy (*procura*) must first be obtained through a notary, empowering the garage to sell the car on your behalf. The buyer then pays ownership transfer fees (see above). At least in this version of second-hand car dealing, the legwork generally has to be done by the garage.

Since 1994 the weakness of the lire, has made Italy one of the cheapest places to buy new cars. However with prices up to 40% lower in Italy than in other EU countries, one company Volkswagen sought to prevent its dealers in Italy from selling cars to other EU nationals who flocked across the border to take advantage of the saving. This was ruled illegal by the European Commission, because under single market regulations, an EU national can buy a product anywhere in the single market he or she chooses to. The EC fined VW an estimated £13m for this impropriety.

For information on importing a car into Italy, see *Setting up Home, Removals*.

Car Tax

A tax stamp (*bollo*) must be purchased for your car and is obtainable either from the post office or the ACI. At the time of press it seemed a new system was imminent to replace the *bollo* (tax stamp) for the driver's licence (*patente*) and the car owner tax (*bollo auto*) with a single *bollo* to cover both.

Insurance

Italian car insurance covers the car, not the driver, and is nearly always third party. Full, comprehensive cover (*kasko*) is available, at a price, upon consultation with the insurance company. Note that insurance is rather more expensive than in other EU countries. Unfortunately, Italian insurance companies are both notoriously slow and mean in honouring claims and be prepared for a hard battle and an even longer wait before a cheque is actually signed, delivered, and in your bank account. This is partly why so many minor road accidents in Italy go unreported.

An insurance broker used to handling the expatriate community's requirements is John Thorpe S.r.l. (Insurance Brokers, Lloyd's Correspondents, Via Dogana 3, 20123 Milan; tel 02-867141; fax 02-809250) and Royal International Insurance (Royal & Sun Alliance) based in Milan, also sell motor insurance through direct marketing in Italy.

Transport

Railways

The Italian railway system, Ferrovie dello Stato (FS) presently runs one of the cheapest railway services in western Europe. This is more remarkable than you might think, considering the substantial reforms that have been made to services over the last decade and which have resulted in a greater network of intercity lines, and a generally modern, fast and reasonably reliable service. Unlike the UK, branch lines reach the remotest areas, with connecting buses that will get you to the most obscure spots. All this smacks of a heavily subsidised rail service and tickets. Unfortunately, even with subsidies the railways still ran up a huge deficit. Part of the solution will be higher ticket prices; even so, the railways will still be excellent value.

Tickets. There are usually formidable queues for tickets at main stations. You can find automatic ticket machines, but these are usually a problem for newcomers. Also, it is compulsory to validate all tickets by inserting them in the yellow machines on platforms which clip and stamp them. Failure to do this makes you liable to a spot fine of 50,000 lire (about £20).

There is a complete national pocket timetable (*Il Pozzorario*) which can be bought at stations and newspaper kiosks for about £5. It has useful maps, and tables to work out costings. Travelling by train in Italy is far preferable to the localized and sluggish bus system.

The *rapido* and *IC* (Inter-city) trains are invariably the fastest and most expensive, stopping only at the major cities. For these a supplement (*supplemento rapido*) is required according to mileage (for example 250km is about £6.50. Remember that tickets for all trains should be bought in advance, and that tickets bought on the train are subject to a surcharge. Reductions of around 50% are available to children under 12 and people over 65

The Milan to Rome rapido train takes under four hours, with an onward link to Naples. There is also a Super Rapido or TEE (Trans-Europe-Express) which has first class only and compulsory reservation. Using the Channel Tunnel from UK the trip to Paris takes 3hrs from where you get the Paris to Milan train.

The *espresso* and *diretto* trains are the next fastest, and reasonably priced, stopping at most large towns. Lastly, and to be avoided if possible, are the slow *locale* trains which seem to stop at every village and country backwater imaginable.

Agents for FS in the UK include Wasteels Travel (121 Wilton Road, London SW1; tel 0171-834 7066) and CIT (50 Conduit Street, London W1; tel 0171-434 3844).

Station Signs

Al Binari/Ai Treni	to the platforms/trains
Arrivi/Partenze	arrivals/departures
Biglietteria	ticket office
Deposito Bagagli	left luggage
Entrata/Uscita	entrance/exit
Orario	timetable
Sala d'Attesa	waiting room
Vietato l'Ingresso	no entry

Phrases

Andata/Andata e ritorno Firenze	single/return to Florence
Il primo/l' ultimo/il prossimo treno	the first/last/next train
A che binario?	Which platform?
C' è un posto?	Is there a seat?
È questo posto libero?	Is this seat taken?

Buses

Italian cities are dotted with bright orange town buses weaving chaotically through the traffic as Italian motorists resolutely refuse to acknowledge the function of bus lanes. Italy has no national bus company but more buses than any other European country. Bus tickets are fairly inexpensive and are obtainable from tobacconists (*tabaccherie*) which have the black 'T' sign displayed, from ticket offices at the bus termini (*capoline*) and from some news-stands, tickets should be cancelled at the ticket machine once you are on the bus.

A single ticket (*corso semplice*) costs between lire 700 and 900 while morning or afternoon tickets, known as half-day tickets (*biglietti orari*) cost slightly more. Season tickets (*abbonamenti*) are also available, although these vary in length and price. A monthly season ticket in Milan for the bus, tram and subway routes (*intera rete*) costs between lire 20,000 (£9) and lire 25,000 (£11).

Buses in the provincial areas of Italy can be a nightmare. Bus services are often severely reduced at the weekends; journeys are long and slow and timetables erratic. Tickets can be bought on the bus and most of them will stop for you if you flag them down along the road and look desperate. Although travelling by train is preferable especially between large cities, the buses and coaches are a reasonable alternative and you may be glad of them if there is a train strike.

The Metro

Both Rome and Milan have metros. The Rome metro (*Metropolitina*) consists of two lines which exist principally to ferry commuters in and out of the centre to the suburbs. Less crowded and less hot than the buses, however, it's worth catching the metro if you're travelling around the city; there are stations at the Colosseum, the Spanish Steps and the Piazza Barberini. A transport map (available from the Piazza dei Cinquecento information booth for lire 1,000) is invaluable when attempting to negotiate you way through the metro system. Books of five or ten tickets can be bought in advance from *edicole* (newsstands) and *tabaccherie* (tobacconists).

In Milan, stations are marked MM and tickets can be bought from the usual places where the black and yellow sign *Biglietti ATM* is displayed. Tickets are also available from stations. A single ticket gives integrated access to other city transport above ground, but only allows one metro trip.

Taxis

Italian taxis are a cheerful canary yellow in colour (like the New York cabs) and more expensive than London cabs. This is partly due to the list of hefty surcharges which are imposed for countless sins: extra luggage, night trips and rides to the airport. Often the meter is 'forgotten', in which case it is worth negotiating a price for the journey in advance rather than recklessly jumping in the cab and finding the price outlandish later.

Air

The Italians indulge in internal flights far more than the British. This is partly due to the distances which separate Italy's most important cities, principally Milan and Rome (flight time about 50 minutes). Alitalia and its sister companies, Alisarda and ATI, fly to eleven major cities throughout mainland Italy and the islands and Air One does flights between Rome and Milan. However, internal flights do tend to be pretty expensive, so bear in mind that passengers of ages 12 to 25 qualify for a 35% discount over normal fares, as do students. There are also reductions of 50% for group family travel, 30% for night travel and children up to two years of age only have to pay 10% of the adult fare while children aged two to twelve pay half fare. Apply to Alitalia for further details.

Like Britain, Italy has its share of little airlines which sprang up following the opening up of the skies to the free market. Unfortunately, all but one of them, Air Dolomiti was running at a loss in 1997. The future for the other five: Air One, Alpi Eagles, Minerva, Air Sicilia and Azurra looks uncertain.

Milan has two airports, Malpensa and Linate which are 46km and 8km respectively from the city centre. Airport buses run between Linate and the Garibaldi Central Station, a journey of about 30/40 minutes. At the time of press, the Italian government was the subject of a protest to the European Commission by eight international airlines for transferring all international flights to Malpensa.

Rome also has two airports: Leonardo da Vinci/Fiumicino, 32 km west of the city for scheduled flights, and Ciampino airport for charter flights.
Buses run every quarter of an hour between Fiumicino and the Termini Station of Via Giolitti; a journey of about an hour. There are also trains which take about half an hour to reach Ostiense station.

Ferries

There are regular ferry connections between the mainland of Italy and the islands and large car ferries run from the ports of Genova, Civitavecchia and Naples to Sardinia and Sicily. There are also ferry connections from the mainland to the smaller Tremiti, Bay of Naples and Pontine islands. The ferries also make international trips from the mainland to Malta, Corsica, Spain, Tunisia, Egypt and Israel. Fares are reasonable although you may have to book well in advance, especially over the summer months, while the number of crossings is greatly reduced during the winter. Serena Holidays which acts as a booking agent for the large Italian shipping company, Tirrenia, can arrange crossings to Sardinia, Sicily, and Tunisia. Serena is charging from £30 one way (from £55 with a car) from Genova to Sardinia at the time of going to press; this service runs daily. For information concerning timetables and prices contact one of the addresses listed below which run ferry services to a variety of islands off Italy:

Aliscafi Snav: Via Carraciolo 13, Naples; tel 081-684 288.
Caremar Molo Beverello: Piazza Municipio, Naples; tel 081-5551 15384.
Siremar: Via F. Crispi 129, Palermo; tel 091-582 688.
Tirrenia: c/o Serena Holidays, 40-42 Kenway Road, London; SW5 0171-373 6548/9.

Banks and Finance

The Banking System

Before becoming involved in the Italian banking system it is advisable to become acquainted with its peculiarities. It is ironic that from the tenth to the fourteenth centuries parts of Italy, including Venice and Lombardy, were responsible for some of the most innovatory banking in Europe and that the Italians virtually brought banking to England (hence Lombard Street in London). Since then alas, history has been reluctant to repeat itself. Italy is generally recognized to have one of the least efficient banking services in Europe. In recent years there have been a number of mergers and acquisitions thus reducing the number of smaller banks. There are now about 987 banks operating in Italy of which 45 are the branches of foreign banks (*filiali di banche estere* or *FBEs*). In the past the phenomenon of the single-outlet bank, meant the customer trying to obtain cash outside the town where the account was held became a virtual impossibility since other banks were certain to refuse to cash a cheque for the customer of another bank. The alternative, the Bancomat network of automatic cash dispensers, which in theory dispense cash to clients of other banks, is so rarely operational that most Italians are resigned to carrying around huge quantities of banknotes. Bank staff are no more cooperative than their technology. Owing to the fact that around 80% of the banking system is state owned, banks are grossly overstaffed and employees have jobs for life; this has produced a similar mentality to that found in the state bureaucracy. History has frequently shown that state industries are inclined to put the welfare of their clients second: a theory borne out by the fact that the average *impiegato bancario* (bank employee) treats customers with haughty disdain.

The frustration of dealing with Italian banks runs a close second to that experienced in close encounters with the state bureaucracy. Bank facades are often impressive, but once inside, the image crumbles: the most simple transaction takes a preposterous amount of time. Queueing is a random affair in Italy, necessitating an opportunistic approach to any window that may become vacant. If you are fortunate enough to attract the teller's attention, the chances are that the bank computer will be down – they nearly always are, or if not, the employee is incapable of working it (technical training is abysmal).

Until recently it was extremely difficult to get a personal loan from an Italian bank and, as in other European countries, issuing a cheque for which there are insufficient funds, is illegal. Italian banking practices are still a far cry from the credit largesse characteristic of banks in the UK. Months of negotiation with an Italian bank and copious paperwork are required for any reasonable overdraft to be granted. Even if the loan is approved, the interest charges will be exorbitant (25% or higher), as are all charges connected with Italian banking. Small wonder then, that Italians are amongst Europe's least keen holders of current bank accounts: about 25% of Italians have such an account, whereas in the UK there are 1.9 accounts per head of the population.

The governing body of Italian banks is the Banca d'Italia (Via Nazionale 91, 00184 Rome). The biggest bank is the Banca Nazionale di Lavoro which is state owned and comes fifteenth in the league table of European banks. Other larger national banks include: Credito Italiano, Banco di Roma, Banco di Napoli, Banco di Sicilia and Banca Commerciale Italiana.

Opening an Account

Anyone who is considering living and working in Italy on a long-term basis will need an Italian bank account. It is however incredibly difficult for a foreigner to open a current account with a bank in Italy without a *residenza* (residence permit). The only option if you are not yet in possession of this invaluable document is to enlist the assistance of an influential Italian who may be able to persuade the bank manager on your behalf, otherwise you will have to manage with Eurocheques until your residenza is granted.

Once an Italian bank account has been set up the customer receives a *libretto di assegni* (cheque book) and will be able to cash a cheque, *incassare un assegno*. When paying by cheque a *carta di garanzia* (cheque guarantee card) is obligatory. For larger purchases a bank draft (*assegno circolare*) is normally required.

Using an Italian Bank Account

The majority of expatriates do not normally choose to transfer all their UK assets into their Italian bank account. There are sound reasons for this: not only are bank charges at least double in Italy, but one is liable to attract the grasping hands of the Italian tax authorities. The consensus seems to be that one should maintain a UK account and transfer the minimum funds needed to Italy to run one's affairs there. If one is maintaining accounts with British banks it is essential to inform the British tax authorities and the bank that one is resident abroad to prevent double taxation.

When calculating the amount of funds needed in your Italian account you should err on the generous side as there are various ways you can be caught out: eg. by bank charges such as lire 1,500 per cheque and automatic adjustments by the gas and electricity companies to your standing orders after the bi-annual meter readings (see Chapter Three, *Setting Up Home*, Utilities). Banks do pay a small amount of interest, usually two or three per cent, on current accounts in credit, but this is a minute concession in the face of the horrendous bank charges. If one is unfortunate enough to issue a bouncing cheque (*un assegno a vuoto*) albeit by accident, it can lead to legal problems, being disbarred from holding any bank account, and even to having your name gazetted in the local press, so one should try to avoid this at all costs. On the other hand pre-arranged overdrafts may be possible, if you can afford the interest.

Transferring Funds from the UK to Italy

For most expatriates transferring funds from the UK to Italy is necessary on a regular basis. It can also, in view of the dinosaur qualities of the Italian banking system, be a protracted process; three weeks is about the minimum, though for those living in Tuscany and Umbria months can elapse before the transfer arrives. Some ways of sending money may be faster than others, for instance the international Swift system by which the transfer is sent direct to the local branch of your bank in Italy rather than to the head office of the Italian bank in Milan, Rome etc. first and then on to your own branch. It is the time transfers spend languishing in the labyrinth of the bank's head office that normally causes the delay. The first step in arranging a Swift transaction is to ascertain from the person in charge of the foreign department of your local Italian bank whether he or she (usually he), will accept transfers direct. One must also check that your UK bank will handle Swift transactions, otherwise it will have to be done through an Italian bank with a UK branch. Under the Swift system the transaction is logged with the precise time and date of the transfer from the UK and it is guaranteed to arrive at the Italian end within two days. With this *via di mezzo* (short cut) in mind, it behoves the prospective foreign resident to select an Italian bank on what services it can provide.

Choosing a Bank

Despite the general condemnation of the Italian banking system, some banks do enjoy a better reputation than others in their dealings with foreigners. These include: Istituto Bancario San Paolo based in Turin, with 500 branches nationwide, and Creditwest, which is the product of a joint venture between the Italian bank Credito Italiano and the UK bank National Westminster. Creditwest has about 30 branches in the Milan, Rome and Naples areas many of which employ staff familiar with the banking needs of expatriates. Some of the smaller, privately-owned banks may also be worthy of closer acquaintance: in particular, Credito Emiliano (Milan, Rome and central Italy), has a policy of encouraging clients from the foreign community.

Useful Addresses

Istituto Bancario San Paolo di Torino: Piazza San Carlo 156, Turin; tel 011-5551.
*Creditwest:*Via Santa Margarita 7, Milan; tel 02-8813.
Credito Emiliano: Via Andegari 14, Milan; tel 02-88261.

Offshore Banking

One of the financial advantages of being an expatriate is that you can invest money offshore in tax havens such as the Isle of Man, the Channel Islands and Gibraltar, thus accruing tax-free interest on your savings. Many such facilities are as flexible as UK high street banking and range from current accounts to long-term, high interest earning deposits. Mortgage facilities are also available . Many of the banks which can provide offshore facilities have reassuringly familiar names. Some building societies have also moved into this field.

Useful Addresses

Abbey National: 237 Main Street, Gibraltar; tel 010-350 76090.
Alliance & Leicester International Ltd.: P.O.B. 226, 10-12 Prospect Hill, Douglas, Isle of Man IM99 1RY; tel +44 1624 663566; fax +44 1624 617286.

Brewin Dolphin Bell Lawrie Ltd. Stockbrokers: 5 Giltspur Street, London EC1A 9BD; tel 0171-246 1028; fax 0171-246 1093. Services include international

portfolio management with offshore facility for those domiciled or resident outside the UK. Contact Robin Lindsay-Stewart.

Bristol & West International: P.O.B. 611, High Street, St Peter Port, Guernsey, Channel Islands GY1 4NY; tel +44 1481-720609; fax +44 1481 711658.

Halifax International (Jersey Ltd): P.O.B. 664, Halifax House, 31-33 New Street, St. Helier, Jersey; tel +44 1534 59840; fax +44 1534 59280.

Midland Offshore: P.O. Box 615, 28/34 Hill Street, St. Helier, Jersey JE4 5YD, Channel Islands.

Lloyds Bank Offshore Centre: P.O. Box 12, Douglas, Isle of Man, IM99 1SS; fax +44 1624 638181.

Nationwide Overseas Ltd: 45-51, Athol Street, Douglas, Isle of Man; tel +44 1624-663494.

Overseas Club: P.O. Box 12, Douglas, Isle of Man, IM99 1SS; tel +44 (0) 990 258079; fax +44 (0) 1624 638181 http://www.lloyds-offshore-bank.com. Also in Jersey and Guernsey. Lloyds TSB merger offers total expatriate financial care.

Woolwich Guernsey Limited: P.O. Box 341, La Tonnelle House, Les Banques, St. Peter Port, Guernsey GY1 3UW; tel +44 1481 715735; fax +44 1481 715722.

Resident Abroad: FT Magazines, Greystoke Place, Fetter Lane, London EC4A 1ND; subscriptions dept: P.O. Box 387, Haywards Heath, RH16 3GS; tel +44 1444-445520; fax +44 1444-445599. Magazine for expatriates.

Taxation

As already mentioned, tax evasion in Italy takes place on a breathtaking scale which has become so widely accepted as part of the Italian system that it is difficult to see how anything can be done about it. The worst offenders are businesses of all sizes, and the self-employed. It has been estimated by the tax inspectors' organization, Il Servizio Centrale degli Ispettori Tributari, that 83% of the self-employed category declare an annual income of less than £4,000. The reason such modesty does not attract the attention of the *Guardia di Finanza*, (a.k.a. *i Finanzieri*, the tax police) is that they are usually in on the fraud at the highest levels. It is probably a mark of their schizophrenia that from time to time, i Finanzieri feel obliged to indulge in advertising campaigns to remind the public and themselves that they are there to root out the culprits, and not to cooperate with them. However despite the enormity of the problem facing them, the Finance Minsistry has been making some war-like moves at least as far as IVA (VAT) evasion and high income earners are concerned, and i Finanzieri have proved more effective than might have been expected in pursuit of offenders.

As regards the foreign resident, the matter of taxation is one area in which the adage 'When in Rome, do as the Romans do' should not necessarily be taken to heart. *L'Evasione fiscale* (tax evasion) is best left to the Italians who are experts and can manage the system much better than foreigners without contacts can ever hope to. In addition any foreigner caught evading personal income or business taxes risks enormous fines. Perhaps worse than this, is being entirely in the power of the tax inspector, whose discretionary powers are as immense as the fine or *bustarella* (bribe), he will deem appropriate. Foreigners become taxable as residents if they are working in Italy for 183 days or longer.

Deciding to pay ones taxes gives rise to its own set of problems, particularly if one is in business or self-employed, as the system is constantly being amended. Unfortunately, new taxes are often brought in without the old ones being cancelled. This induces a permanent state of chaos in the tax system so that it is extremely difficult to ascertain for which taxes one is actually liable. However it is undoubtedly better to pay some taxes rather than none at all. It is probably unwise to proceed without the services of an accountant (*commercialista*) preferably obtained through personal recommendation.

Income Tax

Income tax is known as *Imposta sul Reddito delle Persone Fisiche* (IRPEF) and is levied at varying rates. From 1998 there will be five rates starting at 19% on incomes up to 15 million lire, between 15 and 30 million lire it is 27%; from 30 million to 60 million 34% and up to 135 million lire 40% and the highest rate of 46% levied on incomes over 135 million lire. The previous highest rate was 51% and this has been abolished. As well as the richest being better off, those with children, particularly if both parents are working will benefit from a doubling or more of allowances against income tax. However, once you are earning over 50 million lire you are beginning to lose the benefits enjoyed by those on lower or the highest incomes, even if you have children.

The new IRPEF rates are accompanied by changes to the health contributions paid by employees which make up part of their salary and which are paid straight to the national health service. From 1 January 1998 these will no longer be deducted, as the employer will pay these together with IRAP (see below). This will add about 1% to a salary of 40 million lire.

The way IRPEF is calculated on a gross salary of 40 million lire (about £13,330) would be: you pay 6,900,000 at 43% (see second scale below) and 34% on the remaining ten million lire which comes to 3,400,000 lire. The total IRPEF would therefore be 10,300,000 lire.

Income Tax Table

Income in millions	Tax rate	Amount of tax payable
up to 15mn	19%	19% of whole amount
15mn to 30mn	27%	2,850,000+27% on amount above 15mn
30mn to 60mn	43%	6,900,000+34% on amount above 30mn
60mn to 120mn	40%	17,100,000+40% on amount above 60mn
120mn and over	45%	41,100,000+45% on amount above 120mn

High earners used to pay considerably more income tax in Italy than in the UK, which may account for the national obsession with not paying it. Since no red-blooded, tax-evading Italian would dream of declaring his actual income, the tax authorities devised a cunning, if arbitrary, scheme for assessment based on perceivable assets. For instance, yachts, expensive cars, estates and household staff are all deemed to represent, according to their size and quantity, a specific amount of income. Since Italians are born show offs, there is little chance that they will resort to driving around in battered Lancia's in order to conceal their assets.

There are other peculiarities regarding the Italian tax system: unlike Britain where the tax office will chase you to fill in a tax form, in Italy it is up to the individual to present him or herself at the *Intendenza di Finanza* (local tax office) to fill in a standard tax form (known as a '740') and be given a *codice fiscale* (tax number). A codice fiscale is needed in order to work, and for various transactions such as property and car purchase, rentals and bill payments.

Owing to the fact that Italian personal taxation can be swingeing at the higher levels it is advisable not to have all one's assets in Italy. The alternatives, as already mentioned, are to maintain UK accounts and to consider offshore investment (see above). Owing to the complexity of taxation it is strongly recommended that you take independent, expert financial advice before departing from the UK. A list of such advisors can be obtained from the Personal Investment Authority (1 Canada Square, Canary Wharf, London E14 5AZ; tel 0171-418 5355). The PIA replaces the Financial Intermediaries, Managers and Brokers Regulatory Association (FIMBRA) and LAUTRO.

Local Taxes

As part of Italy's package of fiscal reform introduced in January 1998 *Imposta Locale sui Redditi* (ILOR) was replaced by a new regional tax, IRAP which has to be paid by the self-employed including entrepreneurs, professionals of all kinds, artists as well as companies and organisations. IRAP will also replace health contributions, ICIAP and tax on Parita IVA. It is a tax on services and goods produced, on the difference between the value realised after specified production costs (except labour costs) have been deducted.

The basic rate of IRAP is 4.25% but as with ILOR there is a reduced agricultural rate (3%). The rate for banks, insurance companies and other financial services is 5%. In 1998 and 1999 IRAP will be levied directly into the National Treasury; after that it will be a regionally payable tax.

You will almost certainly need to consult a *commercialista* to work out how the new tax regulations apply to your particular circumstances.

In addition to IRAP there is a new, additional regional tax to allow for the portion of IRAP which the regions need to replace the taxes like ICIAP which have been abolished. The state has limited the new tax to a maximum of 1.1% until 2000 when, since it is a regional tax, the regions themselves will decide the amount of additional local taxes which need to be levied as a subsection of IRAP.

The new taxes will be payable in the same way as income tax with estimated taxes being payable in two tranches in May and November. There are big fines for non-payment and under estimation of the amount due. Late payment is also penalised with fines.

Other Taxes

There is a range of other taxes payable in Italy, most of which have direct equivalents or are similar to taxes payable in the UK.

VAT: Known as IVA or *Imposta sul Valore Aggiunto*. There are three rates (1998) of 4%, 10% and 20%. The standard rate 20%. Most foodstuffs are taxed at 10%. For other goods including most clothing, shoes, records, cassettes and certain alcoholic goods the rate is 20%.

Imposta Comunale sull'incremento di valore degli immobili: (INVIM) is the equivalent of Capital Gains Tax paid on profit from the sale of property. This tax is subject to wide abuse but rarely completely evaded. For further details see Chapter Three, *Setting Up Home*.

Imposta sulle Successioni e Donazioni: Inheritance and Gift Tax. In common with some other European countries, Italian inheritance tax levels vary according to the nearness of the deceased's relatives: direct relatives, eg. spouse or child, pay least, cousins more, and non-relatives the most (see Chapter Five, *Retirement*).

Health Care, Insurance and Hospitals

It would perhaps be a salutory lesson for those who are accustomed to bash the British National Health Service to be sent for treatment in an Italian state hospital.

They would be guaranteed never to complain again. In common with other systems under state control in Italy, the state medical system costs the government (ie. the tax payer) a fortune and is a disaster area to be avoided if at all possible.

Italy has a glut of doctors and produces more medics than any other European country. Many of these, however, are theoretical graduates who may never have seen a surgical procedure or even a corpse! Practical experience is usually gained by becoming the acolyte of a consultant (*primario*) and following the great man or woman on their ward rounds. Despite the erratic standard of Italian medical training, there are some excellent doctors, especially in private clinics. In addition Italy has a clutch of world-renowned specialists including a Nobel prize winner (Daniel Bovet) and a singing heart surgeon with a string of hit records as well as medical successes under his gown (Enzo Jannacci). Simultaneously Italy possesses some of the best doctors and most appalling hospitals in Europe, where treatment is irregular, care haphazard and facilities inadequate. Unsurprisingly, many Italian residents, both nationals and expatriates, take out private health insurance (see below) to cover themselves in the case of long-term, expensive hospitalisation. Note that a list of local national health centres and hospitals is available from your local health authority (*Unita Sanitarie Locali*) in Italy; also most local embassies or consulates should be able to provide a list of English-speaking doctors in your region.

The E111

It is essential that anyone intending to move permanently to Italy register their change of address with the International Services, Department of Social Security (Longbenton, Newcastle upon Tyne NE98 1YX) before leaving the country. They will then be sent the paperwork required to obtain an E111 (allow one month for processing) which entitles all EU nationals whether they are tourists or working abroad to medical treatment by the national health service in any EU/EEA member country. The E111 is valid for twelve months, and is renewable on the proviso that the applicant still makes their UK National Insurance contributions.

Although the E111 covers emergency hospital treatment while abroad it does not include the cost for prescribed medicines, specialist examinations, X-rays, laboratory tests and physiotherapy or dental treatment. Consequently, private insurance should still be taken out for the required period as this will provide financial protection against medical treatment costs which are not regarded as emergencies and which are not covered by the E111.

Leaflet SA29 which gives details of social security, health care and pension rights within the EU is also available from the DSS International Services (see above) and is useful reading for anyone intending to live and work in Italy.

UK National Insurance Contributions

If you start paying into the Italian social security system you become eligible for their benefits. However, if you are planning to return the UK it is advisable to keep up your UK contributions in if you want to retain your entitlement to a UK state pension and other benefits. Class 1 contributions are for those in full-time employment with a British-based employer, but there are alternatives if your employer is not paying: class 2 (self-employed) and class 3 (voluntary) contributions. Class 3 are £6.05 per week (1998). Many UK tax advisors advice you should pay UK NICs if you possibly can. Further details from the Contributions Agency (0191-213 9000) and financial consultants KPMG (0171-311 5000) can advise expatriate employees.

Using the NHS

Anyone who makes social security payments or who receives a state pension, is unemployed, or under the age of 18 is entitled to the dubious benefits of medical treatment on the Italian state health service free of charge. These include free hospital accommodation and medical treatment and up to 90% of the cost of prescription medicines; a contribution (*il ticket*) of 10% is required from the patient. Social security payments, which account for approximately 8% of a worker's gross income, are deducted from the employee's gross salary by the employer.

Foreigners working for foreign firms will almost certainly be insured for treatment under a private medical scheme and thus will be spared the trauma of public health care in an Italian hospital (*ospedale*). The numerous private hospitals in Italy are often run by the church and being both hygienic and efficient prove a pleasant contrast to the state-run hospitals.

Anyone who has become a foreign resident and who wishes to receive treatment under the Italian state system is obliged to register with and obtain a national health number from the local *Unita Sanitaria Locale (USL)*. You will need to produce your permesso di soggiorno and a letter from your employer which states that you are working for him or her. Self-employed or freelance workers should first register with the INPS in Piazza Augusto Imperatore 32, Rome where they will be given the necessary documentation to take to the local USL office together with their permesso di soggiorno. USL addresses can be found in the *Tuttocittà*, a supplement that comes with Italian telephone directories, or alternatively in the local newspaper. Once you are registered with the Unita Sanitaria Locale, the next step is to register with *un medico mutualistico* (general practitioner). The system of free treatment is known as *il mutuo*. Outpatients are normally treated at a *studio medico* or *ambulatorio* (surgery). A private clinic is *una clinica private*.

If you are unlucky enough to find yourself in an Italian state hospital it is essential that your relatives know where you are and that someone visits you regularly to provide you with a regular intake of food. Italian hospitals are notorious for providing inedible food, or none at all. In the latter case the cause is almost certain to be because the kitchen staff have sold off the ingredients or are on strike. However, the food is the least of the patient's worries: only 25% of urgent cases get a hospital bed within a month of diagnosis and 700,000 patients contract further infections in hospital owing to the appalling standards of hygiene.

Some of the better hospitals are in Rome: the Salvator Mundi, the Fatebenefratelli (Via Cassia 600; tel 06-3326 0911) and the Roman American Hospital. In Milan there is the Ospedale Maggiore di Milano Policlinico (via Francesco Sforza 32; tel 02-5501 6723).

Emergencies

If you are involved in or at the site of a serious accident then get to the nearest phone box and dial 113, which will put you through to the emergency services; ask for an *ambulanza* (ambulance). Less serious injuries should be treated at the casualty (*Pronto Soccorso*) ward at the nearest hospital. Alternatively, most major railway stations and airports have first-aid stations with qualified doctors in hand and many of these are reputed to be more effective than the hospitals.

In the event of minor ailments, aches and pains it may well be worth avoiding the chaos of the state hospitals and applying directly to your local chemist (*farmacia*). Chemists are generally extremely highly qualified in Italy, and will probably be able to prescribe something for you. The farmacia are usually open all night in larger towns and cities and if the one you end up at is closed, there should be a list displayed on the door which says which chemists are open that night.

Sickness and Invalidity Benefit

Anyone who is moving to Italy permanently and who claims sickness or invalidity benefit in the UK is entitled to continue claiming this benefit once in Italy. Strictly speaking, to claim either benefit, you must be physically incapable of all work, however, the interpretation of the words 'physically incapable' is frequently stretched just a little beyond literal truth. If the claimant has been paying NI contributions in the UK for two tax years (this may be less depending on his or her level of income) then he or she is eligible to claim weekly sickness benefit. After receiving sickness benefit for 28 weeks, you are entitled to invalidity benefit which is paid at a higher rate with variations above and below this figure.

Although it may seem something of a Catch 22 when you can only claim sickness benefit if you are incapable of working and yet you are only entitled to the benefit through the last two years of National Insurance payments deducted from your income, the benefit is primarily used by people who have had to stop work due to severe arthritis, cancer, Parkinson's etc.

Anyone currently receiving either form of benefit should inform their local branch of the DSS that they are moving to Italy. They will then send your forms to the Overseas Branch of the DSS who will ensure that a monthly sterling cheque is sent either to your new address or direct to your bank account. The only conditions involved are that all claimants submit themselves to a medical examination, either in Italy or the UK, on request.

Italian sickness benefit for workers (*operai*) and salaried staff (*impiegati*) in commerce and industry is paid partly by the employer and partly by the state national sickness fund (INPS). Staff type employees get 100 per cent of their salary (at the employer's cost) for up to six months. For manual workers the amount is dependent on their labour contract and the length of service

Private Medical Insurance

In contrast with the lack of organization in the public sector, the private sector of the health service is amazingly well organized. However, it is also expensive; charges at private hospitals and clinics are a minimum of £150 per day for a room, so private health insurance is a must. If you held a private health insurance policy in the UK, you will find that most companies will switch this for European cover once you are in Italy. With the increase of British and foreign insurance companies offering this type of cover, it is worth shopping around and there is no reason why, if you have not organized this before leaving the UK, you should not do so from Italy. Of course, if you are employed in Italy, you and your family will certainly belong to a health insurance scheme which tops up the state health service, *il mutuo*. The personnel section of your company will advise.

Private health insurance can be arranged through an organization such as BUPA, PPP or Expacare all of which offer international health insurance schemes. BUPA International has designed its Lifeline scheme to offer maximum choice and flexibility. There are three levels of cover: Gold, Classic and Essential all of which provide full refund for hospital accommodation and specialists' fees so you never need to be concerned about unexpected bills for in-patient treatment such as an operation. Cover for emergency ambulance charges and sports injuries is also standard. Gold and Classic offer out-patient treatment which may be a sensible precaution in Italy. The most comprehensive cover is available with the Gold scheme which includes the cost of primary care treatment and home nursing. BUPA International has a 24 hour service centre dedicated to their expatriate members with an experienced team on hand to deal with any queries. Claims are paid promptly in Italian Lira, UK Sterling or any other currencies because with Lifeline you are covered anywhere in the world apart from North America (although additional cover is available for this region). For more information phone +44 (0) 1273 208181.

The PPP offers a choice of three plans, Standard, Comprehensive and Prestige. All plans cover in-patient hospital care with yearly maximum claims per person varying from £500,000 to £1,000,000. Comprehensive provides outpatient cover and nursing at home. Whilst Prestige in addition also covers you for normal pregnancy, stress counselling, disability compensation and annual travel cover. As an indication of premium, the Comprehensive plan starts at £44.20 a month for an under 24-year-old, through to £246.10 a month for someone aged 80. A 10% introductory discount has been applied to the premiums quoted for European cover.

PPP healthcare offers emergency evacuation and repatriation as a standard part of their policies. PPP can also provide immediate cover which is useful for anyone arranging private health insurance at the last minute. They also offer a 30-day, money back guarantee so you have time to ensure you are completely happy with your cover. For more details and a quotation contact +44 (0) 1323 432002.

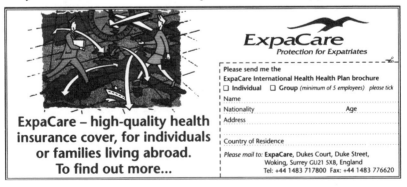
The other major UK insurer, Expacare Insurance Services offers an International Health Plan – Area 1, premium rates (Europe only) provides cost-effective health

insurance for expatriates of all nationalities who are based in Italy; for details contact D.L. Pryor on 01483-717801.

Self-employed expatriates are liable to INPS contributions as a percentage of their annual taxable income. However, if you wish to join the Italian National Health scheme, you are required to pay 7.5% of your taxable income, quite apart from what it may cost to keep your UK pension rights going. It is very doubtful if the benefits achieved by such a contribution in Italy outweigh the disadvantages of possible unnecessary involvement in the Italian tax system and the answer is almost certainly recourse to a private health insurance policy, some of which will even pay GP and dental charges.

The Italian for first aid is *pronto soccorso.*

Useful Addresses
BUPA International: Russell Mews, Brighton BN1 2NR; tel 01273-208181; fax 01273-866583; email: advice@bupa-intl.com; http://www.bupa.com/int.
Expacare Insurance Services: Dukes Court, Duke Street, Woking, Surrey GU21 5XB; tel 01483-717801; fax 01483-776620. Providers of private health insurance for expatriates.
Private Patients Plan: (head office: PPP Healthcare Group plc, Vale Road, Tunbridge Wells Kent TN1 2PL; tel +44 (0) 1892 512 345).
Worldwide Travel Insurance: ASA Inc. USA; tel 1-602 968 0440.

Social Security and Unemployment

Social Security

The Italian state social security system, (*lo stato assistenziale*), is generally regarded as being disastrously inadequate and wasteful. In what has turned out to be a European trend in the latter 1990s, there are massive cutbacks planned for the end of the millennium and into the foreseeable future as the practical necessity of abandoning welfare idealogy continues its decline. At present the Italian system provides the usual array of old age and disability pensions, sickness and unemployment benefits and health and medical care. However, these services are lacking in facilities, sometimes corrupt, always ridden with bureaucracy and mostly inefficient.

The social security system is gradually being merged under the umbrella of the notorious INPS, Istituto Nazionale di Previdenza Sociale (National Insurance and Pensions Fund) which has funds that total well over a quarter of the country's GNP. Health benefits are administered by the USL, Le Unità Sanitarie Locali, (see page 91), the housing system (*la casa*) has steadily deteriorated over the last forty years and the result is chronic overcrowding and housing shortages in the larger Italian cities. The INPS effectively dominates the whole of the pension system, although there also exist several pension funds linked to certain state industries (water, gas, the railways, etc.) as well as private pension plans, which are now growing rapidly. Italians lack reliable pension and medical schemes, amenities like free or subsidized sports facilities, public libraries and meals on wheels, or employment retraining schemes and strongly resent their government's reluctance to produce anything efficient along these lines.

If you have a regular job with an Italian firm you will be paying INPS contributions, the equivalent of national insurance in the UK. The standard rate of social security deducted from an employee's gross salary is low, set at around 10% (compared with 15% in France and 11% in the UK) with the employer's contribution of 43.76% forming by far the greatest chunk of the total offering of 53.75%.

It is possible to keep up national insurance contributions (the equivalent of Italian social security) in the UK on a voluntary basis on moving to Italy. This can be quite a canny move for anyone who isn't working but who hasn't yet reached retirement age. If you do keep your payments up then you will be eligible to claim a UK pension from the age of 60 (for women) or 65 (for men) throughout your time in Italy. However, this will be unnecessary for those who intend to work in Italy as EU regulations ensure that social security contributions made in one member state are counted as a contribution period to the contributor's own country's social security system for the purpose of determining their future benefits from that system.

Unemployment Benefit

Considering Italy's inclusion in the group of the seven most industrialized nations, the country has a chronic unemployment rate. The unemployment figures peaked at 14.2% in 1985 and now stand at 12.4%. Unsurprisingly, unemployment is worst in the poor Mezzogiorno which, although only comprising a total of 36% of the Italian population, accounts for 52% of the total number of unemployed; while unemployment is less than half the national average in the prosperous north. However, Italy's thriving black economy (which contributes, by some estimates, up to 25% of GNP) provides thousands of jobs for those officially out of work and undermines the representational value of these statistics. Moreover, many of Italy's unemployed refuse to do certain jobs, such as street sweeping, washing dishes, making pizzas; leaving such 'menial' chores to the millions of illegal immigrants who scrape a living off the country's black economy. Others indulge in the notorious Italian practice of taking second or third jobs (*il secondo/terzo laboro*), which is a frequently-used means of topping up the often low incomes (as compared to other European countries) which exist in Italy.

Any worker who registers as being unemployed within 45 days of losing employment is entitled to unemployment benefit (*sussidio di disoccupazione*), administered by the provincial unemployment office, the Ufficio di Collocamento. This benefit is presently levied at the pitiful and woefully inadequate rate of lire 1,000 (45p) a day for the unemployed person and for each dependant. Fortunately, the level of benefit rises to lire 30,000 (£13) a day for workers in the industrial and building sector. Family allowances (*assegni familiari*) also exist which cover offspring up to the age of 26 who are still in full-time education.

For anyone who is contemplating a tentative work-finding trip to Italy it may be useful to know that as a national of a full EU member country you may transfer your unemployment benefit claim to Italy for three months while you look for employment there. Benefit can be claimed at the UK rate throughout this period.

Local Government

Running parallel to central government in Italy are three tiers of local government listed in order of ascending importance: *il comune* (the town council), *la provincia* (province) and the twenty *regioni* (regions); the latter comprising the country's largest administrative units. Of the twenty regions, only five have evolved any kind of semi-autonomous powers; Sicily, Sardinia, Trentino-Alto Adige, Friuli-Venezia-Giulia and Valle d'Aosta. The devolution of power in these regions was necessitated by both geographical and ethnic history eg. Trentino-Alto Adige was only annexed to Italy after World War I and with its strong German-speaking contingent and pro-Austria feeling, it remains an uncomfortable Italian annexe with a strong move towards political and administrative independence, mirroring to some extent the long-lived dissension between Northern Ireland and the UK. These five regions are known as *regioni a statuo speciale* and they differ from the other fifteen regions in that their assemblies resemble mini-parliaments which enjoy varying economic and administrative powers. For example, Sicily is the only region of the five which has total control over its own education system. Although legislation passed in 1970 provides, theoretically, for limited powers of autonomy in the assemblies of the remaining fifteen regions, in practice, central government remains very much the dominant force in these areas. Additionally, legislation as recent as 1989 created boroughs in the five main cities of Italy, Milan, Naples, Tome, Genoa and Turin which have a great deal of power over local spending and which are entitled to levy their own taxes.

Each of Italy's 94 provinces has a two-letter sign which forms part of the post-code and is also evident on official documents like driving licences and identity cards. The bureaucratic function of the provinces is obscure, since almost everything they do is duplicated by the other two tiers of local government. A good deal of their budget goes into sponsoring often costly cultural and other prestige projects, which are thought to further their reputation and tourist potential. Finally, the communes, elected once every five years (as are all other tiers of government) deal with all matters of local administration: local taxes, administration of social security services, housing, roads and transport etc. The communes are headed by the *sindaco* (mayor) who is assisted by *gli assessori* (the councillors).

Crime and Police

Crime

Most European countries have experienced a high increase in crime over the last two decades, and Italy is no exception. However whereas in Britain the increase has been in theft and offences against property, particularly cars, in Italy nearly three-quarters of all crime is drug-related. The three areas with the highest crime waves are Latium, the Marche and Campania. The last two in particular have shown a spectacularly rising crime rate based on the statistics for reported crimes of theft and robbery for the fifteen years from 1980 to 1995, these are from 7,200 to 19,700 in the Marche, from 15,000 to 63,600 for Latium and from 6,500 to 47,800 for Campania.

Organised violent crime in Italy is so infamous that it needs little elaboration here: the mafia black spots where murder is a regular occurence, and the vicious kidnappings where the perpetrators have the charming custom of sending the odd ear or finger of the victim to the family as an *aide-mémoire* to pay the ransom. In fact, although kidnapping regularly occurs predominantly in Calabria or Sardina, instances have fallen to a handful a year (in the 60s and 70s, it was up to sixty a year). A law introduced in 1991 forbids victims' families to mediate privately with kidnappers and allows magistrates to freeze the family's assets in order, it is argued, to discourage kidnapping. However, the state is allowed to intervene and has discretion to pay the ransom, which seems rather to negate the law's deterrent value.

Apart from Mafia violence, which is on the increase in well-recognized areas, there is less violent crime, ie. muggings, street violence in general, than in many other Western countries. This may be connected to the fact that drunkenness, which proves a spur to much Anglo-Saxon crime, is very rare in Italy. Indeed the Italians look with consternation upon the hooliganism of drink-inflamed British football supporters. Also little-known in Italy are the type of crazed loners found on both sides of the Atlantic, who blast away a few dozen complete strangers in an orgy of unprovoked gunfire. Private arsenals, except for hunting rifles, are a rarity (except of course amongst the mafia). Until recently, serial killings and crimes against children were a rarity in Italy, but sadly these types of crime are on the increase.

A new crime wave has erupted in the last few years connected with the influx refugees and immigrants from Albania. Milan which is fast becoming the capital of the Albanian mafia. According to local police chiefs the Albanian criminal element is much more agressive and ruthless than other foreign criminals and they are simply murdering the Italian, African and and Arab competition out of the way.

Police

It is unfortunately the case in Italy that the police have a dismal record in beating crime. Around three-quarters of all crimes committed in Italy go unsolved. This is mainly because the bulk of crime occurs in the far south and Sicily – in other words mafia territory. Italy has four main, separate police forces for no other reason than tradition. Liaison between the forces is extremely bad with the result that when representatives of two different ones are called out to the same incident, unseemly scuffles are liable to break out – amongst the police! Owing to the singular ineffectiveness of the police in combatting organized crime in menaced cities such as Naples and Reggio Calabria, private security forces have become a booming industry. Often bizarrely uniformed, they are nevertheless a more effective deterrent against underworld-inspired violence than the regular police are. The official police forces are:

I Carabinieri: The military-associated carabinieri are the largest force, numbering nearly 86,000. They have been striving in recent years to shake off their thick image, and they are generally more personable and helpful than the other forces. Carabinieri are recognizable by their dark blue uniforms (designed by Giorgio Armani) with red stripe and matching peaked cap. Accessories include white belts with matching cartridge holder and holster. They may also carry machine guns (eg. when looking for kidnappers in the Calabrian mountains). Carabinieri squad cars are also dark blue, but with a white stripe. Their dress uniform features an ostrich-feather decorated, bicorn hat, white gloves, sword and cloak. Caribinieri police stations are known as *la Caserna* or *il Comando*. The Carabinieri's responsibilities include stopping motorists in contravention of traffic regulations and administering on-the-spot fines.

La Polizia: There are around three thousand fewer Polizia than Carabinieri, and 5% of the force is comprised of women. Their uniforms are lighter blue than the Carabinieri and have a deep pink stripe. The riot squad section (*La Celere)* who wear green uniforms are not as high profile as they were during the seventies, and are often found guarding important buildings. *La Polizia* have a reputation for uncouthness and being trigger happy. Their plain clothes section are often mistaken for armed robbers. A Polizia station is *la Questura* and Polizia chiefs are *questori*.

La Guardia di Finanza/I Finanzieri: I Finanzieri are the customs police who can trace their origins back to the eighteenth century. Their force level is half that of the Carabinieri. They wear light grey uniforms and dark green berets with a yellow badge. Their reputation reached its nadir when their former head, Generale Raffaele Giudice, was jailed for corruption on a multi-billion dollar scale, but has marginally improved since. When leaving an Italian bar or restaurant it is obligatory to carry your till receipts for 100 metres after leaving the premises in case i Finanzeri wish to inspect it, as a check on whether restaurant owners are fiddling their VAT.

I Vigili Urbani: Vigili Urbani are the local police forces. They are normally dressed in navy blue, with white jackets and a matching helmet. Of all Italian police they are the least professional. Like the Carabinieri, they can stop and fine motorists. They are responsible for checking residence permits, investigating planning infringements and other local matters. In Rome their on-going feud with the Polizia provides regular street entertainment for local citizens.

It is generally agreed that the Carabinieri are the preferred force if one needs to call out the police. The emergency number is 113. Theft being one of the most common crimes in Italy, the chances are that sooner or later you will require the police to make out a stolen goods report (*la denuncia*). It is equally likely that they will be unwilling to do this, which can be very frustrating if you need a denuncia for insurance purposes. It is best to go to a Comando dei Carabinieri, or Questura, in person to exercise your powers of persuasion.

If you are unfortunate enough to be accosted by any type of police, be warned that they expect you to be awestruck. If you show any signs of unwillingness to co-operate, they may arrest you on a charge of insulting a state official. Under Italian law the police have powers to detain you for twenty-four hours without informing a magistrate. You may also be interrogated without a lawyer being present. Owing to the congestion and inefficiency of the Italian judicial system it is legally possible to be held in police custody for up to three years before being brought to trial.

Religion

As the home of the historic administrative centre (the Vatican), as well as the focal point of world Catholicism, Italy has a unique religious heritage that has permeated almost every aspect of Italian culture. Although the Vatican ceased to be a political power in the eighteenth century, its spiritual influence, backed up by the Papal road show, is still capable of producing profound awe amongst the Catholic populations of underdeveloped countries worldwide. In Italy itself however, there exist extreme attitudes of both devotion and profanity to *Cattolicesimo* (Catholicism). The traditional areas of fervour are the poor regions of the south and the area around Venice, while from Emilia Romagna to Umbria has a reputation for sacerdotal antipathy; there is even a pasta named *strangolapreti* (priest-stranglers). The Vatican has often been its own worst enemy; for instance, in its historic feud with the Italian goverment on the basis that it regarded parliament as idealogically unsound and all its members therefore ineligible for Communion; a state of affairs finally remedied by the Lateran pact of 1929 which secularized the state. The Vatican showed equal implacability towards members of the former Italian Communist Party; anyone of that persuasion was excommunicated despite the fact that many of them were fervent Catholics. During the liberal seventies, the Catholic church came in for some sacrilegious lampooning, the most notorious example of which is probably the scene in Frederico Fellini's film *Roma*, in which flashing fairy lights are incorporated in the sacred vestments during a glitzy clerical fashion parade.

In contemporary times, the fundamentalism of the present Pope is worrying for its ineptness in modern times. Unfortunately the effect is potentially devastating. For instance, Wojtyla's commendation of large families while on visits to the faithful in Africa, shows a blinkered disregard for what is probably the main problem facing that continent, namely an ecological crisis exacerbated by overpopulation. Meanwhile, back on home ground, Italian Catholics have reacted to papal dictums with common sense. Despite a religious ban on 'non-natural' birth control and abortion on demand, Italy has one of the lowest birthrates in the world, and one of the most prosperous condom industries.

Away from the developed areas of Italy, religion moves in mysterious ways. Although generally more devout than their metropolitan countrymen the country people mingle Catholicism with older beliefs inherited from pagan times.

English-speaking churches

St Mark's Church: Via Maggio 18, Florence; tel 055-294764. Reverend Richard Major. Founded in 1877 and considered a minor masterpiece of the Pre-Raphaelite movement. Located on the ground floor of the 15th century Palazzo Machiavelli at the above address on the south bank of the Arno. Sunday mornings 9 am Said Eucharist (also Thurs. 6pm & Fri 8pm). Sunday 10.30am Sung Eucharist followed by drinks in the ballroom of the Palazzo Machiavelli is a good way to meet people and if necessary network for jobs. The notice-board in the church foyer is 'full of job and house offers for anglophones'.

American Church of the Anglican communion in Florence; fax 055-294417.

Church of the Holy Ghost: Piazza Marsala, Genoa; tel 010-6552258.

All Saints' Church, Via Solferino 17, Milan; tel 02-655 2258.

Methodist Church (Evangelica Metodista): Via Porro Lambertenghi 38, Milan; tel 02-6072631. Pastor Paul Perry, English-speaking service.

Christ Church: Via S. Pasquala a Chaiai 15b, Naples; tel 081-411842. Also serves Bari, Capri and Sorrento.

Church of the Holy Cross: Via Mariano Stabile, Palermo; tel 091-581787.

Anglican Church of All Saints: Via del Babuino 153, 00187 Rome; tel 06-6794357. Reverend Peter Marchant.

St Andrews Church of Scotland: Via XX Settembre 7, 00187 Rome; tel 06-4827627. Reverend John Ross.

Roman Catholic Church: San Silvestro in Capite, Piazza San Silvestro, 00187 Rome; tel 06-6785609. Father Larry Gould.

Methodist Church: Via Banco di San Spirito 3, 00186 Rome; tel 06-6868314.

Città della Pieve (near Perugia): Anglican worship is offered in the Palazzo Crinelli in Città della Pieve, in the Umbrian hills every Sunday: for details contact Peter Hurd (0578) 29 92 60.

St Peter's Siena: Anglican. Small Victorian Church in Via Garibaldi, 150 yards to the south of the bus stop. Open April to October for a monthly Eucharist.

St George's Church: Campo S. Vio 30123, Venice; tel 041-29195. Also serves Trieste.

Social Life

Business and social life are so intertwined in Italy that anyone who is considering living and working there will almost certainly have to socialize with Italians. The first, indispensable step is to acquire a knowledge of the Italian language (see Chapter Four, *Daily Life*, The Italian Language).

The Italians

As already mentioned, it can be misleading to talk about Italians, since they are clearly less homogeneous than most other European nations and also lack a well defined sense of nationality. There are however some traits that are recognizably Italian: for instance the importance of the family. The closeness of Italian families means that every Italian has a support system from birth. Not only will *mamma e papa* indulge their children's every whim and support them financially *ad infinitum* if possible, but a network of relatives will aid and abet their progress in life. This type of string-pulling was practically invented by the Italians whose word for nephew is *nipote*, hence nepotism. The closeness of the relationship between mothers and sons, *mammisimo*, is generally recognized as another typically Italian trait, whereby mothers do everything for their sons. More than half of Italian men live at home with one or more parents until their mid-thirties. For foreigners, particularly women, becoming romantically involved with Italians usually means taking on an exhausting number of responsibilities across the family network; far more than one would expect from a similar relationship in the UK.

Another manifestation of Italian tribal behaviour is the urge to cluster which is particularly noticeable amongst teenagers, *ragazzi*. This phenomenon is known as *stare insieme* (hanging out). Youngsters usually congregate on streets in groups with no discernable objective other than to operate as a mutual admiration society.

Italians are more than likely to show warmth towards a new acquaintance which contrasts with traditional Anglo-Saxon reserve which means you wait until you know someone better before getting really enthusiastic towards them. This willingness to communicate on the part of Italians is a great help in breaking the ice on social occasions, particularly if you are feeling inhibited about speaking Italian. Being born gesticulators, Italians are very receptive to sign language, which is a gift to foreigners wishing to illustrate their shaky Italian.

Other fairly uniform Italian traits are an obsession with personal cleanliness and *la bella figura* (general turn out), which often leads them to dress beyond their means. Italians also pride themselves on their *xenofilia* approval of foreigners.

Manners and Customs

The Italian concept of individualism can appear by British standards to be incredibly selfish and anti-social. Loyalty and consideration are reserved for the family or those of one's immediate, intimate circle. This contrasts with the northern European idea of having a responsibility to society at large. Thus litter-dropping in Italy is considerably less frowned upon than in the UK, since to Italians it is always someone else's (usually the hated state's) problem. In matters of friendship, it is customary for Italians to go out in a group; one-to-one friendships along UK lines are not common.

Shaking hands is considered paramount at meetings and social occasions. Social kissing is also reasonably prevalent. This European chic custom is nowadays pretty common in the UK but the niceties vary from country to country. In Italy men and women kiss both their own, and the opposite sex on social occasions; two kisses, one on each cheek, not three as in Russia or France. If you do not feel comfortable with kissing then just shake hands. On social occasions it is considered good manners to take presents. Generous to a fault themselves, Italians resent meanness in others, so expensive presents are called for: quality whisky or champagne, generous bouquets, handmade chocolates or other sweet delicacies are some of the acceptable possibilities.

Whilst it is the custom in Britain to go drinking with your friends to the point of excess, often as a way of letting off steam, Italians enjoy social drinking but they regard drunkenness as totally unacceptable behaviour. Whilst you may see heroin addicts by the dozen, shooting up in public in certain areas of the larger Italian cities, you almost never see a drunkard. Italians release pressure by shouting and gesticulating which is probably healthier than bottling it up, Anglo-Saxon fashion, and then indulging in a fit of temper or road rage.

Making Friends

Undoubtedly one of the most rewarding aspects of living and working in a foreign country is breaking down the barriers and forming lasting friendships. Foreigners usually have to work harder at making friends in their adopted country than they would at home because cultural differences and the language problem can constitute formidable impediments. In Italy the effort can be fruitful in the extreme, as, once their hearts are won, Italians can be loyal and generous friends. However, despite Italian enthusiasm on first acquaintance, a major breakthrough is required before the Italian mask of formality drops. As already mentioned in Chapter Four there is a formal and an informal version of address, *lei* and *tu*. It should be noted that lei is considered even more formal than the French *vous*, and thus slipping into tu without being invited to can cause offence. Likewise *ciao* (hello/goodbye) should never be used with lei, use *buon giorno/buona sera* (good morning/afternoon) and *arrivederci/arrivederla* for goodbyes.

For those of you who need a break from forging cross-culture friendships a selective list of expatriate social clubs is given on page 106.

Homosexuality
While the narcissistic habits of the Italian male may suggest otherwise, homosexuality in Italy keeps mainly in the closet as it is frowned upon, largely due to the oppression of the Catholic church – the Pontiff insists that gays are morally disordered. The national left-wing gay and lesbian organisation, Arcigay, based in Bologna, campaigns against hypocrisy (the Vatican staff includes several homosexual noblemen) and the persecution which is inflicted on Italian gays. In the south of Italy you risk being murdered by your own family or the Mafia if you are not heterosexual. Rome has one or two clubs where gays can meet including L'Alibi and L'Angelo Azzurro. The only pink magazine is *Babilonia*.

Entertainment and Culture

As already mentioned, entertainment in Italy is always pursued in groups. The idea of eating out, or going to a film alone would be strange to Italians, who have a group mentality. The foreigner should therefore get into the habit of collecting telephone numbers and ringing round, however slight the acquaintance, to see who might be interested in an evening out. The alternative, if one goes out alone, is to be regarded as eccentric, or even an object of compassion.

The tourist office is a possible source of information on entertainment and cultural events as are the national newspapers *La Repubblica* and *Corriere della Sera* both of which publish listings in their weekly magazines.

Italy has a *patrimonio culturale* (cultural heritage) second to none, and whilst many outsiders believe the Italian government could do more to conserve it, there is no doubting Italian pride in their classical and Renaissance art and architecture. Neither does Italy lack exponents in the performing arts, perhaps most notably in the field of opera, which had a heyday in the nineteenth century, thanks to amongst others, Verdi, Donizetti and Puccini. Likewise the Italian cinematic tradition, together with the French, is universally accepted as one of the greatest.

In common with many other European countries, and certainly the Latin ones, culture in Italy has a general appeal. This contrasts with the elitist reputation of the arts for which Britain in particular is notorious. This may come as a pleasant surprise to foreign residents who can fall back on the arts, especially cinema, as a topic of conversation with Italians of all backgrounds.

Nightlife: Italian city nightlife may not compare with the bright lights of New York, Barcelona or London but the *ragazzi* can do their heads in at the huge discos, especially in Emilia, Turin and Milan which are also some of the venues for rave parties. Elsewhere, as already mentioned the *ragazzi* make do with 'hanging out' in groups which is less effort than making the logistical arrangements necessary for any positive action. Italian teenagers are however, avid consumers of *il fast food* which hit Italy in the form of American hamburger joints, about seven years ago and which continues to blossom there at an increasing rate. For other Italians, bars with outdoor tables are the main form of nightlife, not that the Italians are great drinkers (see above) but they enjoy the company and the gossip. For those who like music with their whisky, retro jazz and other live music clubs exist in most cities. Also popular are video bars showing non-stop rock videos. You can also watch these on television.

Opera and Classical Music: Surprisingly perhaps for a country so closely linked to opera, the season is short – from December to May. There are around a dozen important opera houses the best known of which are: La Scala (Milan), Teatro dell'Opera (Rome), Teatro Communale (Florence) and San Carlo (Naples). Venice's La Fenice was destroyed by fire two years ago, and has yet to be restored. In addition, most provincial towns have an opera season showing productions of a reasonable standard.

Despite a venerable musical tradition, there are few Italian musicians of international renown. The best symphony orchestras are usually attached to opera houses. Compared with other European countries including Britain, the standards of other Italian orchestras are not high. However Italy has three outstanding conductors currently on the international circuit: Riccardo Muti, Claudio Abbado and Carlo Maria Giulini.

Italian National Anthem Most Italians consider the national anthem *Fratelli d'Italia*, (Brothers of Italy) archaic and uninspiring. It was written by the youthful patriot Goffredo Mameli who died while defending the Roman Republic in 1849 and its sentiments are somewhat romantic and high flown for these days. Although meant as an interim anthem it was never replaced. The main current contender for a replacement anthem is reported to be Chorus of the Hebrew Slaves (*Va, pensiero, sull'ali dorate*) from Verdi's Nabucco.

Cinema: Italian cinema provides rich ground for the enthusiast. Over the years Italian audiences have become very discriminating and Italian films have a reputation for being stylish and sophisticated. Unfortunately for the foreign resident whose Italian is not up to following dialogue, films from the English-speaking world are customarily dubbed into Italian. Cinema listings are given in every newspaper. Cinema categories are *Prima Visione* (new release and smart cinema), Seconda Visione (older cinema and re-run films) and Cinema d'Essai (classical world cinema with original soundtrack). Some cities have Cinema all'aperto (open air movies) during the summer. The Pasqunio cinema (Vicolo del Piede 19, 00153 Rome) in Rome may be worth a visit for expats weary of long Italian-speaking days as it shows a good selection of films in English. Dedicated film freaks might like to take advantage of AIACE (Italian Cinema-goers' Association) membership, which entitles patrons to half-price tickets on weekdays (not Fridays). Details can be obtained from local cinemas.

Main Art and Arts Festivals.
Venice Film Festival: The Venice Film Festival is held annually, during the first two weeks of September and is one of the big three, the others being Cannes and Berlin. It is however smaller, and therefore less commercially influential, than the other two. The Festival programme is available from the tourist office a few weeks in advance. Festival premieres are held in the Palazzo del Cinema and the Astra cinemas, and the public can queue for tickets on the day of the performance.
Venice Biennale: The Venice Biennale is a prestigious international exhibition of contemporary art first held in 1895. Now held in even-numbered years from June to September, it has a permanent site is the Giardini Pubblici where exhibits from over forty countries are housed in separate pavilions.
Spoleto Festival dei Duo Mondi: The Spoleto Festival of the Two Worlds is Italy's main international festival of the performing arts including classical music and ballet, held in and around the walled mediaeval town of Spoleto (Umbria), during two months in summer. Further details from the Italian Tourist Office.
Panatenee Pompeiane: The Pompeii music festival is held in the dramatic surroundings of those famous ruins during the last week of August.
Verona Music Festival: One of the oldest Italian annual music and opera festivals, held in the spectacular surroundings of the Roman Arena di Verona from June to August. Further information from the Verona tourist offices: APT, Via Dietro Anfiteatro 6, and Piazza delle Erbe 42.

Sport

The concept of sports like squash and golf as fashionable recreation activity has yet to seize Italy with quite the same force as it has northern Europe and the United States. This objection to after-work exertion is generally held to hearken back to Italy's peasant culture when back-breaking work left no spare energy for active pursuits. The exception to this is probably cycling, of Tour de France type, which is a popular recreation, especially in the north and football which is played by virtually every man and boy.

From a spectator point of view Italian sport, especially football, takes on a much greater importance, outshining both the Pope and Pavarotti as crowd-pulling spectacles with a fanatical following throughout the country. The introduction of football to Italy occurred at the turn of the century, courtesy of British industrialists who imported factory sports clubs as part of their workers' welfare ethos. Sports generally were slow to evolve until Mussolini built many large stadia in the twenties and thirties, thus promoting a body cult whose inspiration came not so much from Classical Rome, but from Nazi Germany. In 1960 Rome played host to the Olympic Games which led to the building of Nervi's Palazzo and Palazzeto dello Sport di Roma. However as in the UK, Italy's would be champions are seriously hampered by a lack of adequate facilities. Unlike Britain, however, sports are not part of the school curriculum in Italy.

The health and fitness boom of the 1980s has also left its mark and tennis clubs and gymnasia have mushroomed. However, one has the sneaking suspicion that the attraction of such places is, for Italians, that they provide a place to hang out and show off their designer sports gear.

Cycling: The Italians have taken to *il ciclismo* (cycling) in much the same way as the French; they even have their own version of the Tour de France, the Giro d'Italia. The majority of the recreational *ciclisti* can be spotted at weekends, crouched over Bianchi or Campagnolo racing bikes in the Po Valley.

Football: To the foreigner Italian football *il calcio* is perhaps best known for its 1982 World Cup win and ability to buy the hottest foreign players for mind-boggling sums and then find they have feet of clay. Maradona livened up Napoli for a while before his cocaine habit led to his being sent back to Argentina, while Lazio (Rome) are probably regretting the day they ever signed up the auto-destructive talents of 'Gazza'. Most of the top league teams (known as *Serie A*) are in the north where big cities have two teams each: Turin has Juventus and Torino, Milan has Internazionale and AC Milan and Rome has Roma and Lazio. The fans *i tifosi* are noisy and boisterous but need only Latin blood not an alcohol transfusion to galvanize them.

Until 1996 Italian football clubs were non-profit organisations. Now that the Italian government has allowed them to raise profits which they desperately need to improve facilities, some have been doing so on the financial markets. The first club likely to be listed on the stock market in 1998 looks likely to be Lazio. With huge profits to be made from football products and Italians keener than most to buy them, many other clubs are likely to follow (provided that they can make a profit which many do not at present). A stipulation of the stock exchange is that any company has to show three consecutive years of profit in order to qualify for stock market flotation.

Tickets can be obtained from local stadia or team headquarters, well before the game and are standing (*in tribuna*), *non numerato* or *numerato*.

Motor Racing: After football, motor racing is Italy's second national sport. Speed and Italians go together. Throughout motoring history the Italians have produced some of the world's most thoroughbred sports cars: Bugatti, Ferrari to name but two. Orignally such cars and the sport of motor-racing could only be afforded by Italian aristocrats. Out of these illustrious beginnings such classic races as the Mille Miglia and the Targa Florio which takes place in Sicily, were born. The best known Italian race circuit is probably Monza, just outside Milan.

English-Language Clubs

Any expatriate who enjoys a busy and fulfilling social life in their host country is well on the way to considering retirement abroad. At any age and in any country socialising involves a certain amount of innovative thinking and new clubs and societies come and go. For retired people, who are at liberty to follow their own interests as far as time filling is concerned there are few countries where there is such a range of historically and artistically based pursuits possible that compare with Italy.

Alternatively, although there is much to be said for forging Italian friendships and creating an authentically Italian social life in your new life abroad (see *Social Life*). However, sometimes relaxation with fellow expatriates is just the way to soothe the frustrations of being only half understood by the natives. Once you are on the expatriate network you will discover there are clubs for for all age groups and professions, some of which are listed below.

Whether you decide to revive a long-neglected passion for Scottish dancing, cultivate a dormant theatrical talent, learn to play bridge, or even if you simply wish to share some of your time and experiences with other expatriates over an espresso or a stronger beverage, then the list provided below should be a good starting point. Other social reference points include International Schools, Churches and Chambers of Commerce. These have been listed in this book (pages 71, 100 and 171 respectively) or they are simple to locate through telephone directories. Please note that although the addresses and telephone numbers provided are correct at the time of going to press, Italian telephone numbers are notorious for their mutability and club secretaries are also liable to fairly frequent changes. A call to Directory Enquiries (12) may help in some cases. The British and American consulates should be able to provide the address of the new-comers club for their area.

Bologna
The British Institute. Contact Mrs Valeria Sarti at Via Santo Stefano 11; tel 051-233882.

Cagliari
Circolo Europeo: Corso Vittorio Emanuele, 404, 09100 Cagliari; tel 070-668159.
Associazione Italia Inghilterra: Via Machiavelli 97, 09100 Cagliari, Sardinia; tel 070-402835; fax 070-402966.

Florence
British Institute Library. Offers a variety of cultural talks; contact Mark Roberts on 055-284031.

Genoa
New-comers' Club: meets at the Hotel Astor (Via delle Palme 16, Nervi, Genoa).
Italo-Britannica Centre for Cambridge Language Courses and examinations. Also houses the British Library (13,000 books in English). Same address as the British Consulate (Piazza della Vittoria 15; tel 010-564833)). The cultural centre also has other activities.
The Anglican Church: (Piazza Marsala, Genoa).

Milan
Benvenuto Club for English-speaking ladies of any nationality: Meet every second Tuesday of the month 10am-3pm at the Circolo A. Volta, Via G Giusti 16, Milan. Contact telephone number: 02-4526880.
The Benvenuto Club – Monza: Meet on the second Thursday of every month from 10am to midday at Monza Sporting Club, Viale Brianza 39. Contact numbers: 039-2494521; or 039-323909.
The Royal Milan & Bordighera Hash House Harriers: Organise fun runs. Contact Robin Duff; tel 0321-94402.

Rome
The American Club: tel 06-3295843.
The American Women's Association: tel 06-4825268.

The Canadian Women's Association: tel 06-36300843 1pm-6pm.
The Commonwealth Club. tel 06-58330919.
The Inter-Embassy Club of Rome: tel 06-33265424.
The Luncheon Club of Rome: tel 06-50913274 & 50912712.
Professional Women's Association: tel 06-8551632.
Rome Labour Party: tel 06-6384227.
United Nations Women's Guild: 06-57056503.

Turin
Esprit Club. Contact Peter Allen (tel 011-8111623).

Umbria
English Speakers' Club. Contact Harry and Barbara Urquhart, San Lorenzo di
Rabatta 1M, 06070 Cenerate; tel 075-690693.

Varese
Bienvenuto Club of Varese. Contact President Hilary Bianchi on 0332-241243 or
Membership Secretary Wendy Neil on 0331-865681.

Food and Drink

Many myths surround the Italians, and their eating habits are no less liable to
exaggeration or misconception than other aspects of their lives. Admittedly,
whether the pasta is cooked *al dente* (just right) or *una colla* (sticky and
overcooked) is a subject treated with an almost obsessional reverence. However,
despite the world-famous ice creams, pizzas and pasta dishes, the Italians boast
one of the lowest incidences of heart disease in Europe (and consume less ice
cream than most of their European neighbours). The basis of Italian eating tends
towards quality, not quantity, and as with all matters of Italian life, is subject to
the rigorous demands of *la bella figura* (cutting a fine figure). Just as drunkenness
is looked upon as a disgusting and unnecessary foreign fetish by the majority of
Italians, obesity is similarly unacceptable, unless accompanied by a corresponding
amount of Pavarotti-like charisma.

Although every Italian region proclaims the excellence of its own cooking, the
region of Emilia-Romagna is thought by some to boast the finest and richest of
Italian cuisine. However, Tuscany is renowned for its high-quality meat and Genoa
for its herb-based dishes while the food of the south is the most spicy. The three
main meals of the Italian day are treated with varying degrees of importance.
Breakfast, (*colazione*) is usually a frugal offering of croissant (*cornetto*) or biscuits
(*biscotti*); although cereals are currently gaining popularity in the Italian market.
Lunch (*pranzo*) is treated as the main meal of the day in the southern regions,
although increasingly, home-cooked food is being superseded by convenience food.
Finally, dinner (*cena*) as in the majority of Mediterranean countries is held late in
the evening, usually between 8pm and 10pm, especially during the summer months.

Traditional Italian restaurants are signalled by the *ristorante trattoria* or
pizzeria signs. Sparse or unpretentious decor is common and does not reflect on
the quality of the food or service as is the case in British restaurants. When eating
out with Italians you should offer to split the bill *alla romana* – divide it by the
number of those present. However, courteous notions of hospitality still persist
and if you have been invited out to dinner, your host or hostess may insist on
paying all of the bill. As far as giving tips is concerned, traditionally service is
added at the customer's discretion, usually at around 10%-15%, although recently
a 10% charge has begun to be included in the total bill.

As mentioned, the Italians are not great drinkers and being drunk (*ubriaco*) carries a special disapproval amongst the majority of Italians which would be thought curious amongst the lager-loving, beer-swilling British pub population. The Italian language does not even possess a word in its extensive vocabulary for 'hangover'. Alcohol sales are flagging in Italy as mineral water (*acqua minerale*) sales escalate nationwide. Italy now ranks only behind France and ahead of Germany and Belgium in annual consumption of the stuff. Another beverage which has taken off in Italy is beer. According to the Italian Statistics Institute, ISTAT, 61% of men and 31% of women now choose beer above wine. This may be a result (or a cause) of the mushrooming of English-style pubs in the larger cites (there are at least 60 in Rome alone). They seem to appeal mainly to the twenty-somethings. By contrast, the annual consumption of wine per head is dropping to such a level that it is now being advertised by the wine marketing board in order to encourage sales. If you prefer wine-bars then look for the signs *vineria* or *enoteca* above the door.

Thus, far from fulfilling the image of a nation of pasta-stuffing, wine-guzzling Pavarotti prototypes, the reality of the Italians' eating habits is far more discerning and infinitely more healthy. The Italians are now spending 10% less of their incomes each year on food than they did a decade ago, and while still providing a role model for every aspiring *buongustaio* (food and drink connoisseur), the national gastronomic motto seems to be, enjoy, but not to excess.

Wine

Most of Italy is wine country and there is no time to do justice to the many varieties here. Suffice it to say that some areas have gone in for professional production and export while others have kept their traditions and best wines a secret from the outside world. The northwest (Piemonte) is famous for its vermouths and spumantes and purplish wines and barolo and barbera grapes. The north-east, particularly the part under Austrian influence has gone in for mass production. Probably the best known wines abroad are those from central Italy, especially the Chianti wines from the Tuscan hills between Florence and Siena. Southern Italy has the Neapolitan wines of Ischia, Capri and red and white wines from the area around Mount Vesuvius. Sicily's best known wine is probably the sweet and treacly Marsala.

Wine label glossary

DOCG – *Denominazione di Origine Controllata Guarantita*: the highest quality, similar to France's appellation contrôlée.

DOC – *Denominazione di Origine Controllata*: the second highest quality.

DS – *Denominazione Semplice* – plonk.

Messo in bottiglia del produttore all' origine/nel' origine: estate-bottled.

Classico: from the central, i.e. best area of the region.

Imbottigliato nello stabilimento della ditta: bottled on the premises of the firm.

Riserva: wine that has been aged for a statutory period.

Wine Colours: *Bianco* (white), *Rosso* (red), *Rosato* (pink), *Chiaretto* (very light red), *Nero* (very dark red).

Secco: dry.

Amaro: bitter or very dry.

Amabile/Abboccato: medium sweet.

dolce: very sweet.

Spumante: bubbly.

Frizzante: slightly fizzy.

Vin/Vino santo: sweet dessert wine made from dried grapes.

Stravecchio: very old, mellow.

Vino liquoroso: fortified wine.

Shopping

Non-food Shopping

Next to tax evasion, the other favourite Italian pastime is shopping. Consumption, especially in luxury goods including *firmato* (designer) clothes, is more conspicuous in Italy than in most other European countries. As class distinctions have all but disappeared in Italian society, everyone aspires to the same high standards. While some are certainly less able to afford designer goods than others, everyone has them. It thus follows that some Italians are prepared to go without decent housing, and the best food, in order to dress the same as the *nuovi ricchi*. It is therefore difficult on a night out in Italy, to distinguish a car mechanic from a high-flying executive as they will both be wearing a Giorgio Armani suit and Gucci loafers. Italians have become addicted to a hedonistic lifestyle that leaves most other Europeans standing. This exhausting pursuit of pleasure and *bella figura* (looking your best at all times) has resulted in the Italians taking the line that nothing but the finest will do.

Italy's preoccupation with fashion, not unexpectedly, means that much shopping revolves around clothes and accessories. Italian suits, knitwear leather goods, jewellery, sunglasses etc. with brand names such as Louis Vuitton, Bulgari, Rayban etc., have an international reputation and cachet.

The Italian love affair with designer labels has rubbed off on other nations and helped to inspire a well-publicized boom in the production of counterfeit brand-name goods much production of which goes on in the Far East. However, in Italy itself, there are hundreds of Mafia-run sweat shops, where illegal, immigrant labour churns out fake *firmati* goods. For instance in December 1997 the Guardia di Finanza impounded a complete shoe factory at Caserta in Campania which was about to begin production of fake Timberland shoes. The foreign resident should therefore beware of improbable bargains.

One way to have your cake and eat it, in this case have designer clothes but not pay the outrageous prices, is to buy from factory outlets. A useful publication *Designer Bargains in Italy* by Dorrie Van Meurs gives details of 200 places where you can do this. For a copy contact Milan (tel 02-93581477) or send 26,000 lire plus 2,000 postage and packing to: Designer Bargains in Italy, via dei Tigli 2, 20020 Arese (MI).

Note that VAT on many goods including most clothes and shoes is 20%.

Food Shopping

Unfortunately the cost of living in Italy is one of the highest in Europe. Food prices especially can come as a nasty shock to foreign residents since many of the items which enjoy an international reputation, such as Parma ham and various cheeses are more expensive to buy in Italy than in Britain. Supermarkets, although not ubiquitous as in the UK, are on the increase. Hypermarkets are even more scarce and represent only 6% of the Italian food market (compared with about 47% in France). Those living in the countryside of Tuscany and Umbria will have to plan their shopping trips to the nearest city carefully, as relying on the village shop for forgotten items can become very expensive.

Pasta is the universal diet of all Italians. However,in the north *polenta* (a porridge made from maize meal); or rice are as common as pasta as a basic constituent of main daily meals. Italian meat is patchy in quality. Pork and famous pork products like *prosciutto crudo*, from the north are excellent but, as in Britain much of the veal (*vitello*) is imported. Beef (*vitellone*) is considered best from Tuscany. In the mountainous regions of the south, prime lamb (*agnello*) is produced. Italians also eat farmed rabbits and fowl, and a variety of small birds that make the British feel squeamish: these include skylarks allodole, blackbirds *merli*, sparrows *passeri* and thrushes *tordi*. These unfortunate songbirds are usually trapped with nets and sold squewered. After grilling, each constitutes a miserable and bony mouthful. Meat is purchased from a *macelleria* and poultry from a *polleria*.

One of the other main dietary constituents, cheese, comes in many delicious specialities a number of which (eg. Parmesan, Gorgonzola and mozzarella) are already familiar to Britons. Parmesan increases in price with age, the most expensive being *stravecchione* (very old). No self-respecting Italian would dream of buying it ready grated. Sheepsmilk cheeses (*pecorino*) are specialities of Sardinia and the Genovese region. If in doubt a cheesemonger (*formaggiaio*) will always let you taste before buying. See below for further details on Italian eating habits.

If there are some consumables that you have grown up with in the UK and for which there is no Italian substitute (Marmite, digestive biscuits, Bird's custard etc.) then there are a few specialist shops like 'Home from Home' (Via Verdi 13, 21043 Castiglione Olona; tel 0331/824373) that stock these and other familiar items.

Shopping Glossary

abbligliamenti	clothes
agenzia di viaggi	travel agency
calzoleria/calzatura	shoeshop/footwear
calzolaio	cobbler/shoe repairer
cartoleria	stationery/bookshop
confezione	clothes
drogheria	grocer
ferramenta	hardware
fioraio	florist
fornaio	baker
fotocopisteria/typografia	photocopying/printing
frutta e verdura/fruttivendolo/	fruit and vegetables/greengrocer
giocattoli	toys
gioielleria	jeweller
ipermercato	hypermarket
latteria	dairy
lavaggio a secco	dry cleaning
libreria	bookshop
macelleria	butcher
merceria	haberdashery
oreficeria	jeweller (lit. goldsmith)
orologiaio/orologeria	watchmaker/repairer
ottico	optician
panificio/panetteria/panettiere	breadshop/bakery/baker
pasticceria	cake/pastry shop
pastificio	fresh pasta
pelleteria	leather goods
pescheria/pescivendolo	fishmonger
rosticceria	shop selling cooked food to take away
salumeria	delicatessen

sarto/sarta	tailor/dress-maker
surgelati	frozen food
tintoria	dry cleaners
vini e liquori	wines and spirits

Public Holidays

Note that on Italian national holidays (*feste*) offices, shops, banks, post offices and schools are all closed. Whether museums, parks, etc, are closed will vary from region to region:

1 January (New Year's Day; *Capodanno*)
6 January (Epiphany; *La Befana*)
Easter Monday (*Pasquetta*)
25 April (Liberation Day; *Anniversario della Liberazione*)
1 May (Labour Day; *primo maggio*)
15 August (Assumption; *Ferragosto*)
1 November (All Saints'; *Ognissanti*)
8 December (Immaculate Conception; *L'Immacolata Concezione*)
25 December (Christmas Day; *Natale*)
26 December (Boxing Day; *Santo Stefano*)

The festival days listed below are held to honour each specific city's own patron saint. Shops and offices usually remain open on these days although it is as well to check with the local tourist board for specific information.

25 April (Venice, St Mark)
24 June (Turin, Genoa and Florence; St John the Baptist)
29 June (Tome, St Peter)
23-25 July (Caltagirone in Sicily, St James)
26 July (island of Ischia in the Bay of Naples, St Anne)
19 September (Naples, St Gennaro)
4 October (Bologna, St Petronius)
6 December (Bari, St Nicholas)
7 December (Milan, St Ambrose)

Retirement

Anyone considering Italy from a retirement point of view will do well to realize that Italy really is the land of frescos, ancient culture and the *bella figura* (personal aestheticism), so if you're after an accessible supply of fish and chips and English beer, try Spain! Many retired Brits in Italy have also retained British homes, splitting their time between the two countries each year. The bulk of retired expatriates have planted themselves in the beautiful country spots of Tuscany and Umbria, (where living and property costs continue their upward spiral) well away from the industrial centres of Milan and Turin. However, remember that for anyone considering the northern regions of Piedmont, Lombardy, Veneto etc., the cost of living in northern Italy is considerably higher than that in the UK and other European countries, so survival dependent on a modest pension would be difficult; if not impossible. There is also a noticeable lack of welfare and after-care services for the elderly throughout Italy.

However, potential retirees will almost certainly find the excellent climate and the easy-going nature of the people, the progressive upgrading of the infrastructure and the lively expatriate community, combined with an ambition to make the most of Italian art and culture are all the excuses needed to justify retirement in Italy. Some of the very real benefits include a quality of life which is often higher than that offered in the UK. Property bargains are still to be found in some of the less-discovered regions of La Marche, Puglia and Liguria.

The Decision to Leave

Most importantly, anyone considering retiring to Italy must be able to afford the move financially. No less vital is to be aware of the stresses involved in moving to another country and the ultimate effect lack of proximity to friends and family will have on you. You have to have the stamina to deal with the move not only practically but also emotionally.

All emigrants must also be prepared to upgrade their level of Italian before arriving in the new country (see *The Italian Language* in the *Daily Life* chapter.

As many decisions to move abroad grow out of a love of the country discovered through past holidays you may have to make the final decision, by making a long stay of say six months (perhaps through home swaps or renting see *Setting up Home*) which should include the winter period if you have not already experienced the colder or emptier months. Ideally the stay should be in the area in which you are most interested so that you can get to know it really well and do your research before moving there. If you have yet to decide which region to move to, you could arrange more than one long stay.

If funds are not a problem, you could buy a second home in Italy and then sell your UK residence and move abroad permanently only after a successful trial period in Italy had been completed.

Residence Requirements

Anyone intending to retire to Italy must first obtain a permit to stay, *permesso di soggiorno*, from the local police station (*Questura*) three months after arrival in

Italy. The *permesso di soggiorno* will be renewed after a five year period and annually thereafter on condition that proof of funds are presented in the form a bank letter or statement to the sum of approximately £12,000 each year. The basic regulations regarding permanent residence both before and after leaving the UK can be found in Chapter Two, *Residence and Entry Regulations*. Additional documents required by the Questura in Italy include proof of retirement or old age pension, indicating the amount received monthly and proof from the bank that you are dealing with in Italy that a bank account has been opened there.

Choosing and Buying a Retirement Home

The main and very obvious point to make regarding buying a retirement property in Italy is to choose something which is both within your financial scope and which, unlike a holiday home, is suitable for year-round living. You will need to keep a firm grasp on reality when it comes to house prices: the lowest prices are often for derelict, isolated farmhouses in need of much renovation work. This may be perfect for someone with plenty of enthusiasm, energy and financial backing with strong hermitic tendencies, but equally inappropriate for someone retiring to Italy to make new friends and enjoy the peace and comfort of a ready-made Italian home. The other extreme is to find yourself tempted by something beyond what you can afford which may become a financial liability. Further information regarding property prices throughout Italy and a list of agents can be found in the Chapter, *Setting up Home*.

Most people will have to budget carefully the expenses involved in moving abroad and will need to take into consideration the running and upkeep costs of the property in question. For instance, the *palazzi* (blocks of flats containing several different apartments) where maintenance and renovation costs are shared on a communal basis may work out more expensive than you think. Some of your budget should be allowed for possible house maintenance costs involved keeping a home in reasonable repair. Proximity to health services and other facilities is also an important consideration for anyone reliant on public transport. Once you have decided on your new home you will need to follow all of the procedures regarding property purchase which are explained in full in *Setting Up Home*.

Avoiding the Con-men

Time after time, expatriates show an inexplicable naivity by involving themselves financially in 'money-making' scams, proposed by smooth-talking salesmen peddling everything from 'precious stones' to dud shares. The temptation to increase a retirement nest egg through seemingly easy means that involve no work is evidently too much for the over-credulous expat to resist. The usual procedure is for a salesman to telephone, introducing him or herself as being a representative from a company with a respectable-sounding name. The conversation somehow turns to shares and stock markets with the unsurprising result that the caller has stock available in a small company which will shortly be on the receiving end of a juicy takeover bid from a large mega-company eg. IBM, ICI, at which time the share price is sure to double. They would so hate to see you miss such a once-in-a-lifetime opportunity and if you send in a cheque today, you won't. Amazingly, people do just this and invariably the brief thrill of anticipation is replaced by a long period of regret. Often their money disappears totally and even if 'Mr Smith' the salesman is ever tracked down, they find they can only sell their shares at a fraction of the price for which they originally bought them. The moral is, if a sharepusher calls, hang up. Nobody but a fool sends a cheque to invest in a company he has never heard of and in response to a phone-call out of the blue. If you do want to invest in shares, consider whether you want to be cautious or to indulge in a more risky scheme and then take truly professional advice eg. from one of the commodity traders/stockbrokers listed in the Directory of Major Employers on page 158 of *Employment*.

Hobbies

Once you have settled into your new home, waded through the lengths of red tape and obtained all the relevant permits and documents, thoughts will necessarily turn to socializing and the pursuit of hobbies and interests for which there are many possibilities in Italy.

Keen gardeners will find that Italy offers a variety of gardening climates and the Italians themselves are renowned as brilliant horticulturalists but not, however, as particularly keen gardeners. You can derive hours of pleasure not only from growing exotic plants and different growing conditions, but also learning the Italian names for the common garden and wild plants: *giglio* (lily), *papavero* (poppy) and *violaciocca gialla* (wallflower) to name but three. Remember that although it is legal to take seeds into Italy, it is against the law to import plants and bulbs without a phyto-sanitary certificate issued by the Ministry of Agriculture (Hook Rise South, Tolworth, Surbiton, Surrey KT6 7NF; tel 0181-330 4411). One potential problem for the keen gardener in Italy is the water shortage which affects most of the country. There are solutions for drought areas (eg. recycling water used in the kitchen and for bathing to the garden).

For those with sporting inclinations, activities abound both strenuous and gentle. Cycling (*ciclismo*) is a particularly popular national sport but if this is too energetic and you would rather be a spectator, there are plenty of spectacles on offer from rugby and football to car racing. For further details on sport see page 104, *Daily Life*.

Lovers of old properties, ancestral homes and formal gardens will find the Italian equivalent of the National Trust, the FAI (Foundation for the Italian Environment) organizes trips to the many places of interest which form the Italy's almost inexhaustible architectural heritage. Although barely twenty years old and with a membership in the thousands (compared to the National Trust's two million), interest in the FAI is growing as the Italians become more aware of the need to protect their heritage if it is to survive in the future. The annual membership cost is lire 40,000 (£18) which entitles members to free entry to all FAI properties and a regular newsletter as well as the outings mentioned above.

Studying is another way of enhancing retirement. The most obvious subjects are those connected with Italy itself, the language and culture. For something more ambitious you can enrol with the Open University in Milan (c/o The British Council, via Manzoni 38, 20121 Milan; tel/fax 02-8138048; e-mail: J.Pollard@open.ac.uk) for any of 150 courses which can lead to a degree.

Useful Addresses

Gruppi Archaeologici d'Italia: Via Degli Scipioni 30/A, 00192 Rome; tel 06-39733786; fax 06-39734449. Season tickets and subscription to the magazine *Archaeologica*.

Entertainment

If you are one of those for whom life without some form of broadcasting provided by the BBC would be unthinkable, whether it be *Letter from America* on the World Service or *Antiques RoadShow* or *One Foot in the Grave* on BBC Prime (the 24-hour television channel for viewers in Continental Europe (tel +44 181 5763061 for details) there is no need to despair. In addition to the sterling entertainment and current affairs programmes of the BBC European television services and the World Service, there is another way for expatriates to keep up with the most recent English-language television viewing and the best of the old ones in their foreign homes. Video Plus Direct (tel 01733-232800) stocks all BBC programme titles that are currently available and also 17,000 video titles currently on general release in the UK. You can order from overseas by contacting the above number or fax 01733-230618 (or e-mail: ORDER@VIDEOPLUS DIRECT.CO.UK). Their complete catalogue of titles can be posted to you abroad for £5.99.

Alternatively, there is BBC radio. Most countries operate an Overseas Service for their own nationals but it is not too biased to say that the BBC World Service (relayed by satellite and broadcast on FM in many parts of Italy) is in a class of its own. British newspapers are expensive abroad, tend to arrive late and are obtainable only in the large towns. Listening to the World Service is therefore the easiest and cheapest way to keep in touch with home. By day, reception is best on higher frequencies (15-21 mHz) but at night the lower frequencies (around 6-7 MHZ) are preferable while early in the morning and evening, the middle bands of 9-11 MHZ provide the best quality reception. The BBC broadcasts throughout a 24 hour period. Programmes and frequency charts can be found in the monthly magazine *BBC On Air*, PO Box 76, Bush House, Strand, London WC2B 4PH; tel 0171-557 2211; fax 0171-240 4899. A subscription to *BBC On Air* costs £24 a year. The magazine lists all overseas radio programmes as well as listings for BBC Prime and BBC World (see above and below) and much additional information such as a wavelength guide, useful tips on reception, suitable radios to buy and similar matters.

BBC World is a 24-hour international news and information television channel which can be received in Italy. For further information contact Customer Services, Telepui (via Piranesi 46, 20137 Milan; tel +39 2 75 76 77). A monthly programme guide is given in *BBC On Air* (see above).

Another possibility for expats starved of true British entertainment is renting English videos, an option available through Atles Videa, whose outlet in Milan is located at Via Varese 8, 20121 Milan (tel 02-29005474) or Economy Book and Video Centre in Rome (Via Torino 136, Rome 00184; tel 06-4746877; fax 06-483661).

For a list of some English-speaking clubs in individual cities, see *Social Life* in the *Daily Life* chapter.

Pensions

Italy is well-known for having one of the highest European rates of expenditure on social security, and in particular pensions which account for nearly 63% of its total social security bill and 14% of GDP. In January 1998, with budget trimming for EMU in mind, the government, after many months of consultations introduced radical changes. These include making pension requirements in the public sector the same as for the private sector i.e. employees in both sectors will have to pay contributions for the same number of years (40) in order to claim a full pension. The changes will be phased in gradually until parity is achieved in 2008. Italy will probably still come out well on top over the UK as regards pension entitlements. This parity of the public and private systems will end the extremely high number of those state workers claiming substantial pensions after 'retiring' early. The so called super pensions (those starting at 3.5 million lire a month) will also have the sliding scale of increments suspended for a year (1998) and partially reduced for the following three years.

One of the reasons that pensions (*pensione di vecchiaia*) were so high was because they were on a sliding scale: rises of 2% of each individual's earnings for every year in which contributions were made. For instance, someone who had worked for 30 years received an Italian pension of 60% of their earnings in the five years prior to retirement; after working in Italy for 15 years, a worker could earn 30% of his or her salary in pension. By contrast, British workers have only been eligible for a full UK pension after approximately 40-45 years of work and this represents only approximately 18% of average earnings. Moreover, the employee's contribution in Italy can be less than 2% of earnings, compared with 9% in the UK. The minimum contribution period to result in entitlement to any Italian pension varies but can be as little as three months. Once a worker has paid contributions for this minimum period, there is an absolute right to receive the pension wherever he or she lives in the EU. The pension is paid by the country in which it was earned at the appropriate pension age. If someone has not worked abroad for the minimum period to entitle them to any pension, then another rule comes into effect and calculates what is called a pro rata pension. This is the theoretical pension they would have earned if they had worked abroad for a longer period which is then scaled down in proportion to the actual time spent working there.

On request, the DSS at Newcastle (International Services, DSS, Longbenton, Newcastle-upon-Tyne, NE98 1YX; tel 0191-213 5000) will send out a form which should then be taken to the nearest social security office (*Unità Sanitaria Locale*) in Italy. The Unità Sanitaria Locale will then make the necessary arrangements for your pension to be transferred to Italy. If you became entitled to a UK pension before leaving for Italy, this can either be paid to you in Italy or in the UK. Alternatively, if you reach retirement age after taking up residence in Italy, again you need only apply to the International Services of the DSS at Newcastle and they will ensure that your pension is delivered to your Italian (or a UK) bank account each month. Anyone who moves to Italy before reaching retirement age should continue to pay national insurance contributions in the UK in order to qualify for a British state pension. Depending on which country you have paid the majority of contributions in, you are eligible to draw the pension in either country. Note that pensions are not frozen at the level they reached on arrival in Italy and instead the pension will rise in accordance with any increases which take effect in the UK. Retired expatriates in most other non-EU countries (with the exception of Mauritius, the USA and Switzerland) are not so lucky as here pensions are frozen at the level levied in the year the expatriate left the UK to retire abroad. The DSS Overseas Branch also publishes Leaflet SA29 (available on receipt of an s.a.e.) which provides details on EU pension and social security legislation.

Italy also offers invalidity pensions (*pensione di invalidità*) – which are widely abused in the south of the country where able-bodied workers are certified as being unable to work in order to decrease the unemployment statistics. There is also something called *la pensione di anianità* (a long-service pension) to which someone is entitled after thirty-five to forty years of work. As recently as 1998 the government brought in new regulations to abolish a scandalous variant on this system, awarding pensions to certain state employees, such as teachers, after only ten years' service (allowing 30 year olds to retire and get another job on the quiet). Political parties also found the generous pension system invaluable for bribing the electorate when it came to voting time. The present government not only has a cleaner image after the corruption scandals of 1993 cleared most of the skeletons out of the closet, but more practically, it is essential to get the budget in trim for European Monetary Union in 1999. One of the first targets for radical reform was the wasteful pensions system.

Although the Instituto Nazionale di Previdenza Sociale (INPS) effectively dominates the Italian pensions system, there also exist several pension funds linked to certain state industries (water, gas, the railways, etc.) and private pension plans, of which there was a dismal shortage of choice only a few years ago, are likely to prove a booming area of investment for Italians..

If you are employed by a UK company but working in Italy you should check how long you are able to contribute to the UK company pensions scheme; normally, employees are able to remain with the UK scheme for at least three years, and with the approval of the Inland revenue, for longer.

Finally, it is worth checking whether your employer's pension contributions, if you are subject to tax in Italy, are taxable in that country. Previously, as a UK taxpayer you would not be taxed on your employer's contributions. Also take advice from an independent financial adviser as to whether it is best for you to continue with a personal pension scheme in the UK and for how long, and what other conditions and/or restrictions apply to the scheme once you are resident in Italy.

The European Commission has recently put forward proposals for a pension directive. Current differences in pension provision between member states are seen as barriers to the total freedom of movement of employees within the Community. The proposals now under discussion are intended to remove the obstacles and to encourage pension provision by employers. These are to include freedom to manage pension funds within the EU, freedom of cross-border investment and cross-border membership of pension fund schemes. The last clause is the one which is causing the most controversy, as it allows for the creation of pan-European funds, and the final outcome is still being awaited.

Note that it is always worth checking on your entitlements to a foreign state pension if you have worked abroad for any length of time. For instance, a British ex-expatriate discovered that she was entitled to a pension of approximately £50 a week and more than £20,000 in payments backdated to her 55th birthday as she had contributed to the Italian state pension scheme for about ten years while working in Rome.

Advice regarding, and administration of, offshore pension funds is available through Bacon and Woodrow Pension Trustees Ltd (Albert House, South Esplanade, St Peter Port, Guernsey, Channel Islands; tel 01481-728432; fax 01481-724082). In the case of offshore pension funds a trust deed is established which is controlled by trustees who may be individuals or a trust company or a combination of the two. However, it is advisable that no individual trustee should be a UK resident in order to avoid complications with the UK Inland Revenue.

Finance

Anyone considering retiring to Italy should take specialist financial advice regarding their own situation. Most people in a position to retire overseas have an amount of capital to invest, or will have once they sell their UK home and it is essential to take good advice on how and where this may best be done. Moreover, those who intend to maintain connections with both the UK and Italy will need advice on how their taxation affairs can be arranged to their own advantage. However, there is no reason why one should not continue with bank accounts or investments already established in the UK and in most cases interest will be paid on deposits paid without deduction of tax where one is non-resident.

Taxation

Tax is payable on any inheritance from a deceased person's estate in Italy. Inheritance tax is levied on all assets wherever they are, in Italy or abroad, that are the property of a resident of Italy at the time of death. If the deceased is not a resident of Italy, inheritance tax is due only on the assets considered to exist in Italy by tax law. As in so many other western European countries, the rates of inheritance tax depend not, as with the British system, directly on the value of the estate, but on the relationship of each beneficiary to the deceased. Also unlike the British system, the surviving spouse is not exempt from inheritance tax, although the tax rates for them and for other beneficiaries who are directly related to the deceased come into effect at 3% on estates valued above 100 million lire. The highest rate for direct relations is 27% estate tax plus 25% inheritance tax on estates valued at over 3,000 million lire. The highest tax rate is for unrelated heirs on the same amount at 60%. In Italy, the beneficiaries are responsible for paying their own inheritance tax (this is not done on their behalf by the estate's executor as in the UK) and the payments can sometimes by deferred or paid by installments, provided the individual is prepared to pay additional interest.

UK pensions paid to British expatriates are subject to Italian tax unless the pensioner is exempted by a double tax agreement or he or she is a former public service employee who worked abroad (in which case the pension is taxable in the UK, although sometimes not liable to any tax at all). The double taxation agreement only taxes pensions in Italy if you are resident there. If your pension is going to be liable for UK income tax or Italian tax, it may be better to elect to take a tax-free lump sum pension option, thereby reducing the level of pension liable to tax. A survey conducted by Price Waterhouse and published in *The International*, found that a UK couple who retire to Italy on a pension of £20,000 with no other income would take home £15,722 of the pension after tax being deducted at the base rate of 25%. This net figure is lower than in France (£18,000), Germany (£17,410) and Switzerland (£18,970), but higher than in all of the Scandinavian countries.

Offshore Banking

From a retired person's point of view, if he or she has a sum of money to be invested or put into a long-term deposit account (for a minimum of 90 days) it is well worth looking at the tax-free interest options which some high street banks, building societies and merchant banks offer on accounts through offshore banking centres in tax havens such as Gibraltar and the Channel Islands. The minimum amount of money required to open a deposit account ranges from £500 to £10,000. The deposit account interest rates work on the basis that the more inaccessible one's money, the higher the rate of interest paid. Interest can be paid monthly or annually and although the account holder will receive much the same gross amount of interest either way (although slightly less on the monthly payments because of the number of transaction charges involves) the monthly payments which bring with them a steady income flow seem invariably more popular with retired account holders. A list of banks which offer offshore banking facilities is given in the *Banking* section of the *Daily Life* chapter.

Social Security

British pensioners who are resident in Italy on a permanent basis are entitled to free or subsidized healthcare under the Italian social security system (*lo stato assistenziale*). However, although free benefits include hospital and emergency treatment, routine visits to the GP or dentist are not included (see below). Those who are retired or who are otherwise eligible for UK social security should apply in Britain as far in advance of departure as possible to the DSS Overseas Branch (address provided above) for form E121, and on arrival in Italy should register with their nearest government health centre.

Health

One serious drawback of the medical treatment provided by Italian social security from a retired person's point of view is that although it provides financial cover for operations and hospital treatment, it does not include funding for general medical treatment such as trips to the dentist or to a general practitioner. Moreover, the Italian social security system caters particularly badly for out-patient and after-care treatment and facilities. Social security will only cover about 75% of a patient's treatment costs, thus the patient has to meet 25% of the costs him or herself or budget for payments for insurance to cover this instead. Those who have worked in Italy and paid into a private top-up scheme, as most people do, have the bulk of this contribution covered: those who are retired and move to Italy, however, may not.

A list of English-speaking doctors is available from the local British Consulate; this will, however, often involve using private facilities.

For details of private health care plan organisations, see *Private Medical Insurance* in the *Daily Life* chapter.

Wills

The easiest and most effective policy for a British citizen resident in Italy is to make a will which follows British (ie. Scottish or English) law, regarding the disposal of his or her estate. If a will involves the dispersal of property both within and without Italy, it is advisable to consult a lawyer (*avvocato*) with experience of both the British and Italian legal systems to avoid legal complications later on. In this case, you may find that it is simplest to make two wills, which deal with UK and Italian assets separately, rather than trying to combine the two. If you wish, you can make an Italian-style will, but unless you have taken on Italian nationality during your time in Italy, this will be executed in accordance with English or Scottish law. British wills also avoid the Italian system of *Legittime*, common to most Western European countries, which gives those directly related to the deceased an absolute right to a share in the estate, regardless of the wishes of the deceased as expressed in the will. Remember that to validate an Italian will you will need to obtain a certificate of law from your consulate which will state that the will is being made under the terms of UK national law which includes a provision for the free disposition of property. Any lawyer will be able to organize this for you.

Death

Death is the unlooked for eventuality which affects us all sooner or later and dying abroad complicates matters slightly in that one's near relations are often not on the spot to deal with the formalities surrounding burial. It is therefore advisable to make your wishes concerning the matter ie. what form of burial is desired and where, known in advance and preferably also written down in a will. Note that burials must take place within 48 hours of death.

All deaths must be registered with the local *municipio* (town hall) within 24 hours. A death certificate is issued by the attending doctor – remember that you will need an international death certificate if the body is to be transported back home. Cremation, particularly in the north of Italy, is fairly common, although practically every Italian commune has its own cemetery in which all residents are entitled to be buried free of charge. There are also British cemetries in large cities like the one at Staglieno in Genoa. Funerals tend to cost anything from one to two million lire (£500-£1,000).

The British Embassy warns that air-freighting a coffin back to the UK is an expensive business. Freight charges depend on weight but the minimum cost is about £2,000; prolonged storage will also add to your costs. The body will have to be picked up once it arrives in the UK; some funeral directors have contacts in other countries who will see to it that the body is safely delivered to its UK destination. It is advisable to get some quotations from Italian undertakers who offer such a service. An alternative is to have just your ashes returned to the UK. Courier companies should handle this if it cannot be done by a friend or relative.

SECTION II

Working in Italy

Employment
Business and Industry Report
Regional Employment Guide
Temporary Work
Starting a Business

Employment

The Employment Scene

With unemployment currently running at 12.4%, annual inflation at 3% (just), industrial growth of 1% (its lowest since 1983), rising living costs and comparatively low salaries by European standards (although managerial staff earn up to 30% more than their British counterparts), working in Italy may not seem initially a brilliant idea. The Italian economy is in recession, albeit mildly, at a time when the USA and Britain have emerged from theirs some years since. It is true that the Italian economy can boom with the best of them, and did in the 1980s. However, this was followed by a decline in the early 1990s. At the time of press, the economy is being trimmed for financial convergence in the form of Economic and Monetary Union (target date 1 January 1999) when the Euro single currency will come into being. However, while there may be niggling doubts and uncertainties about Italy's true financial state, a combination of high quality of life, a sunny climate and a generally dynamic working atmosphere will serve to blot out any background economic concerns. The chronic unemployment in the Mezzogiorno is countered by a higher level of employment in the north. The legendary lack of interest on the part of the Italian tax authorities in reclaiming their share of your earnings may no longer be quite so lackadaisical, but Italy offers a wealth of opportunity to those ready to pluck it. This is borne out by the almost uniform success rate of English companies in Italy. In particular, small business enterprises which enjoy various government tax incentives are thriving (see Chapter Seven, *Starting a Business* for further details). Over 59% of the manufacturing workforce are in companies employing under 100 persons. The majority of these businesses are flourishing and raking in record profits at a time when many small businesses in the UK are struggling to survive bank loans, consumer caution and the disadvantages of competing with bigger companies able to offer greater discounts.

As Italian industry particularly has become ever-more mechanized over the last decade, the number of employees has declined, while the demand for labour in the service industries (commerce, administration, tourism and catering) has steadily increased. Presently, the percentage of Italians employed in agriculture is 8% (much higher than the EU average of 2%) while those in industry make up 33% and the remaining £59.6 are in commerce, administration, tourism, etc.

It is estimated that the development of technological aspects of daily life, although less rapid in Italy than say France or Britain, will be an increasing factor in creating opportunities for distance working or teleworking according to CENSIS, the centre for social studies and policies based in Milan. Less than a dozen teleworking contracts are in place in Italy including two instigated by Dun and Bradstreet, publishers of international business publications. Telemarketing looks set to grow hugely in Italy.

With no limit imposed on the number of foreigners employed by or working in Italian industry, whether you intend to work as employee, employer or entrepreneur, the opportunities available in Italy are constantly diversifying and the time is ripe for foreigners to take the pick of the opportunities now readily available.

Residence and Work Regulations

Unfortunately, Italy's wholehearted enthusiasm for the EU has not dimininished or greatly refined the wearing paperchase required of even EU nationals who wish to work in Italy. If you arrive there with the intention of working, you must apply at the *questura* (police station) for a *ricevuta di Segnalazione di Soggiorno* which allows you to stay for up to three months looking for work. Upon production of this document and a letter from an employer, you must go back to the police to obtain a *libretto di lavoro*, a form of work authorisation which strictly should not be necessary for EU nationals. However, anyone wishing to work in Italy should be prepared to apply for a *libretto di lavoro* as well as a stay permit (*Permesso di Soggiorno*) if intending to stay and work for longer than three months. One English woman who was offered a job EFL teaching in Bari, reported that she had to visit three different government offices about eight times in total. Her health card arrived about six months after the wheels were set in motion.

Note that au pairs, and academics employed by Italian universities are exempt from obtaining the *libretto di lavoro*. Full information on entry regulations to Italy are given in Chapter Two, *Residence and Entry Regulations*. For anyone considering moving to Rome or its environs, the booklet *Notes on Employment and Residence in the District of the British Embassy, Rome* is available free of charge from the British Embassy (Via XX Settembre 80a, Porta Pia, I-00187 Rome; tel 06-482 5551/5441; fax 06-487 3324). This booklet provides basic information on accommodation, medical care, social clubs and obtaining employment in the Rome area.

EC Professional Qualifications Directives

The EC Directive on the mutual recognition of professional qualifications (89/48/EEC) was notified to Member States in January 1989. This Directive (usually referred to as the first diploma directive), dealt with professional qualifications awarded after at least three years of higher education (e.g. doctors, dentists, pharmacists, architects, accountants, lawyers etc.). The second diploma directive (draft directive issued 19 December 1991) dealt with all qualifications that take less than three years to obtain (i.e. all the professions not covered by the first Directive) and was adopted in the summer of 1992. Another definition of the second diploma directive is all professional qualifications which are subject to a regulatory body in the state where they were obtained from now on should be acceptable in any other EU state. This directive, when fully implemented will enable those practising in the so-called regulated professions in their home state, to have their qualifications accepted in all the other member states for the purposes of employment or self-employment. The second directive extended the system and procedures existing before the summer of 1992 (see transitional directives below) and included: qualifications achieved after post-secondary level education involving course of 1-3 years (defined as diplomas); awards made on completion of a course following a minimum school leaving age qualification (defined as certificates); and work experience. The member states implemented the second diploma directive in 1994. This mutual recognition of qualifications may in some instances be subject to certain conditions such as proficiency in the language of the state where the professional intends to practise and length of experience. A copy of the First Directive is contained in the booklet, *The Single Market, Europe Open for Professionals, EC Professional Qualifications Directive* obtainable from the DTI (Kingsgate House, 66-67 Victoria Street, London SW1E 6SW; tel 0171-215 5000). Further details of the qualifications covered by the second diploma directive (everything from hairdressing to insurance broking) can be obtained from the same address.

Prospective job seekers are therefore advised to consult the association relevant to their profession for the exact conditions for acceptance in Italy. You can do this at one of the 40 European Documentation Centres (EDCs) in the UK. To find the address of your nearest one, contact the European Commission, Information Centre, 8 Storey's Gate, London SW1P 3AT; tel 0171-973 1992.

Although some professionals such as doctors and dentists have been able to practise in any EU state for a decade, other professions have proved a stumbling block. In Italy, foreign teachers are not taken on as permanent staff in state schools (though this has been challenged), where staff are civil servants. There may also an *equipollenza* (equivalence) exam (see below) for some professions.

Certificates of Experience: member states, other than the one in which qualifications referred to in the second directive, were attained, may require evidence of one or more years of professional experience. In order to do this the home state can issue a Certificate of Experience. In Britain, those wishing to practise their trade or profession in another EU state can contact the Certificates of Experience Department of the Association of British Chambers of Commerce in Coventry (tel 01203-695688; fax 01203 695844), requesting an application form for a European Community Certificate of Experience (form EC2/GN). The form will be accompanied by a copy of the Directive (see above) applicable to the job. The applicant should check whether he or she meets the terms of the Directive before completing the application form. To be eligible for a certificate you must normally (but not exclusively) have had managerial or self-employed experience for a number of years in the job concerned. The DTI charges £80 for a certificate and a smaller fee for an update/revision. The charge is to cover the costs of checking and authenticating the information submitted by the applicant.

The DTI in London (0171-215 4648) produces a booklet *Europe Open for Professionals* which is regularly updated and is obtainable both from them and the Association of British Chambers of Commerce in Coventry.

UK National Academic Recognition Information Centre (NARIC) provides information on the comparability of overseas qualifications and can be contacted at ECTIS 2000 Ltd (Oriel House, Oriel Road, Cheltenham Glos GL50 1XP; tel 01242 260010; fax 01242 258600; e-mail: 106736.2043@compuserve.com), runs an enquiry service which provides information and advice on the comparability of international and UK qualifications.

Sources of Jobs

Newspapers

UK Newspapers and Directories
The combined effects of the Single Market and the implementation of the EC Professional Qualifications Directives (see above) have not exactly triggered a flood of trans-continental job recruitment, but mobility has certainly increased and become practicable for an increasing number of EU nationals. It is therefore likely that UK newspapers will carry a growing number of job advertisements from other member states including Italy. Most British newspapers including, *The Times*, The *Financial Times*, The *Guardian* and *The European* carry regular job

adverts from other European countries. Every Thursday, the Appointments section in *The Times* provides a comprehensive list of opportunities throughout the market place both in Britain and overseas. The *Times Educational Supplement* (published Fridays) and the Education pages of the Tuesday edition of the *Guardian*, carry prolific advertisements for teaching English abroad. The *Guardian* also has a Europe supplement on Fridays, which includes a job section. A specialist fortnightly newspaper *Overseas Jobs Express* (available on subscription (PO Box 22, Brighton BN1 6HX) contains articles from a range of working travellers and a substantial jobs section under headings including: Education/TEFL, Hotel and Catering, Information Technology and Trade. Recent issues offered the following jobs in France: bilingual secretary, hotel staff, computer technicians and au pair/nanny.

Alternatively, a wide range of casual jobs, including secretarial, agricultural, tourism and domestic work, are advertised in the directory *Summer Jobs Abroad* while *Teaching English Abroad* lists schools worldwide which employ English language teachers each year and *Working in Ski Resorts Europe & North America* includes all the main Italian resorts and tells you how and where to get jobs in them. These publications are available from Vacation Work, 9 Park End Street, Oxford OX1 1HJ; tel 01865-241978; fax 01865-790885.

International and European Newspapers

International newspapers are a relatively new development in newspaper publishing; these publications circulate editions across several national boundaries and usually carry a modest amount of job advertising. Again, the volume of adverts carried and the number of such publications is likely to increase in the near future. Presently, the newspapers to consult include the *The Wall Street Journal, Financial Times, The International Herald Tribune* and *The European*. As well as employers advertising in these papers, individuals can place their own adverts for any kind of job, although bilingual secretaries and assistants, marketing managers and other professionally qualified people seeking to relocate abroad are in the greatest demand. Obviously advertising rates vary, but will be several £s per line, per insertion. For details contact the classified advertising department at the addresses listed below.

The European: Classified Advertising Department, European Liaison, The European, Orbit House, 5 New Fetter Lane, London EC4A 1AP. The European, published weekly in the UK on Thursdays and distributed in every EU country on Fridays. The paper was bought back from limbo by the Barclay Brothers after the Maxwell fiasco.

The Financial Times:, 1 Southwark Bridge, London SE1 9HL; tel 0171-873-3000. The FT is printed in English in the UK, Germany, France, The USA and Japan and distributed worldwide. International appointments appear on Thursdays in all editions.

International Herald Tribune: 63 Long Acre , London WC2E 9JH; tel 0171-836 4802; The IHT international recruitment appears on Thursdays.

Wall Street Journal: The International Press Centre, 76 Shoe Lane, London EC4; tel 0171-334 0008 – European edition published in Brussels : Wall Street Journal Europe, Bld. Brand Whitlock 87, 1200 Bruxelles; tel +32 27 41 12 11. The recruitment section which covers appointments and business opportunities worldwide and appears on Tuesdays.

For information on the Italian press, see below and the *Daily Life* chapter, *Media* section. Some Italian newspapers can be obtained in major city newsagents in the

UK on the day of publication. Alternatively, try major city reference libraries.

Advertising in Newspapers. An advertisement in an Italian newspaper may produce an offer of employment. Smyth International, 1 Torrington Park, London N12 9GG deal with *La Stampa* (Turin daily), and other provincial newspapers. The Milan paper *Il Giornale* is published at Via Gaetano Negri 4, 20123 Milan. Note however, that anyone wishing to insert an advert in the widely-read *Corriere Della Sera* should contact the Italian Publishing Group (4 Wendle Street, 131-157 Wandsworth Road, London SW8 2LL; tel 0171-498 2333) who deal exclusively with this publication. It may also be worth advertising your skills and services in the monthly English-language magazine *The Informer* which has a Classified section in each issue. Anyone who wishes to place an advert with or take out a subscription for *The Informer* should contact the Bureau Service, Via dei Tigli 2, 20020 Arese (Milan); tel 02-93581477, fax 02-9358 0280. The subscription rates are lire 70,000 (about £25) per year for delivery within Italy and 116,000 lire (about £40) per year for anyone living outside Italy. *The Informer* is also available from major international bookshops in Milan, Rome, Arese, Florence, Ispra and Varese and can be accessed on the internet (http://www.mondoweb.it/informer).

Italian Job Publications
The Career Book: usually issued in October by the newspaper *Il Sole 24 Ore* for their subscribers. Contact: Redazione Il Sole 24 Ore, Via Lomazzo 52, 20154 Milan; fax 02-3103426; or 02 341062.

Lavoro Notizie: a fortnightly publication available from Eurocultura (Via Rossi 7, 36100 Vicenza; tel 0444-964770.

Also worth looking is the Friday jobs page of newspaper *Corriere della Sera* and monthly magazines *Campus, Tuttolavoro, Trovalavoro* and *Bolletino del Lavoro.*

British Professional and Trade Publications

Professional journals and magazines are another possible source of job vacancies abroad, from British companies wishing to set up offices elsewhere in Europe and foreign firms advertising for staff e.g. *The Architects' Journal, The Architectural Review, Accountancy, Administrator, Brewing & Distilling International* and *The Bookseller* to name but a few. Anyone in the air transport industry should consult *Flight International* while those employed in the catering trade could try *Caterer and Hotel Keeper* and agricultural workers *Farmers Weekly.* Although published in the UK, some of these magazines are considered world authorities in their field and have a correspondingly wide international readership.

An exhaustive list of trade magazines can be found in media directories, for example *Benn's Media* and *Writers' and Artists' Yearbook* both of which are available in major UK reference libraries.

Professional Associations

UK professional associations are a useful contact point for their members with regard to practising elsewhere in the Community. During the negotiations involved in finalising the EU mutual recognition of qualifications directives, many professional associations negotiated with their counterparts in other member states and can therefore be helpful in providing contacts.

Details of all professional associations may be found in the directory *Trade Associations and Professional Bodies of the UK* available at most UK reference libraries. It is also worth trying to contact the Italian equivalent of UK professional associations: the UK body should be able to provide the address. Alternatively you can consult your trade union for information, as they may have links, however tenuous, with their counterpart organization in Italy. A list of addresses of the more mainstream professional organisations is given below.

Useful Addresses

Architects Registration Council for the United Kingdom: 73 Hallam Street, London W1N 6EE; tel 0171-580 5861.

Association of Professional Music Therapists: c/o Diana Ashbridge, Chestnut Cottage, 38 Pierce Lane, Fulbourn, Cambs, CB1 5DL; tel 01223-880377; 01223-881679.

Biochemical Society: 7 Warwick Court, Holborn, London WC1R 5DP.

British Computer Society: 1 Sandford Street, Swindon SN1 1HJ; tel 01793-417417.

British Medical Association: BMA House, Tavistock Square, London WC1H 9JP; tel switchboard 0171-387 4499; fax for international department: 0171-383 6644. The BMA's International Department gives extensive help and advice to its members wishing to work elsewhere in Europe, and to incoming doctors from other countries.

British Dietetic Association: 7th Floor Elizabeth House, 22 Suffolk Street, Queensway, Birmingham B1 1LS; tel 0121 643 5483.

Chartered Institute of Bankers: 10 Lombard Street, London EC3Y 9AS.

Chartered Institute of Building Services Engineers: 222 Balham High Road, London SW12 9BS; tel 0181 675 5211; fax 0181 675 5449.

Chartered Institute of Building: Englemere Kings Ride, Ascot, Berks SL5 8BJ; tel 01344 23355; fax 01344 875346.

Chartered Institute of Housing: Octavia House, Westwood Business Park, Westward Way, Coventry CV4 8JP. The CIH may be able to help individual members further by putting them in touch with key people/organisations in the EU.

College of Radiographers: 2 Carriage Row, 183 Eversholt Street, London NW1 1BU; tel 0171-391 4500.

College of Speech Therapists: Harold Poster House, 6 Lechmee Road, London NW2 5BU; tel 0181-459 8521.

Department of Education and Science: Elizabeth House, York Road, London SE1 7PH.

Faculty of Advocates: Parliament House, 11 Parliament Square, Edinburgh EH1 1RF; tel 0131-226 5071. Does not have a formal information service which helps members to find jobs abroad but it does maintain close links with other European Bars.

General Council of the Bar: 11 South Square Gray's Inn, London WC1R 5EL.

General Dental Council: 37 Wimpole Street, London W1M 8DQ; tel 0171-486 2171; fax 0171-224 3294.

General Optical Council: 41 Harley Street, London W1N 2DJ; tel 0171-580 3898; fax 0171-436 3525; e-mail: optical@global.net.com.uk

Institute of Actuaries: Napier House, 4 Worcester Street, Gloucester Green, Oxford OX1 2AW; 01865-794144; fax 01865-794094.

Institute of Biology: 20-22 Queensberry Place, London SW7 2DZ; tel 0171-581 8333; fax 0171 823 9409. Can give members advice/contacts in Europe.

Institute of British Foundrymen: Bordersley Hall, Alvchurch, Birmingham B48 7QA; tel 01527-596100; fax 01527-596102.

Institute of Chartered Accountants in England & Wales: Chartered Accounts' Hall, P O Box 433, Moorgate Place, London EC2P 2BJ; tel 0171-920 8100; fax 0171 920 0547. Is able to offer members advice on working within the

EU. The institute also has an office in Brussels which may be contacted by its members on a freephone number 0500 893369.

Institute of Chartered Foresters: 7A Colne Street, Edinburgh EH3 6AA; tel 0131-225 2705.

Institute of Chartered Secretaries and Administrators: 16 Park Crescent, London W1N 4AH; tel 0171-580 4741; fax 0171-323 1132.

Institute of Chartered Shipbrokers: 24 St Mary Axe, London EC3A 8DE.

Institute of Civil Engineers: 1 Great Ceorge Street, Westminster, London SW1P 3AA; tel 0171-222 7722; (web: http://www.ice.org.uk). Also has an international recruitment agency: Thomas Telford Recruitment Consultancy (0171-987 6999; ext. 2441).

Institute of Marine Engineers: The Memorial Building, 76 Mark Lane, London EC3R 7JN; tel 0171-481 8493; fax 0171-488 1854; (Internet: http://www.engc.org.uk/imare). Provides its members with contacts and information through its network of branches throughout Europe.

Institute of Mining and Metallurgy: 44 Portland Place, London W1N.

The Institution of Electrical Engineers: Michael Faraday House, Six Hills Way, Stevenage, Herts SG1 2AY; International department tel 01438-767272; fax 01438-742856. Helps members who wish to travel or work abroad with details of the IEE representative in their new location who will then help them to find employment etc. Sometimes a job seeker company is used to help members find jobs abroad.

Institution of Gas Engineers: 17 Grosvenor Crescent, London SW1X 7ES.

Library Association: 7 Ridgmount Street, London WC1E 7AE; tel 0171-636 7543; fax 0171 436 7218.

Chartered Institute of Marketing (CIM): Moor Hall, Cookham, Maidenhead, Berks SL6 9QH; tel 01628-427500; fax 01628 427499; e-mai: marketing@cim.co.uk (website: http://www.cim.co.uk).

Pharmaceutical Society of Northern Ireland: 73 University Street, Belfast BT7 1HL.

The Registrar and Chief Executive, United Kingdom Central Council for Nursing, Midwifery and Health Visiting: 23 Portland Place, London W1N 3AF; tel 0171-637 7181.

Royal Aeronautical Society: 4 Hamilton Place, London W1V OBQ; fax only 071-243 2546.

Royal College of Veterinary Surgeons: Belgravia House, 62-64 Horseferry Road, London SW1P 2AF; tel 0171-222 2001; fax 0171-222 2004.

Royal Pharmaceutical Society of Great Britain: 1 Lambeth High Street, London SE1 7JN; tel 0171-735 9141; fax 0171-735 7629.

Royal Town Planning Institute: 26 Portland Place, London W1N 4BE; 0171-636 9107; fax 0171-323 1582.

Employment Organizations

EURES

Eures (short for European Employment Services) is a computerised, pan-European job information network accessible through job centres which have a specially trained Euroadvisor. Through them, you can find out about jobs in Italy. The idea is that you contact the Euroadvisor nearest you in your own country, and with their help use the EURES system (which has computer links with job organisations in seventeen European countries) to track down a suitable vacancy in another country, e.g. Italy, that is on the EURES network. In Britain you can access EURES at Jobcentres. Details can also be obtained from the Overseas

Placing Unit (Level 4, Skills House, 3-7 Holy Green, Off the Moor, Sheffield S1 4AQ; tel 0114 2596051.

Italy has 22 Euroadvisors (*euroconsiglieri*) mainly to help Italians wanting to work abroad. In Italy, EURES comes under the logo *Sportelli Eures* can be accessed in various offices; e.g. in Lazio (Rome), EURES is care of l'Agenzia per l'Impiego, (Vicolo d'Aste n. 12, tel 4393870).

At any one time there is a total of about 5000 vacancies of all types from unskilled to executive and professional posts are registered on EURES which can be used free by employers. At the time of press, job seekers were not able to register their details and requests for work on the network, but this may change, so it is worth asking about doing this.

UK Employment Agencies. Details of employment agency members of the national organization, the Federation of Recruitment and Employment Services Ltd (36-38 Mortimer Street, London SW1X 8PH; tel 0171-323 4300) can be obtained direct from their London address. The agencies listed deal mainly with specific sectors eg. electronics, secretarial, accountancy etc., and will only recruit qualified and experienced staff. Alternatively, some 400 recruitment agencies can be located through the *CEPEC Recruitment Guide* which is available in reference libraries or from the Centre for Professional Employment Counselling (Lilly House, 13 Hanover Square, London W1R 9HD: tel 0171-629 2266) for £37 including postage and packing. The *Recruitment Guide* lists agencies which arrange jobs, predominantly for graduates and professionals, within the UK and sometimes abroad.

Italian Employment Agencies. The state-run *Ufficio di Collocaménto Manodòpera* is the only employment and recruitment agency which is allowed to operate officially in Italy. Germany, France and Spain have all adopted similar closed-door policies towards private employment agencies, which may only legally function as temporary employment bureaux. Those who are interested in temporary work should contact these agencies which are listed in the Italian *Yellow Pages*; bearing in mind, however, that there is little point in applying if you are not proficient in Italian.

Chambers of Commerce

The main function of the Italian chambers of commerce (*Camera di Commercio Industria*) is to promote business and trade in their area but they may well do a sideline in providing information on potential employees to interested companies. The British Chamber in Milan (Via Camperio 9; tel 02-877798; fax 02-86461885) actually does this. For a small fee they will lodge your CV on their files, usually for a determinate period and circulate your details to likely employers. They hold information on member companies but you will probably have to pay them for this unless you become a member.

Anyone setting up in business or self employment in Italy has to register with the local chamber of commerce on arrival; there are local and regional chambers of commerce in virtually every town and city. Their main task is to provide enthusiastic support for local industries and companies and, on request, will provide details of these and a list of government incentives for new industry (see the section, *Government Incentives*, in the Business chapter).

Application Procedure

To avoid disappointment it is as well to accept that if your speculative letter of employment successfully negotiates the shambles of the Italian postal system, your application is still only at the very earliest stages in the job-hunting process. Remember that the Italians are notoriously bad at answering letters and faxes and that each application will have to be accompanied by copious amounts of persistance and patience, if not goodwill. However, after accepting these drawbacks as inherent in postal applications, proceed with the utmost enthusiasm and determination. The list, *Directory of Employers* on page ??? is a good source from which to base a speculative job hunt list and if you feel that the letter would be more effective in Italian (ie. be understood) then the Institute of Translation and Interpreting (377 City Road, London EC1V 1NA; tel 0171-713 7600; fax 0171-713 7650; e-mail: iti@compuserve.com) provides a good service of freelance translating, putting callers in touch with translators who will provide a fluent translation for a fee of approximately £70 per thousand words. Keep your letters formal, clear and polite and to the point; a flood of personal history will not be greeted appreciatively. Always send a cv, whether the letter is speculative or in response to an advertised vacancy.

For advice on how to compile and CV, refer to the publication *The Right Way to Write Your Own CV*, John Clarke (Paper Fronts) and *CVs and Written Applications*, Judy Skeats (Ward Lock). Agencies which prepare CVs (usually for the cost of approximately £25 for a one-page graduate CV; the shorter the better) can be found under the heading *Employment Agencies* in the local *Yellow Pages*. After the CV has been written, any abbreviations, etc. which may confuse a foreign reader should be modified. Don't send any original certificates or documents with an enquiry or application as it is extremely unlikely that you will ever see them again.

If you are offered an interview, remember that first impressions and appearances are always important. Whatever the number of interviewers, you will usually find that the meeting is formal as a casual approach to interviews is an Americanism not yet in vogue with most Italian employers. As for dress, try to look smart, as the Italians inevitably are. However, it is probably wisest to err on the side of conservatism, at the risk of looking like you've just been on an unfortunate shopping spree in Marks and Spencers, rather than attempting, and more often than not failing, to beat the Italians at their own game (ie. the notorious *bella figura*) which involves looking one's best at all times). Remember that handshaking is popular throughout Italy with both men and women and that it is polite to shake hands both on arrival and departure. As with any job in any country, it is best to find out as much background information as possible about the company and the position for which you have applied in advance of the interview. An interest based on knowledge and hard facts is bound to impress a potential employer.

Useful Address

Studio Papperini: 114 Via Ugo Ojetti, 00137 Roma; tel 06-86895810; fax 06-86896516. Comprehensive relocation service headed by Giovanni Papperini a solicitor specialising in immigration and nationality law. Based in Rome, but operates throughout Italy. Offers a pre-move service and cost effective, tailormade package to suit employer or employee.

Temporary Work

Agriculture

Casual labouring jobs in Italy are harder to come by than in some other Mediterranean countries. This is because vineyard owners traditionally employ migrant workers from North Africa and other Arab countries who are prepared to work illegally and for a pittance throughout the duration of the grape harvest (*vendemmia*) each year. Opportunities for grape picking are best in the north west of the country, for example in the vineyards lying south east of Turin in Piedmont and in the north east in Alto Adige and to the east and west of Verona. The harvest takes place in September and October. There are other possibilities for fruit picking earlier in the year, but again there will be stiff competition for the limited number of jobs available. Strawberries are picked in the region of Emilia Romagna in June and apples from late August in the Alto Adige region and in the Valtellina, which lies between the north of Lake Como and Tirano. Jobs are also available picking grapes and tobacco leaves in Tuscany in September each year.

The Val di Non apple harvest around Cles in the river valley of the Adige, north of Trento, is a mecca for migrant workers and is a veritable cultural melting pot of Italians, blacks, South Americans et al, and picking begins around 20-25th September for about four to five weeks. Women normally get the sorting jobs (hourly wage 9000 lire) and the men earn slightly more picking. The object seems to be to get the harvest gathered in record time, so expect to work ten hours a day with no days off. If lunch and accommodation are provided there is a standard deduction and most farmers eat lunch with their pickers. And yes, Italian workers *do* sing operatic arias in the orchards while they work.

The International organisation WWOOF (Willing Workers on Organic Farms) has its Italian adherents and further details can be obtained from WWOOF in your own country. In the UK send a s.a.e. to WWOOF (19 Bradford Road, Lewes, Sussex BN7 1RB. Membership costs £10 a year and includes bi-monthly newsletters with adverts for helpers in the UK and abroad. You can buy a list of organic farms from the European Centre for Eco Agro Tourism (postbox 10899, 1001 EW Amsterdam, Netherlands) for £5/8$ in cash. However, this list is aimed at promoting agro tourism, (i.e. paying stays on farms) and it is merely a suggestion that you can use it for contacts who might let you work and learn about organic farming in return for keep.

For those with a professional interest in farming, the International Farm Experience Programme (YFC Centre, National Agricultural Centre, Kenilworth, Warwickshire CV8 2LG) arranges courses combining language tuition and work experience on farms for five months beginning in February and July. Five weeks at a language school are followed by four months on a farm. Free board and lodgign throughout the language course and wages at local rates while on the farm are provided. Applicants must be aged 18-26 and have at least two years of practical farming experience. Travel costs and insurance are subsidised.

The Italian organisation SCICA – Sezione Circondariale per L'Impiego et il Collocamento (Via Maccani 76 38100 Trento; tel 0461-826433 & 826434) organises agricultural jobs and training placements in the Alps.

Au Pair

There is always a demand for au pairs (known as *alla pari* or *i babysitter* in Italian), and also for qualified nannies. The rules for au pairs are slightly confused in that they are not in general eligible for a *libretto di lavoro* (see *Residence and Entry Regulations*) but must apply for a stay permit (*permesso di soggiorno*) if they are staying for longer than three months. They must also register at the local registry office (*Ufficio Anagrafe*) which must be done before they can for instance, open a bank account in Italy. Non-EU or EEA nationals are not eligible for a *permesso di soggiorno* and must therefore must arrive in Italy with an exchange or cultural visa.

In general, the conditions of work for an au pair among the affluent Italian middle classes who take them are reasonably good. They get board, lodging and pocket money of about 100,000 lire per week. Mothers helps work longer hours a week and get about 120,000-170,000 lire. Au pairs are expected to devote a certain amount of time to their hosts' offspring, to attend a part-time language course at the local school and to be an active member in the family's social milieu. In Italy particularly, au pairs tend to be embraced into the bosom of the host family and to the uninitiated this can be an overpowering and bewildering experience. Most people seem to adapt to the Italians' demonstrative and vociferous ways and whatever else this arrangement may involve, it is unlikely that you will ever feel alienated or lonely in the midst of Italian family life. As the Italians who can afford au pairs tend also to be the ones who can afford luxury holiday villas on the coast, keep your fingers crossed for a trip to the seaside in the holiday month of August and one to the Italian Alps in the skiing season.

The majority of European au pair agencies deal with Italy and so you should have no trouble arranging a job there. Remember that it is illegal for any agency to charge a registration fee to clients; the latter are only liable to pay a commission of about £40 once a job has been organized and the contract actually signed. After the expiry of your first three months au pairing in Italy, you have only to visit the local police station (*Questura*) with a member of the host family to sign that he or she is willing to take responsibility for you; proof may also be required that you are actually attending a language course. Au pairs are then granted a three-month extension which must be renewed for a further three months on its expiry. The publication, *The Au Pair and Nanny's Guide to Working Abroad* is an invaluable source for those looking for an au pair job abroad and is available for £9.99 from Vacation Work in Oxford (tel 01865-241978).

Useful Addresses

Agencies in Italy

L'Aquilone Au Pair Bureau: Via Giovanni Pascoli 15, 20129 Milan; tel 2-29529639; fax 2-29522175; e-mail: aquilone@azienda.net UK co-operating agency: Avenue Au-Pairs, The Gables, 44 The Avenue, Hatch End, Middlesex HA5 4EY; tel 0181-421 5452.

A.R.C.E: (Attivitá Culturali con l'Estero), via XX Settembre 2/44, 16121 Genova, Italy; tel 10-583020; fax 10-583092.

Au Pair International: Via S. Stefano 32, 40125 Bologna, Italy; tel 051-267575; fax 051-236594.

Intermediate: Via Bramante 13, 00153 Rome 13; tel/fax 6-57 47 444.

Sunshine Agency: Viale Principessa Mafalda 14, 90149 Palermo; tel/fax 91-454870.

3 esse Agency: Via F. Baracca 18-1, 21013 Gallarate (VA); tel/fax 0331-771065.

Agencies in the UK

Au Pairs Italy: 46 The Rise, Sevenoaks, Kent TN13 1RJ; tel 01732-451 522. Has been specialising in Italy since 1975 and has a large number of contacts and 'regular' families.

Abbey au Pairs: 8 Boulnois Avenue, Parkstone, Poole, Dorset BN14 9NX; tel/fax 01202-732922.

Anglo Continental Au Pairs Placement Agency: 21 Amesbury Crescent, Hove, East Sussex BN3 5RD; tel/fax 01273-705959.

Anglo Pair Agency: 40 Wavertree Road, Streatham Hill, London SW2 3SP; tel
    0181-674 3605; fax 0181-674 1264.
English-Italian Agency; 69 Woodside, Wimbledon SW9 7AF; tel 0181-946 5728;
    partner agency in Turin: The English Agency, Via Pigafetta 48, 10129 Turin;
    tel/fax 011-597458.
English Solutions: 11 Marlborough Place, Brighton BN1 1UB; tel 01273-608311;
    fax 01273-772747. Specialises in Italy
European Connections: 25 Eastgate House, High Street, Guildford, Surrey GU1
    3BY; tel/fax 01483-574035. Deals only with Italy.
Girls About Town Au Pair Agency: 15 Maxim Road, Grange Park, London N21
    1EY; tel 0181-364 0034; fax 0181-364 0354.
Students Abroad/Global Nannies: 3 Kneller Road, New Malden, Surrey KT3
    5ND; tel 0181-330 0777; fax 0181-330 0345.

Teaching English

Italy is one of the European countries which has a steady demand for Teachers
of English as a foreign language. There are hundreds of language schools in
Italy as any *pagine gialle* (yellow pages) will confirm, and between them they
employ thousands of teachers. Moreover, it is not just the inhabitants of the
large and sophisticated cities of Rome, Florence and Milan who long to learn
English; small towns in Sicily and Sardinia, in the Dolomites and along the
Adriatic all have more than their fair share of private language schools and thus
offer a variety of teaching opportunities. As you might surmise from the above
range and distribution of schools, there is some variation of standards. At the
elite end there are the 27 schools which are AISLI (Associazione Italiana
Scuole di Lingua Inglese) members and which are administered from the
Cambridge Centre of English in Modena (Via Campanella 16, 41100 Modena).
AISLI has very strict regulations and its schools are ultra-respectable. However,
it would be a mistake to assume AISLI represents the best schools: for instance
neither the British Institute in Florence, nor International House in Rome are
members.

However, just because there are hundreds of schools does not mean jobs are
that easy to come by. In some cases supply outstrips demand and although things
are picking up again after the recession, it is difficult to get anything other than
short-term contracts and freelance work as the cost to employers of full-time
employees is prohibitive. The best way of finding private teaching jobs on the
spot is to head for any of the the 31 university towns and put up notices that you
are offering conversation lessons. Since all Italian university students have to take
some type of English course, many are eager to be taught by a native speaker. For
other teaching work, it is worth looking in the English language papers eg. the
Daily American or *When in Rome* and the Italian newspapers, *Messaggero* in
Rome or *La Pulce* in Florence for adverts. For speculative applications you you
will find a list of language schools listed under *Scuole de Lingua* in the Italian
Yellow Pages; the best time to look is September/October time or just after
Christmas. Do keep in mind, however, that your chances are much improved if
you have some kind of TEFL qualification, either the RSA Certificate or a shorter
TEFL training course. If you decide a TEFL course in Italy, contact International
House in Rome (Viale Manzoni 57, 00165 Rome) which offers month-long
courses for about 2,430,000 lire, and also has a useful bulletin board which
advertises teaching jobs throughout Italy.

If you don't have any teaching qualifications it is still possible to talk your way
into a job, bearing in mind, however, that competition tends to be keenest in

Rome, Florence and Venice, so non-qualified job-seekers would be advised to avoid the major cities. However, reports suggest that the number of schools willing to employ unqualified teachers is declining so private conversation lessons are probably a better bet. As mentioned above, the publication, *Teaching English Abroad* (1997 Vacation Work, £10.99) is an invaluable source of reference for anyone considering teaching in Italy. Another publication *Teaching English in Italy* (1995) by Martin Penner, an EFL teacher at International House in Rome contains details of only about 60 schools but has lots of useful background information on red tape etc. It is published by In Print Publishing of Brighton at £9.95 and available from Bailey Distribution (tel 01797 366905). Also, try the *Education* section of *The Guardian* on Tuesdays, the *Times Educational Supplement* on Fridays and the fortnightly *Overseas Jobs Express* (see page 126), all of which are regular sources of TEFL jobs.

The standard teaching wage in 1996 was 1,500,000 lire net monthly; for freelance workers 15,000 – 20,000 hourly. Do not expect subsidised or free accommodation, though some help may be given in finding it.

Useful Addresses

TEFL schools in Italy:

Benedict School: Via Salara 36, 48100 Ravenna; tel 544-38199; fax 544-38399. Eight to 12-month contracts, renewable.

The British Institute of Florence: Piazza Stozzi 2, 50123 Florence; tel 55-239 8866/284033; fax 55 287056; e-mail: british@fol.it

British Schools Group: Via Lucullo 14, 00187 Rome; tel 06-488 0333). Has about 65 member schools.

British s.r.l.: Via XX Settembre 12, 16121 Genoa; tel 10-593591/562621; fax 10 562621.

Cambridge Centre of English: Via Campanella 16, 41100 Modena; tel 59-241004. Member of AISLI (see above).

The Cambridge School: Via Mercanti 36, 84100 Salerno; tel 89-228942; fax 89 252523.

CLM-BELL (Centro di Lingue Moderne/Bell Educational Trust): Via Pozzo 30, 38100 Trento; tel 461-981733; fax 461 981687. Member of AISLI.

The English Centre: Via P Paoli 34, 07100 Sassari, Sardinia; tel 79-232154; fax 79 232180. Member of AISLI.

Lord Byron College: Via Sparano 102, 70121 Bari; tel 80-5232686; fax 80-5241349. Eight-month renewable contracts.

Modern English Study Centre: Via Borgonuovo 14, 40125 Bolgogna; tel 51-227523; fax 51-225314.

Oxford School of English: Administrative office: Via S. Pertini 14, Mirano, 30035 Venice; tel 41 5702355; fax 41 5702390.

Regency School: Via dell'Arcivescovado 7, 10121 Turin; tel 11 562 7456; fax 11 541845; e-mail regency@mbox.vol.it

Summer Camps: Via Roma 54, 18038 San Remo, Liguria; tel/fax 184 506070. Teaching English to children. Must have genuine love of children, high moral standards and ability to teach English and organise activities including drama.

Wall Street Institutes/St. Louis School: Corso V. Emanuele 30, 20122 Milan: tel 2 760 01435/760 06731. Has about 50 Italian franchise schools. List available from head office in Spain (Torre Mapfre, Marina 16-18, 08005 Barcelona).

Washington School: Via del Corso 184, Rome 00186; tel 6 679 3785; fax 6 678 1512.

TEFL Training in the UK:

Bell Language School Cambridge: 1 Redcross Lane, Cambridge CB2 2QX; tel 01223-247242; fax 01223-412410. Four weeks (130 hours). Also part-time courses (Tues and Thurs evenings) October to June. Six full time courses per year. Can advise on host families.

Berlitz (UK) Ltd: 9-13 Grosvenor Street, London W1A 3BZ; tel 0171-915 0909; fax 0171-915 0222. Does not run TEFL courses but comulsory method training for its own method lasting one to two weeks. This can be taken in the country in which the employee is successfully interviewed rather than in the country where they will be working.

inlingua Training Courses: Rodney Lodge, Rodney Road, Cheltenham, Glos GL50 1JF; tel 01242-253171; fax 01242-253181. Either five weeks in Cheltenham or three weeks in Italy plus two weeks in Cheltenham.

ILC Recruitment (International Language Centres): 1 Riding House, London W1A 3AS; tel 071-580 4351; fax 071-631 0741.

International House: 106 Piccadilly, London W1 9FL; tel 071-491 2598.

Linguarama: New Oxford House, 16 Waterloo Street, Birmingham B2 5UG; tel 0121-632 5925. Also at 28-32 Princess Street, Manchester M1 4LB; tel 0161-228 3983 and Oceanic House, 89 High Street, Alton, Hampshire GU34 1LG; tel 01420-80899; fax 0161-236 9833. Possibility of a placement in a Linguarama school abroad (e.g. Italy) on successful completion of a course.

Lynda Hazelwood Services: Charlton Park, Keynsham, Bristol BS18 2ND; tel 01452 532449/0117 986 0688; fax 01452-530305. Runs TEFL training courses by distance learning and has contacts with Italian schools.

Tourism

Italy's buzzing tourist industry is a major source of local employment providing jobs for six to seven per cent of the population. It is often difficult for foreigners to gain access to this cosy little arrangement since even the so-called menial jobs available in major resorts in other European countries have a readily available pool of impeccably turned out, well-trained, multi-lingual locals. This can be rather frustrating if you have set your heart on working in, and gaining an insider's knowledge of Florence, Venice, Rome, Pisa etc. An alternative is to work for a British tour company. Even this is problematic owing to restrictions on the employment of non-Italians. Some companies have exploited a legal loophole and called themselves art and cultural associations in order to employ non-Italians. The main tourist areas apart from the cities are the coastal resorts of Rimini and Pescara (on the Adriatic), Portofino and San Remo on the Italian Riviera and Capri (island), Sorrento and Amalfi (south of Naples). However, finding any kind of work through tourism is going to be difficult.

Apparently your chances improve if you speak German and there is an agency which specialises in vacancies in the tourist industry in northern Italy (Agentur Messner, Stadelgasse 9, 39042 Brixen; tel/fax +39 471 80 12 22).

If your knowledge of Italian fails to get you a job with a local employer, your skill may be more valued as a campsite courier with one of the major British camping holiday organizers such as Canvas Holidays. You can also try Italian-run campsites and holiday villages run by Club Valtur (the Italian Club Med) which have a large staff to run the on-site restaurants, bars and shops. The two main campsites in Rome (the Tiber and the Flamignio) take on English help before the season begins in the early summer of each year. If you have a background in the hotel trade or childcare you could try Forte's village in southern Sardinia which caters largely for families.

Useful Addresses

British tour companies/campsites operating in Italy:

Canvas Holidays Ltd: 12 Abbey Park Place, Dunfermline, Fife KY12 7PD; tel 01383-644018. Campsite couriers April to end of September.

Club Med: 106/110 /Brompton Road, London SW3 1JJ; 0171-225 1066. Has two villages in Sicily and two in Sardinia and another three in mainland Italy.

Eurocamp plc: Overseas Recruitment Department; tel 01565-625522. Has a about 40 sites dotted around Italy: on the Ligurian coast, in the Dolomites, on the Adriatic Coast, Sardinia, Amalfi Peninsula and Tuscany.

Garoto Tours: 0171-430 1378. Small operator, occasionally employs office staff to meet and greet and who can speak Italian.

Haven Europe: 1 Park Lane, P O Box 216, Hemel Hempstead HP2 4GJ. Campsite couriers and children's staff for campsites.

Mark Warner: Telephone 0171-393 3179 (24-hour). All kinds of staff (managers, accountants, receptionists, watersports instructors, nannies, handypersons etc) for beachclubs in Capo Testa on the northern Sardinian coast and Punta Licosa, about two hours south of Naples.

Venue Holidays: 21 Christchurch Road, Ashford, Kent TN23 7XD. Employs summer season reps at campsites on the Venetian Riviera.

Welcome Hotels & Resorts; Via Bologna 498, 44100, Ferrara; tel +39 532 977105; fax +39 532 970238. Computer application person and telephone marketing person. Must be Italian and English speaking. Needs to translate text from Italian to English to put on the computer for tourist readership. Bed and breakfast and £25 weekly. Minimum two weeks June to August.

Any EU national aged 18-27 with a vocational qualification in Leisure and Tourism (but not a university degree) should look into EU-funded schemes for work experience in another EU country. At unpredictable intervals they offer attractive summer packages of a month's language tuition followed by three months' experience working in the Italian tourist industry for a merely nominal cost. Details are available from Pro-Europa (59 High Street, Totnes, Devon TQ9 5PB; 01803 864526).

There are Italian agencies that place people in hotel jobs, but you would have to be Italian speaking to deal with them. You could try the following:

Italian job finding organisations and hotels

Alberghi Consorziati: 61032 Fano; tel 0721-827376. A consortium of hotels that recruits summer workers for the establishments along the beach resort of Fano (near Pesaro).

Albergo Ristorante Colibri: Via Cristoforo Colombo, 17024 Finale Ligure (Savona).

Associazione Albergatori di Rimini: Viale Baldini 14, 47037 Rimini; fax 0541-56519. Organisation which recruits seasonal staff for Adriatic hotels.

Blue Hotels SRL: Via Porto Portese 22, 25010 S Felice d/Benaco (Brescia). Hotel chain with establishments in Lake Garda, Sardinia, Umbria, Arezzo, Tuscany and Lazio.

Club Mediterranee Servizio Risorse Umane: Largo Corsia dei Servi 11, 20122 Milan; tel 02-778261; fax 02-7786261. Worldwide organisation has villages in Italy including Sardinia.

DIEFFE Animation: Corso Vittorio Emanuele 749, 80122 Naples. Organisation that recruits personnel for tourist villages and cruise ships on the Tyrrhenian coast (Naples).

Grand Hotel Cesenatico: Cesenatico, Forli International tourist Hotel on the coast between Ravenna and Rimini recruits summer staff.

Hotel Cavallino d'Oro: 39040 Castelrotto (BZ) Sudtirolo; tel 0471-706337; fax 0471 707172. Hotel in picturesque town in the Dolomite mountains. All year round resort.

Relai Ca'masieri: Trissino (Veneto); tel 0445-490122. Hotel needing seasonal staff.

SCICA Azienda del Lavoro: 38054 Fiera di Primiero (Trento); tel 0439 762232. Recruits all types of service staff (bar, dining room, kitchen etc.) for hotels of San Martino di Castrozza, Passo Rolle and Lagorai.

SCICA Agenzia del Lavoro: 38066 Riva del Garda; tel 04464 552130. Agricultural and hotel jobs in the lake Garda area.

Team Bagarre SRL: Via Palladio 12, 20135 Milan; tel 02-58302765; fax 02-58305824. Organisation that recruits couriers and representatives for the Italian tourist industry.

Valtur S.P.A. Risorse Umane: Via Milano 42, 00184 Rome; tel 06-4706271; fax 06-4706300. Tour operator that runs a series of tourist villages on Italy's Mediterranean coast. Employs couriers etc.

For other potentially useful addresses, e.g. hotels – see the list of 'Major Employers' at the end of this chapter.

Jobs Glossary

aiutocuochi/aiuto-cucin	assistant chef/kitchen assistant
baristi	bar persons
camerieri/e di sala	waiters/resses
cameriere di piano	chambermaids
commessi/e	shop assistants
cuochi	chefs
lavapiatti	washer-upper
portieri	porters

Winter Resorts

The winter playgrounds of Italy in the Alps, Dolomites and Apennines offer on-the-spot opportunities. Many of the jobs are part-time and do not pay well, but if they come with free accommodation and a ski pass, at least you can improve your skiing technique for free at famous resorts like Cortina and Courmayeur. The Veneto region of Italy is a good area to target as it is in easy reach of the eastern Dolomites and boasts a number of ski resorts, including Cortina d'Ampezzo (near Belluno), Asiago, Canarei, Alleghe and Santo Stefano di Codore. Other resorts include La Villa, San Cassiano, Pedraces, Corvara and Colfosco in the province of Bolzano. The winter season lasts from Christmas to Easter and most mountain resorts have a summer season mainly July and August. Remember that jobs in ski resorts do get snatched up very quickly and the earlier you apply the more likely you are to get a job; Mark Warner told us that they recommend people to apply as early as June for the winter season. If you speak Italian you can call round the resorts in person. Note that if you work for an Italian employer you are likely to work much longer hours than if you work for a British tour company.

Italian Job Organisations

SCICI: 38054 Fiera di Primiero (Trento); tel 0439-762232. Recruits a range of personnel for the hotels of San Martino di Castrozza, Passo Rolle, Lagorai.

SCICA Azienda del Lavoro di Tione: Recruits trainees for hotels of the Tione area, Madonna di Campiglio.

British Winter Sports tour operators

Equity Total Travel: Dukes Lane House, 47 Middle Street, Brighton, East Sussex BN1 1AL; tel 01273-886878; fax 01273-203212. Goes to 19 resorts in Italy.

Winterski: 38 Ship Street, Brighton BN1 1AB; tel 01273-204541. Specialises in

Italian resorts: Marilleva, Pejo, Sauze d'Oulx and Tonale.

Interski: Acorn Park, St. Peter's Way, Mansfield, Notts NG18 1EX; tel 01623-456333; fax 01623-456353. School group organiser that employs up to 250 ski instructors for the resorts of Courmayeur, Aosta/Pila and La Thuile.

PGL Ski Europe: Alton Court, Penyard Lane, Ross-on-Wye, Herefordshire HR9 5NR; tel 01989-768168; fax 01989-563162. Organises school travel groups to Italy.

Voluntary Work

There are many Italian organizations that accept volunteers during the summer months to help with various projects. These can revolve around helping to relieve social deprivation, wildlife preservation, archaeology and restoration and ecological research projects. Most of the organisations below charge the volunteer a participation fee which covers board and lodging. Paid volunteer work, or work for keep is harder to come by. The following organisations can be contacted directly for further information.

Abruzzo National Park: Viale Tito Livio 12, 00136 Rome; tel 06-35403331; fax 0635403253. Volunteers spend fifteen days working with other young people who are interested in protecting flora and fauna in an outpost of the Abruzzo National Park. Participants collaborate with the operators, researchers, technicians and guards of the Park in activities such as assisting and educating visitors, maintenance and research. Volunteers should have experience of working in this field and be able to spend time in the mountains living in rough conditions. Accommodation and a contribution towards food costs are provided.

Archeoclub d'Italia: Via Sicilia 235 00100 Rome; tel 06-488 1821. Information about archaeological work camps.

Brown Bears, Central Italy: CTS, Via Nazionale 66, 00184 Rome; tel +39-6 4679317; fax +39-64679252. Volunteers needed to help researchers in the Abruzzo National Park, the only habitat of a sub-species of Brown Bear. Volunteers must be able to walk for long periods during the day.

Centro Camuno di Studi Preistorici: Piazza S. Maria 8, 25040 Braone, Brescia; tel 0364/433621.

Communita' di Agape: Centro Ecumenico, 10060 Prali (Torino); tel +39 121 807514; fax 0121-807690. This organization recruits volunteers to work alongside the permanent staff to help run this ecumenical centre for national and international meetings. Applicants should be at least 18 years old and be available to work for a minimum of one month over the summer. Knowledge of Italian would be an advantage; board and lodging is provided.

CTS-Centro Turistico Studentesco e Giovanile: Via Nazionale 66, 00184 Rome; tel +39-6 4679317; fax +39-6 4679252; (e-mail: ctsambi@mbox.vol.it - www: http://www.cts.vol.it/). The largest Italian youth association. Organises research activities and expeditions which use paying volunteers to work in the field and fund different projects carried out by scientists. Some of the projects are in Italy in the Alps, Appennines and National Parks. Membership is required to join the expeditions. Further details from the above.

Emmaus: Via Castelnuovo 21/B, Segretariato Campi Lavoro, c/o Parr, 50047 Prato; tel 0574-541104; fax 055-6503458. Social and community work camps.

Europe Conservation in Italy: Via Bertini 34, 20154 Milan; tel 02-33103344; fax 02-33104068. Volunteers are needed to work on archaeological excavations for a minimum of two weeks between July and September – six hours per day, six days per week. Board and accommodation are available for approximately

£140 per week. Previous archaeological experience is desirable. Placements involve lectures and excursions but no fares or wages are paid.

Gruppi Archaeologici d'Italia: Via Degli Scipioni 30/A, 00192 Rome; tel 06-39733786; fax 06-39734449. Work camps, season tickets and subscription to the magazine *Archaeologica.*

Kalat Project: Via S.Maria di Capua, 91100 Trapani, Sicily; tel/fax +39 923 873844. Environmental and archaeological camps in summer during July and August. Field School £300 (44 hours of field work plus 30 hours of lessons and lectures plus six excursions to the most important archaeological and environmental sites of western Sicily/or work camps £50 (72 hours of field work plus eight hours of lessons and lectures and three excursions).

Legambiente: Via Salaria 403, 00199 Rome; tel +39 6 862681; fax +39-6 86218474; (e-mail: mc7273@mclink.it; www: http://www.legambiente.com). Non-profit organisation. Volunteer opportunities include work camps, currently these are: restoration and protection camps on small islands off Sicily, bear research project in the Appeninnes, underwater archaeology and ecology in Sicily etc.

LIPU (Lega Italiana Protezione Uccelli): Vicolo San Tiburzio 5, 431 Parma; tel 0521-233414; fax 0521-287116. The Italian equivalent of the RSPB publishes a list (in Italian) of their programme of summer working holidays. Camps last one or two weeks and cost from 430,000 lire per week.

La Sabranenque: Centre International, rue de la Tour de l'Oume, 30290 Sainte Victor la Coste, France; tel +33 4-66 500505. Restoration of villages, sites and simple monuments using traditional building methods in Altamura, southern Italy and the hamlet of Gnallo, northern Italy. Work includes walls, paths and small houses. Two to three weeks during July and August. Cost to volunteer is £180 per three-week project for board and accommodation.

Mani Tese: Via Cavenaghi 4, 20149 Milan; tel 02-48008617; fax 02-4812296. Collects and recyles objects for profit to finance department projects. Their summer projects include a study of development issues for which a knowledge of Italian is necessary.

Mediterranean Fin Whale Programme: Tethys Research Institute c/o Aquario Civico, Viale Gadio 2, 1-20121 Milan; tel +39-2 72001947; fax +39-2 72001946. Volunteers to assist with study of Fin Whales during the summer in the western Ligurian sea and off Corsica. Volunteers must be able to swim and their tasks are varied from helping run the camp to collating data and observing.

MIR – Movimento Nonviolento: Via Assietta 13/A, 10125 Turin; tel 011-532824; fax 011-549184. Work camps.

OIKOS Via Paola Renzi 55, 00128 Rome; tel 06-5080280. Environmental organisation that has, since 1979 organised work camps to conserve a large area of mediterranean scrubland to the south west of Rome.

Organizzazione Internazionale Nuova Acropoli: Piaza Regina Margherita 7, 67100 l'Aquila; tel 0862-61051. Environmental protection organisation that organises a fire prevention work camp in the mountains of the region and in the Gran Sasso park.

WWF Italia: Ufficio Campi, Via Canzio 15, 20131 Milan; tel 02-29513742; fax 02-29513860. Publishes a list of annual *campi* (work camps) in magazine form – in Italian only.

Aspects of Employment

Salaries

Each industry in Italy has a national labour contract stipulating minimum wage and salary levels. However, workers in the North would never dream of being offered (let alone accepting) work paid at the minimum wage level and it is only in the most depressed areas of the Mezzogiorno where the minimum wage is a working reality. A major bone of contention betwen employers and unions contines to be Italy's adherence to the *scala mobile* when negotiating salary levels. Although the scala mobile, whereby wages are indexed to inflation, no longer passes on 100% of inflation but instead around 47% of the official inflation rate, the principle remains and the unions are reluctant to forgo it.

Although Italian salaries have a reputation for being lower than the European norm, this does not account for the number of Italians who hold a second or third salaried job. Managerial jobs (*dirigenti*) in particular are well paid with a managing director earning a top-of-the-range salary level of approximately 150 million lire (£70,000) each year. Marketing, personnel and financial executives can expect to earn from 80 million lire (approximately £40,000) each year while executives slightly lower down the hierarchical scale (eg. accountants, purchasing offices etc.) earn roughly 40 million lire(£20,000) each year. Office staff and manual workers (*operai*) usually earn from £7,000 each year, depending on the area and individual qualifications. In southern Italy, however, be prepared for all of these salary rates to be somewhat lower.

Peculiar to the West European countries is the practice of employers distributing from two to a maximum of four extra payrolls each year. All employees are entitled to an additional month's renumeration (the so-called 13th month) payable in December. Furthermore, the collective bargaining contracts for certain concerns provide for additional payments. For example, in banking, monthly salaries are paid 16 times a year and, in the petroleum industry, 15 times. In commerce, a 14th month salary is payable in June of each year. These extra payments unsurprisingly comprise one of the greatest perks for UK nationals planning to work abroad. Remember, however, that often the base salary offered is simply divided by fourteen, fifteen or sixteen, rather than twelve so any feeling of extra wealth is unfortunately illusory.

Working Conditions

The standard working week in Italy is 39 although the average comes out at 38.6 hours (compared with 43.9 average in Britain). In reality only the serious industrial workers do a 39-hour week and cinema workers slightly more at 40 hours. Italy's civil servants spend only 36 hours a week producing paperwork, along with journalists, postal and railway workers. The police forces' lot is 37 hours. Overtime cannot be demanded of any employee and is paid at a rate of between 130% and 150% of the normal hourly rate, depending on the number of hours worked and whether it is on a weekend or holiday. However, many unions do not permit overtime and are not convinced either that the proposed 35-hour week (which is supposed to create more jobs), is at all a good thing. This was one of Prime Minister Prodi's election promises and it followed the initiative set by France which has committed itself to the idea. Presumably, Italians would like to see how it works there first.

Italian business hours vary from the Mediterranean working day of 9am-1pm and 3pm-7pm (maintained particularly in the south) to the more familiar 9-5 working day, followed by most of the larger companies and institutions. As in France, most Italian businesses simply close down for the entire month of August as the country takes its month-long summer holiday. Every employee is entitled to an annual holiday of between five and six weeks, depending on the length of service, in addition to the ten statutory days of holiday (see *Daily Life Holidays*) which are celebrated nationally.

Hidden Jobs

There are about 24,378,000 individuals who are working in Italy and of these approximately one sixth or almost four million of them are working black (*lavoro nero*) in other words they are unrecorded and do not pay tax or social security payments. This unofficial workforce is comprised of housewives, retired people, the 'unemployed' (those on redundancy funds and work mobility schemes), students, and people who already have another job (11%). Having two jobs (but only declaring one), is more common in the north whereas in the south, illegal work is virtually a permanent form of employment. The result of such a huge percentage of illegal workers is a boon to the Italian economy and general prosperity, as companies and businesses have benefitted from irregular workers boosting their productivity and profits.

Pensions

One of reforms aimed at getting Italy ready for EMU has been an assault on Italian pensions which until 1997 represented the highest percentage of GDP (14%) out of six European countries including France, Germany, the UK and Ireland. In 1994 the number of pensions being paid out reached the rather startling number of 21,273,763 with the pensioners slightly outnumbering workers at 1.03 pensioners per worker. One of the main problems tackled by the reforms was the number of people receiving pensions in Italy before reaching the maximum retirement age. Included in this was the fact that civil servants had the right to receive a pension of approximately 20 million lire a year after 16 years service.

Reforms introduced in January 1998 meant that for private sector workers to qualify for a long service pension they must be at least 54 years old (57 by 2002) with a minimum of 35 years of contributions. Public sector pensions will be brought into line with private ones gradually over a period of years until by 2004 they will have the same age and period of contributions limits. A more ruthless measure is that anyone who was expecting to retire in January, July and October 1998 have had their pensions deferred for a year. The notorious *scala mobile* (sliding scale) where pensions were increased in line with cost of living, has also been suspended for a year and then will undergo a gradual reduction over a period of three years. For instance on the pension minimum of 3.5 million lire (about £11,166) the monthly reduction will be about £23 or about £292 pounds annually.

Business Etiquette

Anyone used to Northern European or North American business practices will find the Italian way of doing things somewhat less thrusting. Contrary to what is probably your usual practice, the Italians consider it uncivilized to race through a deal in one day and positively barbaric to hustle at a working lunch. Instead, once you have realised that business is likely to be indivisible from pleasure and likely to induce a flurry of lunch and dinner invitations at which you should make an effort to converse in as much of the national language as you have succeeded in mastering, you are going to do better at it than you think.

Although seemingly relaxed and easy going, most Italian offices and all business procedure is far more intensely hierarchical than we are used to. This is largely because of the Italian's status-conscious psyche and to err on the side of safety it is often wise to adopt the blanket title of Signor or Signora, rather than breach the familiarity of Christian names. Women may also come across sexism of some kind when working in Italy; this is dealt with in more detail in the section *Women in Work* below.

Trade Unions

Italy's four main trade unions (*sindacati*) are grouped by political identity rather than profession. The CGIL, Confederazione Generale del Lavoro is predominantly Communist with a Socialist minority faction, while the UIL, Unione Italiana del Lavoro has a strong affiliation with the Socialists. The CISL, Confederazione Italiana Sindacati del Lavoro, is Christian Democrat while the CISNAL is affiliated with the right wing Italian social movement. There are also trade unions formed on the basis of an industry or sector of economic activity, mainly in the public sector and transportation industry. The most important of these are the General Confederations of Industry, Commerce and Agriculture. Although harbouring a history of radicalism and turbulence during the post-war decades of the 50s and 60s, the 80s saw a taming of the Italian trade unions to some of the most peaceable and compliant in Europe.

Union membership is not compulsory in Italy and membership figures have fluctuated considerably from 60% membership at the union's most militant post-war period in 1947 to an all time low of 33% membership in 1967. However, after the UK, Italy remains the most strongly unionized country in Europe.

The unions tend to work through a cycle of relative peace (with the exception of sporadic strikes on such national issues as housing, schools, unemployment etc.) until the negotiation for the renewal of the two or three yearly labour contracts (*il rinnovo del contratto*) comes around. Then whole sectors of different industries are protesting simultaneously in the arduous negotiation process; a situation not eased by La Confindustria's (the Italian employer's confederation, the equivalent of the CBI) insistence on deliberately allowing the contract expiry dates to overrun to gain bargaining power over the unions whose workers are technically without contracts during this interim period.

Women in Work

The statistics about the female working population in Italy show that with roughly an identical female population as the UK, slightly fewer (more than 40%) of women work overall. If you take the age band 30 to 49 this percentage jumps to 60% of women in the north of Italy compared to 45% in the south. Amongst the youngest age band 15 to 24, unemployment is 59% in the south and 25% in the north. Amongst the age group 25 to 34 the southern unemployment rate is 35% and in the north it is lower than the national average for both sexes at 11.2%. Since women in Italy are having children at an average of about 26 years, this means that they are working at a time when their children are growing up and when family demands are considered at their peak.

However, Italian women tend to earn substantially more than their British counterparts; 84% of the equivalent male wage, as opposed to 69% in the UK.

The position of women in the Italian work place is ambiguous. Italian females have yet to penetrate the highest and most elite echelons of Italy's political and business establishments; as yet there is no Italian equivalent of France's Edith Cresson or the UK's Margaret Thatcher. However, increasingly, women are reaching the forefront of the major professions (journalism, medicine, law and architecture in particular) and commanding the respect which their influential positions warrant. However, Italian male chauvinism is a resilient dinosaur that working women still have to contend with. Many of these old-fashioned Latin prejudices are connected to the woman's perceived role within the family. Moreover, the Italian social services are not geared to the working mother; there is a serious shortage of free nursery schools and of company and state-funded crèches. Ironically then, it is often only those who can afford babysitters and private nursery school fees who are able to have a career or even work outside the home if they wish to.

In 1991 Italy passed law 125 on Positive Action for the Achievement of male female equality at work (*Azioni positive per la realizzazione della parita uomo donna nel lavoro*) designed to remove all obstacles and give women free access to professions and types of work where they were under-represented and introduced the concept of indirect discrimination, where discrimination is unseen but evidenced by the facts. If a women were to bring a case against an employer the onus would be on the employer to demonstrate that there was no discrimination and not the other way around. Law 125, also allowed for the setting up of a series of organisations to oversee the administration of the law.

Also in 1991, a special law 215 was passed aimed at helping women to start their own businesses. Further information can be obtained from local chambers of commerce, regional cooperative and artisan associations and Centri Bic (Business Innovation Centres).

Useful Addresses for Women

Ufficio Speciale della formazione Professionale: via Capitan Bavastro, 94 Rome; tel 06-57902505. Provides professional training courses for women, regardless of age, designed to provide the skills that employers are looking for. Further details can be obtained from the above address. Needless to say, the courses will be conducted in Italian.

Telefono Rosa: via Tor di Nona 43, Rome; tel 06-6832690/820/675. Monday to Friday from 10am to 1pm and 4pm to 7pm. Women's association that can offer advice to working women e.g. sexual discrimination and harassment.

Differenza Donna: tel 06-5810926/5811473. Women's organisation. Help and advice to working women.

Contacts for business start-ups by women:

Terzario Donna presso Confcommercio, Rome: 06-3574206. Business enterprises advice for women.

I Comitati Impresa donna presso la CNA (Confederazione nazionale dell'artigianato): Rome; tel 06-47496268.

Impresa Femminile Singolare: c/o Federlazio viale Libano 62 Rome; tel 06/549121.

La Societa per l'Imprenditorialita Giovanile: via Mascagni, 160 Rome; tel 862641.

Business and Industry Report

The 1980s saw a decade of enormous economic and industrial success for Italy. After entering that decade with the highest strike record in the West, lame-duck industries and layer upon layer of ill-concealed political corruption, Italy succeeded in emerging from them as the capitalist world's fifth strongest economy, poised to overtake France into fourth position. However, the successes of the manufacturing industry during this time belied an ominous lack of any overall economic policy and a national debt greater than the country's GDP, with a budget deficit running at over 12%. By mid-1990 to 1991 Italy's recession marked the end of one of the longest and most prosperous periods of expansion ever experienced by the industrialized economies since the reconstruction years following the Second World War. In 1993-94 the recession was still biting with rising unemployment (25% in the south). However, in the last couple of years there has been not only a political upheaval that saw the ignominious demise of the Christian Democrats in a sea of corruption allegations, but an economic one as Italy tightens its welfare belt ready for joining the single currency for which she is on course. There is still high unemployment, but the economy is showing definite, if undramatic signs of a turn-around.

High-tech industries in Italy have grown greatly in recent years due to increased demand and to the availability of skilled labour. Other fast-growing sectors include telecommunications, electrical appliances and the machine tool (industrial robots) industry. Within the service sector, business services and financial services and insurance companies in particular are expanding. Further information on the Italian business scenario is provided in the chapter *Starting a Business*. Many of the multinational companies which dominate Italian industry provide good potential for UK job hunters. These companies are to be found predominantly in the motor vehicles (Fiat, Ford, Renault) and electrical appliances (Merloni, Zanussi, Electrolux) sectors.

The level of state-run industry in Italy has gone from being the highest in the EU thanks to a massive sell off in recent years that has brought deregulation in that most dynamic of sectors, telecommunications. There is still however a large state interest in a variety of industries, especially those which are considered of strategic importance, such as raw materials, transport, defence, power generation, telecommunications and banks. Istituto per la Ricostruzione Industriale (IRI) is Europe's largest single company (excluding oil companies) and directly or indirectly employs over 500,000 people and controls over 1,000 companies including three major banks, RAI (the radio and television network), Alitalia (airways) and companies belonging to groups such as Finsder (steel), Finmeccanica (engineering), Fincantieri (shipbuilding) and Telecom Italia (electronics). Istituto Ente Nazionale per Idrocarboni's (ENI) interests include oil, raw and derived chemicals, petrochemicals, mining, energy engineering and services, textiles and financing. It has a share in some 285 companies, employing around 100,000 people. Finally, Ente Participazioni & Finanziamento Industria Manifattureriera (EFIM) has shares in 137 companies employing 60,000 workers. Its subsidiaries include aluminium, glass, food, engineering, transport and railways, aircraft and diesel engines companies. Although state-controlled industry includes many well-managed and technologically-advanced concerns, it is suffering from huge accumulated debts and the effects of political interference and mismanagement in past years. The origins of all three mega-companies date back to the years following the Second World War, when the state intervened to rescue many companies with the proposed objective of selling them back into the private sector once they had been restructured and revitalized. This, however, rarely happened. Recently, some companies have been sold back into the private sector.

Small businesses have dominated Italian industry over the last decade, and comprise one of its most distinctive features. Only 19% of the workforce is employed in companies which have more than 500 staff and over 59% of the manufacturing workforce is employed in companies where the total number of workers is less than 100. By contrast, these percentages for Britain and Germany are nearly a complete reverse. At the last count there were approximately three million registered small businesses functioning in Italy. Thus, small businesses are responsible for a large share of industrial output, especially in sectors where size is not a strategic feature, eg. the retail trade, clothing and furniture and other areas requiring not large investments but substantial entrepreneurial ability. Most businesses in Italy are owned by a family or a partnership; this is typically true of farms, most retail and service establishments and many small manufacturing concerns. Gaps in the market exist (eg. health food shops, DIY outlets, fast food, small garages) and are there to be taken advantage of by expatriates with hands-on experience of the relevant market in their own country. See the Chapter, *Starting a Business* for more ideas for new businesses. Although it will take perseverance to find a gap and to establish a presence in the Italian market, once you have made contacts and established your foothold the rewards, both financial and in terms of job satisfaction, can be immense; the time to act is now.

The widely-held belief that the whole of the Mezzogiorno is an area lacking potential for industrial development and to be avoided at all costs on account of Mafia infestation is mistaken. Admittedly, some areas in the far south, eg. Sicily and Calabria, are not ideal areas for industrial investment, dominated as they are by organized crime and hampered by a ludicrously inadequate system of infrastructure, communications and transport. However, some areas of the south – the mountain region of Abruzzi, Puglia and parts of Molise – have factories which function as efficiently as in the north, while benefitting from impressive government tax and credit incentives. In 1990, Fiat announced a major new project at Melfi in Basilicata; about 2,700 billion lire will be spent on an integrated bodywork and assembly plant to employ about 7,000 workers.

Finally, the opportunities of the single market are being taken very seriously by Italy (as her wholehearted endorsement of EMU shows) even if her observance of EU directives is not quite so assiduous. Forty percent of the cases before the European Court for non-implementation of European directives are against Italy. However, harmonising trade will probably be a lot easier for Italy than harmonizing banking standards and practices which still lag behind as do financial services providing private pensions and life assurance.

The following section provides an alphabetical guide to the most important Italian industries. The current prosperity or otherwise of each industry is discussed with a view to its employment and business potential for the expatriate. The most powerful companies in each sector have been listed wherever possible and the Italian contact addresses for these and many other Italian and international companies can be found in the *Directory of Major Employers* on page 158.

Aerospace

The aircraft and defence electronics group, Alenia, was formed in December 1990 from the merger of the Selenia electronics and Aeritalia aircraft subsidiaries of IRI and is Italy's leading aerospace group. In December 1997, Italy joined the

UK, Germany and Spain in approving participation in the Eurofighter programme. The governments of these countries have agreed to buy these aircraft and Italy's order is for 121. However, despite general buoyancy at the time of press there is cause for gloom in the defence business owing to a decline in other orders from the military services as defence budgets continue to shrink. Funding difficulties for the Italian air force have put a ceiling on the number of Tornado jets being purchased and there are doubts about how many other aircraft will be needed.

Bright spots on the industry's horizon include aerospace electronics, concentrated in the former Selenia group, which continues to flourish. Alenia in particular has also expanded on the space side. Combined with Aerospatiale and Alcatel Espace of France, it spent has spent millions of dollars on a stake in Space Systems/Loral, the satellites business controlled by Loral, the US defence group.

On the commercial aviation front, Alitalia the national carrier is seeking an state subsidy to finance its reorganisation plan. However, dubious management practices have resulted in a delay in the subsidy going through and the airline is the subject of investigations.

The profitable small airline, Air Dolomiti has taken over the lucrative Naples to Germany connection from Lufthansa. The proposed route is Naples-Bologna-Munich.

Agriculture

Italy has a total land area of 30,127,874 hectares of which 24% is classified as mountainous (ie. above 600m or 700m according to region). Forty-five percent is hill land and the remaining 31% is plain. Average rainfall is 43 inches in the north, 37 inches in the centre and 33 inches in the south. There are more than 3,200,000 agricultural holdings, with an average farm owning 7.2 hectares of land of which 4.8 hectares is usable. The main agricultural area is the large fertile Po Valley, which is responsible for about 40% of Italy's total grain production. Other important, though less fertile plains are on the Tyrrhenian coast from Pisa down towards Naples and the coastal plains in Puglia.

About 8% of Italians work in agriculture which is considerably higher than the EU average of 2% which means that there is no shortage of experienced workers for agricultural enterprises.

About half of the value of Italy's total agricultural output is derived from Mediterranean produce grown largely in the southern regions: wine, olive oil, and especially fruit and vegetables; Italy is the most prolific grower of fruit and vegetables in Europe. The remainder of Italy's agricultural output is farmed in the north and mostly comprises meat, dairy products and cereals. Farms in the south tend to be smaller, more labour intensive and much less fertile than those in the north. Additionally, the level of mechanization and investment is lower in the south, communications are relatively poor and marketing less developed. Agricultural contribution towards the GDP fluctuates but represents about 7% on an average year, with total sales exceeding 50,000 billion lire. Sugar beet, grapes for wine and maize are the three largest agricultural crops in Italy, while sheep, pigs and cattle are the most profitable forms of livestock. About 7.4% of the population is employed in agriculture, of which 63% are self employed and 35% are women. However, the interest in agriculture and the opportunities offered within it have declined and Italy's youth are now opting increasingly for the more attractive conditions offered by industry.

The Automotive Industry

The Italian automotive industry is led by Fiat of Turin which has dominated Italy's home market for the last decade. The success of this mega-corporation, the largest in the private sector, is mainly due to the popularity of new models such as Uno, Panda, Regata, Prisma Seicento and Tipo. Other major manufacturers include the Fiat subsidiaries: Autobianchi, Lancia, Nuova Innocenti, Alfa Romeo and high class makes, which account for only minimal shares of the market, such as Maserati, Ferarri and Lamborghini. Fiat had a 12.8% share of the European car market in 1997 which made it the second most successful car maker in that year. The home market, i.e. Italy was the fastest growing car market in the first half of 1997 which may have something to do with the government's policy of offering a subsidy to owners of dilapidated cars if they buy new ones.

This is a far cry from 1991 when Fiat laid off between 20,000 and 50,000 workers for one week each month when foreign competition and the recession dampened within the Italian market.

Japanese-badged cars (many of which are constructed in Europe) have begun, for the first time, to pose a threatening presence in the home market. Ford and Renault have also made vast inroads into the Italian market From 1991 to 1995, Fiat spent 6,000 billion lire (£2.76bn) on research and development and a further 22,000 billion lire on investment in processes and products in the automobile sector.

The joint venture between Piaggio and India's Greaves organisation will produce 'Ape' three-wheeled vehicles at a new plant at Baramati from 1998. The motorcycle industry has held steady, unlike the UK market, in the face of the Japanese challenge. The DIY sector in particular has been the centre of increased interest, with the number of outlets selling parts and accessories growing. However, the market in motorcar accessories is not especially significant as there are only few outlets and these stock a limited range of automotive products. The majority of Italians live in flats in crowded towns and cities which have few facilities and space permitting personal servicing or repairing. Moreover, many small garages follow a flexible pricing policy and overall, DIY is still perceived as being too much pain for too little gain by the majority of Italian motorists.

Chemicals

The outlook for the Italian chemicals sector is not a rosy one. If the industry is to catch up with its principal rivals and to be a competitive international force in the next millennium, it will have to carry out large-scale structural reforms within the next few years. The chemicals sector has always been subject to political manipulations and has suffered directly as a result of this. Moreover, the industry has moved against international trends by becoming more rather than less state-controlled and by relying heavily on the domestic market for sales and plant location. The industry is now dominated by the chemicals subsidiary of the state-controlled ENI, EniChem. EniChem is the only major chemicals group to be in the red. In an effort to turn around the grave situation, EniChem had to weather a strong union protest to its closure of some plants in the south and a permanent cut of some 4,500 jobs. It has a 50,000 strong workforce. Almost 55% of new investment is in the south, Sardinia and Sicily.

However, EniChem still represents 3.4% of world chemical production and 12.11% of that of Europe. The industry employs approximately 230,000 workers and the other major chemicals force, the privately-owned Montedison company is currently in a stronger position than its larger and more powerful rival. Major foreign multinationals with a strong presence in the Italian industry include Unilever, Esso, Dupont, BASF, Ciba Geigy, Hoescht, ICI, Henkel and Alusuisse.

The highly successful Menarini group reported a 7.1% rise in profits in 1997 compared with 1996. It makes over 40% of its sales abroad and has spent in the region of 100 billion lire in developing foreign interests. The group's current priority is to open up a market in the UK.

Many small/medium sized companies also flourish in this sector; 60% of Italian chemicals companies employ less than 50 staff.

Clothing and Textiles

Italy is one of the world's largest textile and clothing producers but now, with increasingly strong competition from low-cost producer countries (notably, Portugal, Romania and certain countries in the Far East) and a turndown in the home market, Italy is striving to maintain its position and reputation within the market. Biella and Prato in northern Italy are the two centres of the Italian textiles trade. Some of the most powerful Italian textile companies include Marzotto, Montefibre, Gommatex, Snia-fibra, Lanerossi and Legier Industria Tessile. However, after nearly three decades of spectacular growth the industry is facing its first crisis. Over the last five years the largely family-run, small textile businesses typical of the trade have had to tighten their belts and reduce production by 30%. The number of textile companies has fallen from 17,000 to 12,999 and employment levels have dropped from an all-time high of 60,000 jobs in the 1980s to the current, depressed level of about 10,000. In an effort to cut costs, the industry employs an immigrant and largely illegal work force (mostly Chinese and North African).

The unpredictability of the fashion business is partly responsible for these cutbacks, combined with the small size of the majority of the companies which means that financial structures are weak (only 65 companies have payrolls of more than 50 people). Moreover, as mentioned above, the Portuguese textile industry has emerged over the last decade as a major competitor, and more recently Romania and a number of Asian producers as well. Today some 35% of activity is still concerned with recycling textiles and producing for the mass market. Roughly half of total productivity is taken up with supplying the ready-to-wear business and department stores; while the remaining 15% focuses on the production of upmarket fashion garments. However, the textiles industry is under no serious threat of extinction and some of its greatest supporters even argue that the decline in the number of companies during the last five years is a part of a dynamic process whereby the industry is being strengthened and modernized.

Italian designers are also struggling. A centuries-old artisan tradition in working endless variations of fabric and leather, added to extensive recent research on novel ways of treating or developing various fabrics, allows Italian designers to adopt a unique look which constantly eludes and frustrates foreign designers. However, as competition from new rivals (eg. USA, Germany and Japan) grows more intense and the pressure is maintained from traditional rivals (eg. France), Italian designers are exploring all available avenues in order to survive and prosper; market flotation, expansion into other manufacturing fields via franchises – even the financial market. Some of the largest Italian clothing manufacturers of international renown are Benetton, Max Mara, Stefanel, Miroglio Tessile, Linea Sprint and Confezioni di Matelica. The top Italian fashion designers include Valentino, Versace, Armani, Ferre, Trussardi, Krizia, Enrico Coveri, Laura Biagiotti, Missoni and Mario Valentino.

Computers

The Italian computer industry, in line with the industry worldwide, has experienced a dramatic downslide in orders and profits over the last few years. This is largely due to the sharp decline in demand for personal computers and Olivetti, the champion of Italy's computer industry, whose survival and profit performance relies heavily on personal computers, is just about in the black again after nearly seven years of losses. This is a far cry from 1990 when it made a 60.9 billion lire profit. Olivetti's rescue plan included moving some of its production plants to cheaper plants in Singapore and Mexico amidst an inevitable fury of protest from trade unionists and politicians alike. Olivetti plans to try to build the order-invoking and profit-building government links enjoyed by the French and German computer industries with their respective governments. Moreover, with the European computer industry as a whole being forced to tighten its belt in the face of US and Japanese competition, the European computer giants, Bull in France and Siemens-Nixdorf of Germany with Italy's Olivetti may even come together on certain European information technology ventures. The very fact that these erstwhile rivals are now contemplating collaboration shows just how deeply the world computer industry has sunk into recession.

A potential growth area for the industry in Italy is in software and services, where margins remain relatively high compared with the downturn in demand in mainstream computer manufacturing. Finsiel, the software subsidiary of the IRI and the main agent for the Italian public sector in software development is another powerful force in the Italian computer industry.

Electrical Household Appliances

Italy's white goods sector counts among one of the country's greatest successes in terms of innovation, productivity, quality and sheer financial success. Italy is responsible for approximately 40% of total European production of electrical appliances – as is obvious if you walk around any European showroom admiring the rows of sleek washing machines and dryers sporting 'Made in Italy' tags. The success of the industry is not only due to low labour costs. Innovative thinking and personal leadership by the industry's giants eg. Lino Zanussi and the Fumagalli brothers (from Candy), were responsible for the industry's meteoric rise to fame and success in the 1950s and 1960s. The industry's export market is thriving and exports represent nearly three quarters of the market. In particular, the Eastern European market is one which presents future potential for Italian exports. Italy's white goods producers have already sold more than half a million appliances to former eastern bloc countries. The home market is also thriving, helped by the Italians' propensity (by British standards anyway) to feverishly change their entire kitchen armoury with great regularity; approximately every seven years.

The industry's largest companies include Merloni (the largest Italian-owned company in the industry whose brands include Ariston, Indesit and Colston), Zanussi (now owned by the Swedish Electrolux group), Elettrodomestici, Ocean, Rancilio, Framec and Nilox.

Food and Beverages

Although Italy is traditionally regarded as being an agricultural country, self sufficient in food stuffs, food and agricultural produce is the largest single item on

Italy's import bill and seems to be increasing. The average Italian family spends 28% of its income each year on food. The following unlikely assortment of goods are recognized as potential growth areas: health food, breakfast cereals, high quality biscuits, processed sliced cheese, pork, mayonnaise and beer. The general trend of this industry is one of increased profitability achieved through the application of high technology production methods and the adoption of high-quality advertising campaigns. Olivetti, IBP (Buitoni Perugina), Gardini, Barilla, Galbani, Sagit, Ferrero and Parmalat are some of the largest Italian food companies. European and American multinationals have also made large inroads into the Italian market. The main Italian beverage companies include Martini & Rossi I.V.L.A.S., Fransesci Cinzano and Gio Butoni.

High Technology

Italy features well in various advance technology sectors eg. robotics, radar systems and aerospace. Fiat's Comau subsidiary makes industrial robots which are used worldwide (General Motors is a major client), as well as in Italy where they have successfully automated much of the Fiat auto production line and the gigantic Benetton warehouse stock systems. Italy's hi-fi industry is fairly buoyant – Brionvega radios, Seleco TV's and Autovax car stereos all have as good a name as imports from Northern Europe or Japan, as does the entire Olivetti office equipment range.

Iron and Steel

Industrial development in Italy is a very recent phenomenon and the iron and steel industry dates back as far as 1958. This was when new ventures mushroomed while existing industries underwent a solid period of consolidation and marked a boom period in the iron and steel industry which lasted until the arrival of 1974 and recession. The industry has never really returned to its former heights although steel-pipemaking is doing well and the Marcegaglia group announced at the end of 1997 that it will be building a new 500 billion lire factory for pipes and steel plate at Ravenna. In 1993 the European Commission elected to cut the EU's capacity for 'hot steel' production by subsidizing shut-downs. In Italy this resulted in a 43.8% shutdown up to 1996. Generally speaking however, there has been a shift in focus away from the manufacturing to the service sectors in industry, Italy's current fastest-growing sectors are all steel users eg. the machine tool, automobile, industrial equipment and household electrical appliance sectors. Some of the largest Italian steel companies include Italsider, Techint, Terni Acciai Speciali, Nuova Deltasider, Dalmine and ATB Siderugica.

Italian iron and steel foundries invested a combined total of 722 billion lire in plant and equipment during 1997 to help fend off increasing competition from outside Italy.

Housing and Construction

In recent years the construction sector has been troubled by high interest rates and strict legislation on rents and building permits. The result has been an unsatisfied demand for both rented and owned accommodation and a proliferation of illegal building work. However, subsidies are available to facilitate access to finance and thereby encourage construction activity.

Machine Tool Industry

Despite a slight downward trend in the home market shared with the majority of Italian industries at this time, the machine tool sector continues to thrive. Italy has been successful in ousting the USA from its position as fourth largest machine tool producer in the world. The machine tools industry is comprised greatly of small-sized industries (the watchword of Italian industry) which are able to meet the requirements and adjustments of individual demand; about 85% of the industry's 450 firms have payrolls of less than 100 workers. Especially successful are the metal-bending equipment firm Pedrazzoli and the food-processing machine firm, Braibanti. The industry is represented by the national machine tools, robot and automation manufacturers' association, UCIMU. The association's membership of nearly 220 companies accounts for about 80% of total industry-wide turnover. The industry's particular stronghold is its export market which increased by 1.2% last year; Germany, France, the US and Russia provide the main outlets for the export market. UCIMU considers that Italian machine tool makers are well positioned in Europe, particularly in the German, Spanish and French markets. In addition, the industry has good sales networks in Portugal, Switzerland, eastern Europe and Russia.

Mining

Italy is poorly endowed with mineral resources, although sizeable quantities of pyrites, lead, zinc, magnesium, bauxite and coal are mined. Europe's only significant deposits of sulphur are found in Sicily, but extraction is uneconomic. Output of metallic materials has been in long-term decline, although surveying is now being intensified. Domestic coal production accounts for less than 10% of total consumption of coal.

Oil and Gas

ENI's two distribution subsidiaries are Agip Petroli and IP, which together hold 48.5% of the Italian market. Agip and IP have 7,730 outlets and 4,760 respectively. The largest non-Italian oil company is Esso, followed by MonteShell (a conglomerate of the privately-owned, home-grown Montedison and Shell) and Mobil, while the three largest Italian concerns are Isaoil, Erg and Api. All non-Italian oil companies are required to follow the rigid regulatory framework laid down for all ENI state subsidiaries. This code involves regulations on the opening and closing times of service stations which are, however, due to be liberalised and extended from 1998. Finally, permits are required for station modifications, including changes to the types of fuel handles, storage, the provision of additional services eg. the sale of soft drinks, snacks and sweets and the introduction of self-service facilities.

Regional Employment Guide

In Chapter One, *General Introduction*, the main cities and regions of Italy were discussed with a view to residence. In this section, the same regions and major cities are covered, but this time with a view to the employment prospects available in the major industries in each area. The information provided will give some idea of the industries which are dominant and the types of jobs which are most readily available in each area.

Lombardy, Emilia-Romagna, Trentino-Alto Adige

Unlike most of northern Italy, which was predominantly agricultural until the end of the Second World War, Lombardy boasts an industrial history which dates back to the nineteenth century. Although Rome attracts many foreign business men and professionals as the country's capital, Milan, the regional capital of Lombardy, functions as the true economic and financial centre of Italy. A major trading and manufacturing centre for centuries, Milan has maintained a business tradition which positions it at the forefront of the European business scene. The income which Milan generates is responsible for more than 12% of the Italian gross industrial product and employs more than 10% of the Italian industrial workforce. Greater Milan alone, with a population of more than four million, has more than 70,000 industrial units employing more than a million people. The most important of the confusingly wide range of industries to be found in Milan include steel, heavy engineering, machine tools, transport equipment, chemicals, oil refining, plastics, textiles, clothing and shoes, electronics and domestic appliances. The food industry as a whole is especially strong in Milan and throughout the entire region.

The industrial importance of Emilia-Romagna has escalated over the last fifty years. At one time solely agricultural, the region, particularly in and around Bologna and Modena, has become extremely influential industrially, particularly in the areas of light engineering, food processing and ceramics. The city of Modena is now estimated to have the highest per capita income in Italy while the 3.9 million citizens of the region as a whole have come to enjoy the second highest per capita incomes in Italy. With an unemployment rate of 3.8% set against a national average of just over 12%, the region has the rare problem of facing a shortage of labour. The region boasts 45,000 highly successful small and medium-sized businesses operating in agriculture and food products, industry and tourism. Modena's contribution is in the form of farm machinery and luxury sports cars. Bologna is famous for its electronics, packaging and mechanical industries while Forli is an important fruit and vegetable processing industry. Ravenna is an important port as well as being the home town of the Ferruzzi Group which has a whole range of interests from oil seed, cement and sugar production to a controlling interest in one of Italy's largest chemical companies, Montedison. The total group turnover rivals that of the Fiat group.

Trentino-Alto Adige, the alpine area to the north of Verona, has succeeded in implementing a miracle of long-term planning and efficient administration over the past two decades. The largely German-speaking population enjoys a wide-ranging regional autonomy from Rome and its mountain farming population is actually increasing and prospering while everywhere else in Europe such populations are in decline and the indigenous farming population leaving their homes in droves. The Trentino-Alto Adige area is often favoured by large German and Japanese companies setting up in Italy, both for its northern European mentality and its easy accessibility and efficient infrastructure. The highly developed infrastructure of the area includes an efficient motorway system, the Munich-Verona railway line and a gas piping system which covers almost all the industrial development zones of the region. This region also offers highly attractive tax and investment incentives which, though less weighty than those offered in the south, can be approved by the efficient local bureaucracy in a very short period, often in little more than three months. Incentives include significant tax concessions, cheap land, subsidized infrastructure development and training courses with the prestigious University of Trento.

Together the three regions produce a total of 41% of Italy's gross industrial production. A large portion of this derives from the small and medium-sized manufacturers which are the hallmark of Italian industry. Statistics on the size of registered firms show that the great majority of firms employ under 50 people and many others fewer still.

Piedmont and Aosta

Piedmont forms Italy's main industrial and commercial heartland and the Valle d'Aosta, although not a major international trading market, is important as a tourist area and attracts an average of 6.5 million visitors each year, chiefly in the winter months of the ski season. The Valle d'Aosta also exports over 75% of its annual production figure of 3,200 million kw of electricity to meet the industrial demands of Piedmont. As Italy is sadly deficient in indigenous sources of energy, substantial investment to achieve a further 25% increase in the hydro-capacity of the region is forseen over the next decade.

The region of Piedmont boasts a wealth of distinct, diverse and prosperous commercial features within its six provinces. From the Fiat-based automobile industry of Turin to Olivetti computers at Ivrea, textiles in Biella, wine, soft fruits and agricultural produce from Cuneo, Asti and Vercelli and light precision engineering in Alessandria and Novara, the area is richly endowed as a source of potential wealth. Piedmont has succeeded in motivating its industries through a level of automation and technological innovation which necessitates a labour force of only 1.8 million – less than 9% of the Italian total. Turin is however moving away from its almost exclusive industrial base towards finance, service and technology. The area encompassing the cities of Turin, Ivrea and Novara has been designated Italy's 'Technocity' to signify the wide range of new industries developed in the region ie. robotics, aerospace, telecommunications, computers, bioengineering and new materials. The Technocity is responsible for half the national production of robots, 30% of its computers and almost three quarters of the aerospace sector.

Notable industrial presences in the Technocity area include Aeritalia (aerospace and aviation), SKF (ball and roller bearings), Microtechnica (aviation and space research), Prima Industria, Bisiach and Carm (robotics), BICC/CEAT (cabling) and Pirelli (tyres). As far as the other major provincial towns are concerned, Biella is a prime textile centre with 70% of national capacity in wool combing. Ivrea is the home of Olivetti, famous for its office machinery, computer and communications products while the province of Cuneo is one of the largest market gardening areas of northern Italy. The soil and climatic conditions which exist here are ideal for the cultivation of a wide range of vegetables and soft fruits while Alba and Asti are renowned for their high-quality wines. As part of Technocity, Novara is notable for its hi-tech, precision engineering companies, many of which serve the industrial needs of Milan. Alessandria and Valenza are famous for their jewellery trade while Vercelli is noted for its rice and maize cultivation.

Useful information

Honorary regional secretary of the chamber of commerce: Jocelyn Holmes, Musci & Holmes Architetti, Via Genola 3, 10141 Torino; tel 011-331216; fax 011-331216.

Turin airport: tel 011-5676361/2 (flight info.); tel 011-5676372/3 (tickets). Approx. 15km from city centre. Bus link to rail station Porta Nuova about every half hour;

Turin railway stations: Porta Nuova (tel 011-5613333) and Porta Susa (tel 011-538513).

Tourist Info: I.A.T. tel 011-535901.

Liguria

Liguria essentially forms the Italian Riviera. Genoa saw the start of the industrial revolution in Italy, albeit almost a century after Britain's. The region produced the first motor car, the first military field tank and the first aeroplane. The region's traditional wealth stems from its steel, port handling and ship building industries in the port city of Genoa as well as from the tourist industry in the whole region. However, all of these sectors are now in difficulty and perhaps this history of success has also bred a dangerous complacency among the inhabitants of Liguria. The region must now seek a new way forward by trying to attract high-tech industries and new investment to Genoa.

The old port at Genoa is now obsolete, as are its original functions and a new port is being created with the main emphasis on container handling, ferry activities and improved handling of a still active oil and petrochemicals sector. This will hopefully compensate for some of the thousands of jobs to be lost when the remnants of the failing steel industry (the area's largest employer for thirty years) are finally dismantled as ILVA, a branch company of the state-controlled IRI intends to close down its remaining plants in Genoa after the last few, loss-making years. The situation is sadly similar in the ship building industry as Fincantieri, again a subsidiary of IRI has borne heavy financial losses (mainly due to a cutback in military budgets and hence orders) and is also trying to get out of the business. Tourism, once the main money-spinner of the whole region, accounting for some 4,000 billion lire in annual turnover is now also in decline. Visitors to the region are mostly Italians rather than foreigners. The fact that the Italian Riviera has to some extent lost its fashionable reputation of the past, has reduced the number of visitors to the region overall.

However, on the more positive side of life in Liguria, Genoa came sixth in a recent country-wide quality of life assessment – ahead of Milan, Rome and Turin. The purchasing power of the local population is high, boosted by a large number of wealthy people who are in retirement or who own holiday homes in the region. Although there were some disappointments in overall economic performance, this can be attributed mainly to the poor performance of state sector industries, and regional GDP is almost in line with the national average.

The oil and associated petrochemicals industries located in and around Genoa still survive and are doing surprisingly well and the small industries sector is also holding up well. Interestingly, some 30% of businesses registered with the Genoa chamber of commerce are run by women. Finally, the highly developed infrastructure of the area includes an efficient motorway system, the Munich-Verona railway line and a gas piping system which covers almost all the industrial development zones of the region.

Veneto and Friuli-Venezia Giulia

The concentration of economic activity is not entirely limited to the north-western regions of Italy. In the past 25 years the Veneto region in Italy's north-east has become one of Italy's most successful business regions, especially with small to medium-sized companies producing high quality, hand-crafted goods such as shoes, clothes, spectacle frames, medical equipment and mechanical components. This is the territory of Benetton, Stefanel and Carrera Jeans. Other commercial activities include speciality cakes and foods, printing and publishing, natural stone, wine, banking, light and heavy engineering, advertising, consultancy and research. Verona is the area's commercial hub and is strategically placed to take advantage of the good communications to central Europe. Verona is also home to

Italy's third largest exhibition centre. Verona focuses on pharmaceuticals, transport, engineering and publishing, while Vicenza is famous for its tanning, textiles, industrial jewellery, ceramics and steel and mechanical engineering. Names of international stature in the area include Benetton in the Treviso province, the Vicenza-based Marzotto (the biggest wool manufacturer in Europe). This region was largely agricultural until after the Second World War, the main exceptions being the textile, jewellery, tanning and ceramic manufacturing industries around Vicenza which date back to the eighteenth century. Treviso specializes in textiles, sportswear, ceramics and mechanical engineering and Venice in glass, heavy industry and fishing. Padua is known for mechanical engineering, finance and services distribution

The Friuli region is made more attractive to potential investors by the various financial and tax incentives offered here by the Government. However, most likely due to the area's somewhat isolated position geographically, investments by foreign and Italian companies were slow to build up but are now booming. Ironically, the area's position tucked into the north-east corner of Italy was traditionally its downfall, but now looks set to become its biggest advantage in years to come with its strategic closeness to the rapidly changing economies of Eastern Europe. The industrial area of Porto Marghera in the Venice lagoon was established in the 1920s and ship building takes place along the coast near Trieste. However, now these traditional, large industries are at least equalled in importance by a firmament of young medium and small enterprises, producing an extensive range of capital and consumer goods. Belluno is noted for its spectacle manufacturing industry and Pordenone for its white goods and steel engineering sectors; Zanussi have a large base in Pordenone. Pordenone is the main town in the province of the same name and is a dynamic economic and cultural centre. There is an annual international business Fair (*fiera*) held in September and throughout the year there are many other events based around various sectors: machine tools, horticulture, food and catering, electronics and hi-fi, optical equipment, design and more. Significant trends in the region include a much stronger decrease in the number of agricultural workers than the national average and a much higher rate of increase in industrial workers. Thus, the economic outlook is rosy and industrialists and traders, aware of the blossoming of opportunities which the EU has brought, are ready to collaborate with British firms.

Useful information

Honorary regional secretary of the Chamber of Commerce – Pordenone: Susan
  Clarke, Overseas Language Consultancy, Corso Vittorio Emmanuele 54,
  33170 Pordenone; tel 0434-523460; fax 0434-523460.
Airport (Marco Polo, Venice): tel 0141-2609260.
Railway station: tel 0434-520616.
Tourist Information: 0434-21912.

Tuscany, Umbria & Le Marche

About 57% of the total population of these three regions is concentrated in Tuscany, of which Florence is the much-famed and tourist-infiltrated capital. Close to Florence at Prato is the centre of the largest textile area in Italy which involves some thousand companies and nearby at Santa Croce sull'Arno is Italy's largest tanning industry which supplies the local shoe and leather industry. Other important industrial areas include Pisa, Lucca (home to a large paper-making industry), Livorno (which boasts the main Italian container port) and Empoli (renowned for its glass and pottery). Other important industries in Tuscany include steelworks, electronics, furniture, medical equipment and the famous Chianti wine and olive oil as well as Carrara marble. Umbria, home to approximately 23% of the regional population, is mainly agricultural although important steelworks exist at Terni and ceramic production near Perugia. Le Marche is again predominantly agricultural although the prospering Merloni group (producer of white goods) is based in this area.

Useful Information

Honorary Regional Secretary of the Chamber of Commerce: Ralph Griffiths, Consul, British Consulate: Lungarno Corsini 2, 50123 Firenze; tel 055-284133; fax 055-219112.

Florence railway station: tel 055-288765.

Airport: tel 055-373498. About 10km north-west of Florence.

Lazio, Abruzzo & Molise

This area is significant for the strong presence of service industries, especially Lazio. The three regions together account for 11% of the GNP but 12.1% of total national expenditure on goods and services, of which Lazio accounts for over 10%. Rome, besides being the administrative and governmental capital of Italy is also home to the main offices of the state holding companies, IRI, ENI, and EFIM which collectively account for approximately 40% of industrial production in Italy and 85% of Italy's basic industrial infrastructure. The head offices of the main Italian banks are also found in Rome, as are the majority of state agencies and public utilities eg. RAI, the state television company; ENEL, the national electricity board; CNR, the national research council; the Italian State Railways and the Southern Italian Economic Development Board (Agenzia per la Promzione dello Sviluppo des Mezzogiorno). Industrial activity in the capital is low in comparison with the service industries. However, a number of towns near the capital have become centres of intensive industrial production eg. Frosinone, Latina, Aprilla, Pomezia, Civita Castellana and Rieti which specialize in the electronics, telecommunications, light engineering, pharmaceuticals and chemicals industries.

Useful Information

Honorary Regional Secretary of the Chamber of Commerce: Simon Oddie, Enterprise Oil Exploration, Via due Macelli 66, 00187 Roma; tel 06-699561; fax 06-69956600.

Airports: Fiumicino tel 06-60121; Ciampino tel 06-724241.

Tourist info: 06-4871270 or 4824078.

The South Italian Mainland

The four southern regions of the Italian mainland are Campania, Puglia, Basilicata and Calabria. The total working population is around 4 million and unemployment is high, over 20% in some parts.

Calabria and Basilicata comprise approximately 20% of the area's population, are relatively undeveloped with few industries and remain largely dependent on agriculture and increasingly on tourism. Campania has the largest concentration of industry in the south and this region's economic growth has been only slightly below the national average over the last few years. Campania's main interests include traditional industries such as food processing, canning, tanning and leatherwork, ship building and steel railway rolling stock and chemicals, but also more advanced and potentially prosperous sectors such as aerospace, electronics, telecommunications and motor vehicles. The latter are the areas in which there has been the greatest amount of new investment in recent years, largely by the major national companies. The older industries, and particularly the myriad small artisan-type industries which abound in the Naples area, have however, been slow to invest in new technology and risk being left behind by Western rivals.

In Puglia, the highest concentration of population is around Bari, which also has a high concentration of relatively small but energetic industries and every year the *Fiera del Levante* is held, while in Foggia, there is a agricultural fair. Taranto is a major steel producing centre, with a number of ancillary industries but is having to cut back production to meet EU directives. The main agricultural products of the region are hard wheat, wine, olive oil, chestnuts and hazlenuts, tomatoes, vegetables and fruit (citrus fruits and kiwi fruit in particular). Agriculture accounts for 18% of the total local gross product and around half the population still depends directly or indirectly on agriculture. Though the number of people directly engaged in agriculture is declining, land holdings still remain relatively small. The average per capita income in the south is now much lower than in the north and the disparity in wealth between the north and south are widening. However, there is no lack of money in the south and a large consumer market exists even for luxury items. There are approximately 4,000 wholesalers and 99,000 retailers in Campania; 4,500 wholesalers and 42,000 retailers in Calabria and 700 wholesalers and 11,000 retailers in Basilicata.

Useful Information

Honorary Regional Secretary of the Chamber of Commerce: Giuseppe Giordano, Via dei Bruzi 1/F, 25100 Matera; tel 0835-339790; fax 0835-334093.

Bari Airport: 080-5835111.

Tourist Info: Bari tel 080-5235186; Matera tel 0835-331983.

Directory of Major Employers

Airlines & Airport Operators

British Airports Authority (BAA) Italia: BAA GESAC-Capodichino Airport 80014 Napoli; tel 081-7896528; fax 081-7896021.

British Airways Plc: Corso Italia 8, 20122 Milano; tel 02-809896; fax 06-809898.

Cathay Pacific Airways Limited: Via Barberini 3, 00187 Roma; tel 06-4741297; fax 06-5533113.

British Banks

Abbey National Mutui Spa: Via Cicerone 58, 00198 Rome, RM; tel 06-3214910; fax 06-3221536.

Banca Woolwich Spa-Servizio Finanziario: C.so Sempione 39, 20145 Milano; tel 02-349791; fax 02-34979210.

Barclays Bank Plc: Via Moscova 18, 20121 Milano; tel 02-63721; fax 02-63722925.

Baring Brothers (Italia) Srl: via Brera 3, 20121 Milano; tel 02-809271; fax 02-809007.

Midland Bank Plc: Via dela Moscova 3, 20121 Milano; tel 02-62525200; fax 02-62525333.

National Westminster Bank Plc International Businesses; c/o Cred. Italiano, Via Broletto 16, 20121 Milano; tel 02-88622213; fax 02-877426.

National Westminster Bank: via F Turati, 16-18, 20121 Milano; tel 02-6251; fax 02-6572869.

Italian Banks
Banca Agricola Milanese: Via Mazzini 9/11, 20123 Milano; fax 02-8693745.

Banca Commerciale Italiana: Piazza della Scala 6, 20121 Milan; fax 02-88502173.

Banca di Roma Spa: Piazza T Edison 1, 20123 Milano; tel 02-7229.1; fax 02-72292471.

Banca Toscana Spa: Via del Corso 6, 50122 Firenze; tel 055-43911; fax 055-4391742.

Banco Ambrosiano Veneto – Relazione Esterne: Piazza Ferrari 10, 20100 Milano; tel 02-85941; fax 02-72395137.

Banca Commerciale Italiana: Piazza della Scala, 6, 20121 Milano; tel 02-8850; fax 02-88502173.

Banca Popolare di Novora Scrl: Via Negroni 12, 28100 Novara; tel 0321-662736; fax 0321-662017.

Centro Banca-Banca Centrale di Credito Popolare Spa: Corso Europa 20, 20122 Milano; tel 02-7781.

*Monte dei Paschi di Siena:*U.S.I.E. Sett.Serv. V. le Toselli 60, 53100 Siena; tel 0577/294589; fax 0577-44772.

Chartered Accountants
Arthur Andersen Spa: Via della Moscova 3, 20121 Milan; fax 02-6572876.

Coopers & Lybrand Spa: Via delle Quattre Fontane 15, 00184 Rome; tel 06-4818565; fax 06-48146365; also Via Vittor Pisani 20, 20124 Milano and Corso Vittorio Emmanuele 97. 10128 Torino.

Deloitte and Touche Spa: Palazzo Carducci, Via Olona 2, 20123 Milano; tel 02-88011; fax 02-433440.

KPMG Peat Marwick Fides Snc.: Via Vittor Pisani 25, 20121 Milano; tel 02-67631; fax 02-67632278.

Moores Rowland Italia: Via Monte Rosa, 3, 20100 Milano; tel 02-4986350; fax 02-4818143.

Price Waterhouse Spa: Corso Europa 2, 20122 Milan; tel 02-77851; fax 02-7785240.

Reconta Ernst & Young SaS di Bruno Gimpel: Via Torino, 68, 20123 Milano; tel 02-722121; fax 02-72212037.

Chemical, Cosmetics and Pharmaceutical Companies
BP Italia Spa: Milano Fiori Palazzo E/5-Strada 6, 20090 Assago; tel 02-822741; fax 82274223.

Chem-Plast Specialities Spa: Piazza Vetra 21, 20123 Milano; tel 02-838751; fax 02-58313528. Printing inks, paint and adhesives.

Croda Italiana Spa: Via P Grocco 917/919, 27036 Mortara PV; tel 0384-92701; tel 0384-91973. Lanolin.

Glaxo Wellcome Spa: Via A Fleming 2, 37135 Verona; tel 045/9218111; fax 045-9218388. Industrial chemicals and pharmaceuticals.

Nuncas Italia Spa: Via G. di Vittorio 43, 20017 Rho; tel 02-9317961; fax 02-9317930. Industrial chemicals: cleaning products and perfume products for home and person.

Segix Italia Srl: Via del Mare 36; 00040 Pomezia; tel 06-911801; fax 06-91180224. Manufacture of pharmaceutical products.

Shell Italia Spa Direzione PA/CNG: Via Chiese 74, 20126 Milano; tel 02-661601; fax 02-66101407.

Smithkline Beecham Spa: Via Zambeletti, 20021 Baranzate Milano; tel 02-38061; fax 02-3501882.

Solplant Spa: Via Santa Sofia 21, 20122 Milano; tel 02-58306030; fax 02-58306037. Agro-chemicals.

Tecres Spa: Via dell'Industria 22/24, 37012 Bussolengo; tel 045-6700929; fax 045-7157227.

Unilever Italia Spa: Via N Bonnet 10, 20154 Milano; tel 02-623380; fax 02-6552310. Cosmetics, accessories.

Zeneca Spa: Palazzo Volta: Via F. Sforza, 20089 Basiglio; tel 02-904541; fax 02-90755615.

Electrical Equipment/Electronics
Arteleta International Srl: Via P. da Volpedo, 57, 20092 Cinissello Balsamo; fax 02-6122573. Electromedical apparatus.

Control Techniques Spa: Via Brodolini 7, 20089 Rozzano, Milano; tel 02-575751; fax 02-57512858. Electronic speed and position controls.

Innovative Technologies Italia Srl. Via Mazzini 12, 20123 Milano; tel 02-875949; Importer of consumer electronics and distribution throughout Italy.

Kontron Instruments Spa: Via Fantoli 16/15, 20138 Milano; tel 02-580851; fax 02-5060918. Electromedical equipment.

3G Electronics Srl: S Gallo Gorgatti, Via Boncompagni 3/A, 20139 Milano; tel 02-5390441; fax 02-5690243. Electronic equipment and components.

Rank Taylor Hobson Spa: Strada Provinciale, 28 Vigentina no 6-8, 20090 Opera, Milano; tel 02-57606424. Construction of precision optical and electronic equipment.

Selcom Srl: C.so Vittorio Emmanuele II, 92, 10121 Torino; tel 011-5621495; fax 011-562994. Electronic systems for security.

Tecnimex Srl: Via A Corti 28, 20133 Milano; tel 02-235924; fax 02-238412. Industrial electronic equipment.

Computer Consultants
Collett Adrian Graham: Via Agadir 18b, 20097 San Donato Milanese, Milan; tel/fax 02-55601211.

Convention Service Srl: Via F.lli Bettinelli 4, 20136 Milano; tel 02-89400463; fa 02-8940063. Consultant, software management, safety & security.

Data Professionals Marketing Srl: Via Gian Giacomo Mora 14, 20100 Milano; tel 02-89401223; fax 02-89401197.

De Morgan Michael: Corso di Porta Romana 94, 20122 Milano; tel/fax 02-58322371.

Eicon Technology Srl: Via Aldo Moro 54, 24040 Lallio Bg; tel 035-204300; fax 035-204400. Computer communications.

Mathema Srl: Via Q Sella 3, 20121 Milano; tel 02-6691051; fax 02-6693929.

Mondoweb Srl: Via Cappelletta della Giustiniana 49, 00123 Roma; tel 06-3036084; fax 06-30311095.

Orlandi Flavia: Via Amedei 6, 20123 Milano; tel 02-86453273; fax 02-86453273.

S.T.A. Sas: Walter Pelizzari, Via Carnia 29, 20132 Torino; tel/fax 02-2840116/26; fax 2-2840116.

Siosistemi Srl. Via Cefalonia 58, 25124 Brescia; tel 02-930440.

Estate Agents & Property Consultants
AICI: (Italian Association of Real Estate Consultants) Via Ninno 5, 20123 Milan; tel 02-310231; fax 02-872913.

E.T.G. Immobili Srl.: Piazza Emanuele Filiberto 11/G, 10122 Torino; tel 011/5212202; fax 011-5211777.

Healey and Baker: Via Turati 25, 20121 Milano; tel 02-29005169; fax 02-653254. Property consultancy.

Jones Lang Wootton Srl: Via Meravigli 3, 20123 Milano; tel 02-72023883; fax 02-72023769. International real estate consultants, surveyors and valuers.

Property International Srl: Via Correggio 55, 20149 Milano; tel 02-4983295; fax 02-48194170. Estate Agency and relocation services.

SBC Warburg Italia Sim Spa: Via Santa Maria Segreta 6, 20123 Milano; tel 02-725271; fax 02-7527773.

Studio Immobiliare-Real Estate Mina Mothadi: Residenza Sagittario, Milano 2, 20090 Segrate; tel 02-2640582; fax 02-26410393.

Vigano'Giorgio Srl.: Via Maggiolini 2, 20122 Milano; tel 02-76003914; fax 02-783618. (brokering, property management, valuation).

Financial & Business Consultants and Financial Services

Citicorp Finanziaria Spa-CITIFIN: Via Della Moscova 3, 20121 Milano; tel 02-20121; fax 02-63192325.

ISMA Srl: Via Alfieri 7, 20089 Rozzano Milano; tel 02-57511275; fax 02-57512604. Business and credit consulting.

Pizzocaro Massimo: Piazza Duomo 3A, 27100 Pavia; tel 0382-28561; fax 0382-303187.

Scottish Equitable Italia Spa: Via Spadari 7, 20123 Milano; tel 02-8055746; fax 02-8057118. Investment, life and pensions.

Insurance Brokers

Biondaro Vittorio: Via Roma 4/B, 37047 San Bonifacio, Verona; tel 045-7611230; fax 045-6102385.

Carlo Comi: P.O. Box 293, 20052 Monza; tel 039-9960791; fax 039-9960791.

Italcar Spa: Corso Magenta 32, 20146 Milano; tel 02-86450081; fax 02-89010047.

J&H Marsh & McLennan Italia Spa: Palazzo Carducci, Via Olona 2, 20123 Milano; tel 02-485381; fax 02-48538300.

John Thorpe Srl.: Via Dogana 3, 20123 Milano; tel 02-867141; fax 02-809250.

Johnson & Higgins Spa.: Viale della Liberazione 18, 20124 Milano; tel 02-669981; fax 02-450928. Insurance brokers.

Profins Srl: Via Zurigo 2, 20147 Milano; tel 02-416106; fax 02-48302265.

UTA Spa: Via Padova 55, 10152 Torino; tel 02-6690622; fax 02-66985961.

Insurance Companies

Commercial Union Italia Spa: Viale Abruzzi 94, 20131 Milano; tel 02-27751; fax 02-2775454.

General Accident Fire & Life Assurance Corporation Ltd.: Via SS Giacomo e Filippo 15, 16122 Genova; tel 010/84041; fax 010-816417.

Generali Assicurazioni Spa: Piazza Duca degli Abruzzi 2, 34132 Trieste; tel 040-29551.

La Fondiaria Assicurazioni Spa; Piazza della Liberta 6, 50129 Firenze; tel 055-47941; fax 055-476026.

Lloyd Italico Assicurazioni Spa. Via Feschi 9, 16121 Genova; tel 010-53801; 010-541221.

Lloyd's of London: Italian representative Mr Barry Gibson, Via Sigieri 14, 20135 Milano ; tel 02-55193121; fax 02-55193107.

Mondial Assistance-Sias Spa: Via Palmiro Togliatti 1625, 00195 Roma; tel 06-439981; 06-43998300. 24-hour assistance for motor, medical insurance. Telemarket.

Norwich Union Vita Spa: Via Battistoti Sassi 11/a, 20133 Milano; tel 02-748101; fax 02-70120880. Life assurance.

Royal & Sun Alliance Assicurazioni: Via Martin Piaggio 1, 16122 Genova; tel 010-8330.1; fax 010-884989.

Royal International Insurance Holdings Ltd.: Via F.lli Gracchi 27, 20092 Cinisello Balsamo; tel 02-660791; fax 02-66011565.

SAI – Societa Assicuratrice Industriale Spa: Corso Galileo Galilei 12, 10126 Torino; fax 011-6647749.

Language schools and language consultants/services

AB Westminster Language Sas: Via Lupi di Toscana 3, 25032 Chiari BS; tel 167017258; fax 48843935. Language institute.

Advanced Language Services Srl: Via Podgora 10, 20122 Milano; tel 02-5054289; fax 02-5050402. Specialised language learning.

Anglo-American Centre – Cambridge Srl: Via Mamelli 46, 09124 Cagliari; tel 070-654955; fax 070-670605. English language training.

British Institute of Florence: Pal. Lanfredini, Lungarno, 50125 Firenze; tel 055-284031. Teaching and cultural institution.

British Institute of Rome: Via Quattro Fontane 109, 00184 Roma; tel 06-4881979; fax 06-4825222. English language and literature teaching, Cambridge University examination centre.

The British School: Via Taramelli 52, 24121 Bergamo; tel 035-249150; fax 035-249150. School of languages.

British School of Turin: Via Giolitti 55, 10123 Torino; tel 011-884141; 011-884242.

Canning Italia Srl: Corso Magenta 43, 20123 Milano; tel 0248015840; fax 02-48015877. English courses for business, industry and the professions.

Connor Language Services: Piazza Piemonte 8, 20145 Milano; tel 02-4695819; fax 02-4695807. Language courses for businesses.

English Language Centre Snc: Località IL GALLO, 55060 San Martino in Freddana, LU; tel 0583-38060; 0583-38198. Professional and Technical language services.

International Language School Srl – Rome: Via Tibullo 10, 00193 Roma; tel 06-68307796; 06-6869758. Language courses, interpreting, translations.

Language password di Anna di Ciolo & C. Sas: Via Leonardo da Vinci 255A, 20090 Trezzano sul Naviglio, Milano; tel 02-48403721; fax 02-48403225. Translation and interpreting services.

Regent Italia Srl: Via Fabio Filzi 27, 20124 Milano; tel 02-67070516; fax 02-6693929. Company language training.

Winkler Srl: Centro Dir. Colleoni-Palazzo Orione 1, 20041 Agrate Brianza, Milano; tel 039-636261. Linguistic services, language courses, translations, interpreting.

Legal Studios/Practitioners/International Law Firms
Milan

Cipolla Avv.Anna Maria: Via Corridoni 8, 20122 Milano: tel 02-55017767; fax 02-5461039.

Contardi Avv. Nicoletta: Piazza Grandi 1, 20129 Milano; tel/fax 02-70001939.

Dobson & Pinci: Via Santa Radegonda 16, 20121 Milano; tel 02-809816; fax 02-86464548. International law firm.

Grippo, Associati et Simmons & Simmons: Corso Vittorio Emanuele 1, 20122 Milano; tel 02-725051; fax 02-72505505. International law firm.

Holden Julia: Via dei Foscari 3, 20148 Milano; tel 02-86463844; fax 02-

864463892. Solicitor (Trade marks, patent law, intellectual property).
Macfarlane D.B. Via Visconti di Modrone 32, 20122 Milano; tel 02-76006425; fax 02-799564. Solicitor.
Serra Antonio: Corso Porta Nuova 2, 20121 Milano; tel 02-6572866; fax 02-6572715. Avvocato.
Studio Associato Legale Tributario: Via Cornaggia 10, 20123 Milano; te; 02-85141; fax 02-89010199.
Studio Avvocati Capurro-Marchini-Michetti-Roj: Piazza Cavour 1, 20121 Milan; tel 02-6592741; fax 02-6595822. International law firm.
Studio Bernoni: Piazza F Meda 3, 20121 Milano; tel 02-783351.
Studio Cajola: Via G Rossini 5, 20122 Milan; tel 02-709305; fax 02-780177.
Studio Camozzi & Bonissoni: Viale Majno 17, Milano; tel 02-76027542; fax 02-76021816.
Studio Legale Associato Corrado, Russo, Padova, Cherubini: Piazza Castello 24, 20121 Milano; tel 02-72003457; fax 02-72003469.
Studio Legale Baldi: Via Visconti di Modrone 8/1' 20122 Milano; tel 02-76008711; fax 02-76014033.
Studio Legale Barberi Mauro: Piazzetta Guastalla 10; 20122 Milano; tel 02-55182412; fax 02-55187301.
Studio Legale Bruni-Gramelini e Associati: Corso di Porta Vittoria 28, 20122 Milano; tel 02-5454149; fax 02-5457495.
Studio Legale Canessa & Fava: Via Rugabella 1, 20122 Milano; tel 02-867476; fax 02-860056.
Studio Legale Camelutti: Corso G Matteotti 10, 20121 Milano; tel 02-76002042.
Studio Legale Cavasla, Scamone e Associati: Via Mario Pagano 65, 20100 Milano; tel 02-48011171; fax 02-4812914.
Studio Legale de Berti & Jacchia: Foro Bonaparte 20, 20121 Milano; tel 02-809486.
Studio Legale Dui e Associati: Via Morozzo della Rocco 8, 20100 Milano; tel 02-4816385; fax 02-4816726.
Studio Legale Fabozzi: Via Ansperto 7, 20123 Milano; tel 02-86451645; fax 02-8693706.
Studio Legale Mastracchio: Viale Vittorio Veneto 24, 20141 Milano; tel 02-6552656; fax 02-6575509.
Studio Legale Sutti: Via Montenapoleone 8, 20121 Milano; tel 02-762041; fax 02-76204805.
Studio Legale Villa, Guiso, Broglio & Mameli: Avenue Guido Broglio, Corso di Porta Vittoria 28, 20122 Milano; tel 02-55017889; fax 02-55188994.

Rome
Amenta, Biolato, Corrao, Longo, Ridola: Via del Babuino 51, 00187 Roma; tel 06-3233001; fax 06-3234238.
Grimaldi e Clifford Chance: Via G Rossini 7; 00198 Roma: tel 06-8072251; fax 06-8078201.
Studio Legale Associato Frere Cholmeley Bischoff: Via B Buozzi 47, 0019 Rome; tel 06-8080133; fax 06-8080134. Studio Legale Internazionale.
Studio Legale Associato Puopolo, Sistilli, Geffers: Via Panama 74, 00198 Roma; tel 06-8411611.
Studio Legale Rosauer: Via Umbria 7, 00187 Rome; tel 06-4758415.
Studio Legale Sinisi, Ceschini e Mancini: Via Francesco Carrara 24 Roma; tel 06-3221485.
Studio Legale Ughi & Nunziante: Via XX Settembre 1, 00187 Roma; tel 06-476841.

Florence & Genoa
Castagnoli Avv. Alberto: Corso A. Podesta, 11/8, 16128 Genova; tel 010-590700; fax 010-5533113.
Studio Legale Contri: Via Pico della Mirandola 9, Florence; tel 055-579259.
Studio Legale Afferni Via Assarotti 5, Genoa; tel 010-885635/6/7.
Studio Legale Contri: Via Pico della Mirandola 9, 50123 Firenze; tel 055-579259; fax 055-578605.

Management & Business Consultants
Arthur Anderson Spa: Via Della Moscova 3, 20121 Milano; tel 02-6572876.
Coopers & Lybrand Spa: Via Vittor Pisani 20, 20124 Milano; tel 02-67831; fax 02-6704533.
IGD/Milani Associati: Via Vivaio 21, 20121 Milano; tel 02-76022421; 02-74022442.
Studio Caramanti & Ticozzi: Via Felice Casati 20, 20124 Milano; tel 02-29521641; fax 02-2047517. Studio comercialista.
T.D. Erikson (MA Oxon): Via Bevignani 9, 00162 Roma; tel 06-47818469; fax 06-8604182. English-language training consultancy.

Oil and Gas Companies
British Gas Italia Spa: Piazza Cavour 2, 20121 Milano; tel 02-777941; fax 02-77794440. Gas and energy engineering and consultancy.
BP Italia SpA: Milano Fiori Palazzo E/5-Strada 6, 20090 Assago; tel 02-822741; fax 02-82274223.
Castrol Italiana Spa: Via Aosta 4/A, 20155 Milano; tel 02-336251.
Enterprise Oil Exploration Ltd. Sede Secondaria: Via dei Due Macelli 66, 00187 Roma; tel 06-699561; fax 06-6995600.
Shell Italia Spa-Direzione PA/CNG: Via Chiese 74, 20126 Milano; tel 02-661601; fax 02-66101407.

Stock Brokers:
Robert Fleming SIM Spa: Via Manzoni 12, 20100 Milano: tel 02-760311; fax 02-76008107.
SBC Warburg Dillon Read, Italia SIM Spa: Via Santa Maria Segreta 6, 20123 Milano; tel 02-725271; fax 02-72527773.
(SIM – Società Intermediazione Mobiliare)

Tourism (Tour Operators, Travel Agents, Hotels and Tourist Authorities
AFI Hotels Ltd Spa: Via Mazzola 66, 00142 Roma; tel 02-516001; fax 02-510115.
Aer Lingus Plc.: Galleria Passarella 2, 20122 Milano; tel 02-76000080; fax 02-76006391.
Appuntamenti nel Mondo di Arimar Tours Srl: Piazza Velasca 5, 20122 Milano; tel 02-89010908; fax 02-89010925. tour operator
 Arimar Club de Safaar: Via della Vigna Nova 24, 50124 Firenze; tel 055-283429; fax 055-283432.
Arimar Tours – Appuntamenti nel Mondo Srl: Via Raya 106, 00184 Roma; tel 06-4741241; fax 06-4744671. tour operator.
Bonaparte Hotel Group Radisson SAS Scandinavia Htl. Mi.: Via Fauchè 15, 20154 Milano; tel 02-336391; fax 06-89501233. Hotel company.
British Tourist Authority: Corso V Emanuele II,337, 00186 Rome; tel 06-68806464; fax 06-6879095.
Clio Viaggi della Silene Srl: Via Beccaria 5, 20122 Milano; tel 02-76001763.

Delaville Spa: Via Sistina 67/71, 00187 Rome; tel 06-6733; fax 06-6784213. Hotels.
Delta Hotel Srl: Via Emilia, 2/a, 20097 San Donato Milanese; tel 02-5231021; fax 06-6784213. Hotels.
Ente Danese per il Turismo: Via Cappuccio 11,20123 Milano; tel 02-72022323; fax 02-860712.
ERC Srl: Via Ripamonti 89, 20139 Milano; tel 02-57403653; fax 57419065. Travel agent.
Excelsior Hotel Galia Spa: Piazza Duca d'Aosta 9, 20124 Milano; tel 02-6785; fax 02-66713239.
Forte Sales Srl: Via F Filzi 28, 20124 Milano; tel 02-66981881; fax 02-6700696.
Hotel Villa Lupis: Via San Martino 34, 33080 Rivarotta di Pasiano; tel 0434-626969; fax 0434-626228. 4 star hotel, restaurant and conference centre.
Jolly Hotel President: Largo Augusto 10, 20122 Milano; tel 02-7746; fax 02-783449.
Matta John: Castello Vicchiomaggio, 50022 Greve in Chianti, Firenze; tel 055-854079. Holiday apartments, restaurant.
Organizzazione Trasporti Internazionali Marittimi Milano (O.T.I.M) Spa Organizzazione Trasporti Intern. Marrittimi: Via P Lambertenghi 9, 20159 Milano; tel 02-6882641; fax 02-6073827. International expeditions, maritime charter, travel agents.
Quark Hotel All Suites: Via Lampedusa 11a, 20141 Milano; tel 02-84431; fax 02-8464190. Hotel, Congress Centre.
Radisson Sas Bonaparte Hotel: Foro Bonaparte 51, 20121 Milano; tel 02-8560; fax 02-8693601.
Terramare Spa: Via Melchiorre Gioia 63, 20124 Milano; tel 02-67074703; fax 02-67075823. Tourist services.

Miscellaneous
Cable and Wireless Spa: via Ferrante Aporti, 26, 20125 Milano; tel 02-26818.1; fax 02-26141504.
Christie's of London: Piazza Navona 114, 00186 Rome; tel 06-6872787; fax 06-6893080 (fine art auctioneers).
Enterprise Oil Italiana Spa: Via dei due Macelli 66, 00187 Roma; tel 06-69561; fax 06-69956600. Petroleum exploration and production.
Ferranti International: (Elmer), Viale dell'Industria 4, 00040 Pomezia; tel 06-912971; fax 06-9125390 (defence equipment).
Flexibox Spa: Via di Grotta, Perfetta 353, 00142 Rome; tel 06-5940503 (transmission couplings).
General Motors Italia Spa: Piazzale dell'Industria 40, 00144 Roma; tel 06-54661. Commercial motor vehicles.
Grimaldi Compagnia di Navigazione Spa: Via Marchese Campodisola 13, 80133 Napoli; tel 081-496111; fax 081-5517401. Maritime transport for motor vehicles, containers etc in Europe, Africa and South America.
Harbour Club Milano Srl.: Via Cascina Bellaria 19, 20153 Milano; tel 02-48204001; fax 02-40910888.
Homesat International Srl: Via dei Longobardi, Resid, Tralci 752; 20080 Basiglio, Milano; tel 02-90756090; fax 02-90753564. Satellite TV Distribution and Communication Products.
IGD Milani Associati: Via Vivaio 21; 20121 Milano; tel 02-76022421; fax 02-76022442. Management consultant: specialist in Corp ID, Communications, trading for multinationals.
Imx Italy Srl: Via G di Vittorio 307/1, 20099 Sesto san Giovanni, Milano; tel 02-2421398; fax 02-22476559. Mail services.

Innovative Technologies Italia Srl: Via Mazzini 12, 20123, Milano; tel 02-875949. Import of consumer electronics products and distribution throughout Italy.

Intercontinental Srl: Via Veracini 9, 20124 Milano; tel 02-67073227; 02-67073243.

J & A Consultants Italia Snc: Piazza San Fedele 4, 20121 Milano; tel 02-86915041. Project management – construction.

Jaguar Italia Spa: Via Aurelia 866 Roma; tel 06-665001; fax 06-66415880. Import of motor vehicles.

JCB Spa: Via E Fermi 16; 20090 Assago, Milano; tel 02-4880374. Commercial earth moving vehicles.

LLG Italy Spa: Via bonnet 6B, 20154 Milano; tel 02-29003565; fax 02-29004696. Reinsurance broking.

Linpac Plastics – Verona Srl: Via Monte Pastello 40; 37057 San Giovanni Lupatoto; tel 045-9216411. Production of packaging for fresh foods.

Longman Italia Srl: Via Felice Casati 20; 20124 Milano; tel 02-29401392; fax 02-201151.

Lucas Automotive Spa: V Lazzaro Palazzi 2/A, 20124 Milano; tel 02-29524541; fax 02-2043108. Accessories, instruments and lamps for automobiles.

Lucas Ricambi Spa: Via Valtellina 5/7, 20092 Cinisello Balsamo Milano; tel 02-66010176. Auto parts.

Master Consulting Group Srl: via Fontana 5, 20122 Milano; management consultancy.

Open University: c/o The British Council, Via Manzoni 38; 20121 Milano; tel 02-8138048; fax 02-8138048.

P & O Container Europe Srl Strada 4, Palazzo A, Scala 7, 20090 Assago, Milano; tel 02-575681; fax 02-57512614. Worldwide container shipping.

P & O Ferrymasters Srl.: Via Tofetti 118, 20124 Milano; tel 02-55211573; fax 02-57303091.

Philips Spa: Piazza IV Novembre 3, Ufficio.Bil.Civilist, 20100 Milano; tel 02-67521; fax 02-67522084. Production and sales of consumer domestic electrical goods, medical instruments and lighting products.

Reckitt & Colman Italia Spa: Via Grosio, 10/8, 20151 Milano; tel 02-3012800; fax 02-3012800. Commercial chemical products.

Reuters Italia Spa: V.le Fulvio Testi, 280, 20126 Milano; tel 02-661291; fax 02-66101498.

Rover Italia Spa: Via Cesare Pavese 305, 00144 Roma; tel 06-500851; fax 06-50085200.

Saatchi & Saatchi Advertising Spa: Corso Monforte 52, 20122 Milano; tel 02-4984041; fax 02-2840116.

Salvage Association (London): Via Ravasco, 10-Torre Nuova, Carignano, 16128 Genova; tel 010-540848. Marine surveyors to London Insurance market.

Siba Srl: Via Tortona 33, 20144 Milano; tel 02-4299243; fax 02-4299233. Water treatment plants, construction and operation.

Siemens Spa: Casella Postale 17154, 20170 Milano; tel 02-66761; fax 02-66762212. Electronics.

Simms Barry: c/o Bechtel - Tecnimont Spa: Viale Monte Grappa 3, 20124 Milano; tel 02-631399031; fax 02-63139911. Oil, gas, energy.

Sotheby Italian Srl: Piazza di Spagna 90, 00187 Rome; tel 06-6841791; fax 06-6796167 (art).

Thomas Cook Italia Ltd: Viale Marche 54, 00187 Roma; tel 06-48782316; fax 06-48782330. Financial services.

Starting a Business

The Single European Market has made Europeans from EU countries increasingly aware of the possibility of starting a business in another Community country which can prove a rewarding experience for those who have the appropriate skills and know how, and who are aware of the support and resources at their disposal and the nature of the challenges (mainly bureaucratic and cultural), that they are up against. Many Britons who are considering living in another EU state will be doing so with the idea of running their own business there. They will most probably already have a successful business, or professional career in the UK and be looking to Europe for other or greater opportunities. The possibilities if not limitless are certainly as wide-ranging and and in some areas (e.g financial services, consultancies, high quality consumer goods) more promising than they are in Britain: self-employment as a medical or dental practitioner, artist, mechanic, manufacturer, retailer, personal trainer or farmer are just some of the successes notched up so far.

Italy is the land of the small business; there are over three million of them, 99.5% of which employ fewer than 50 people. Estimates put the number of new enterprises started annually at an astonishing 300,000. This explosion of entrepreneurial activity is linked to the difficulty in finding an employer willing to offer long-term job security which has resulted in many people going into business for themselves whether they have an aptitude for it or not. Small wonder is it then that this exceptional volume of entrepreneurism leads to a high failure rate. Studies show that the majority of Italian businesses fold in the first five years of their existence. In fact, in 1997, the number of firms that ceased activity, exceeded the number newly registered.

Part of the reason for this high failure rate is that while Italy encourages people to set up businesses, the necessary support structures including bank finance and even training for potential entrepreneurs is lacking. Another problem is the bureaucratic assault course to be negotiated before nailing up a nameplate, emblazoning a logo or evening opening a shop. Getting finance may not be that easy either: Italian banks have had a policy for not lending to any but well-established businesses. There has been some recent progress on bank support for start-ups and banks are now permitted to lend in the medium-term for commercial projects (though they are bound to be searchingly scrutinised). Some banks, notably Credito Italliano have a corporate finance and mergers and acquisitions department.

However, Evidently, the process is not for the faint-hearted. Problems that you might encounter getting a business up and running in your own country are heightened in foreign country where you have to cope with unfamiliar bureaucracy, culture, language and business practices.

To sum up: to the prospective foreign entrepreneur Italy offers two extremes: on the one hand Italians are some of the world's best business people and are excellent to deal with. On the other hand, Italy's red-tape is one of the world's worst. Depending on the area, it can take up to a year, and cost thousands of pounds spent on various fees, trips to Rome and the town where you will be based, to complete all the formalities, many of which seem tediously repetitive. No wonder that some foreigners take the headache out of the process by employing one of the increasing number of professional advisors and relocation agencies, the majority of which are based in Milan where some boast of having you up and running in 40 days. The services offered by each vary from helping to form a network of contacts to completing the formalities necessary to start trading, and from complete corporate relocation (including finding accommodation for foreign executives and arranging domestic telephone, gas and electricity connections) to helping find offices and staff for your business.

As already mentioned, it would be unthinkable to attempt going into business in Italy without learning the language, mainly because being a commercial success in Italy probably relies more on socializing than in other countries. The ability to communicate in Italian is therefore imperative for anyone contemplating an Italian business venture. It is also important to have a sound business plan, to carry out an in depth feasibility study, to have a thorough knowledge and experience of the type of business you are intending to run, personal stamina and determination and the capacity to handle risk. And finally, as they say in Italy *pensare in grande, cominciare in piccolo* (think big, start small).

The following sections outline the various processes involved in setting up different types of businesses.

Procedures Involved in Starting a New Business

The predicament facing Britons who wish to operate a business in Italy is whether to acquire an existing business or to originate their own. There are arguments for both options. Taking over an existing concern avoids the bureaucracy involved in setting up from scratch. On the other hand it is often difficult to ascertain with certainty the exact financial state or standing of the package you are acquiring. If the package includes staff, then Italy's protective labour laws may make a shake up, or dismissal of staff extremely difficult. On balance there is probably more to be said in favour of starting up an entirely new business.

Preparation from Scratch

Before launching yourself into the necessary formalities for setting up a business in Italy, exhaustive preparation is essential. For instance thorough research should enable you to determine accurately whether a proposed business has a reasonable prospect of succeeding. This often means finding a gap in the market that the Italians have not yet exploited. A prime example of niche-making is that of Abbey National, which having noted the lack of an Italian equivalent of building societies, is now happily ensconced in northern Italy and has ten branches selling mortgages to Italians. Other financial areas include private pension providers and car insurance which are likely to expand hugely in Italy with recent financial deregulation. There is also scope in providing all these services for the expatriates (see *Ideas for New Businesses* below).

Preparation is not only about spotting a gap in the market. Other considerations include whether or not the prospective business person feels that he or she can relate to the Italians. The best way of finding out is undoubtedly to spend as much time there as possible, on holidays, business prospecting trips etc. making friends and useful contacts who will form your network of advisors and allies when you finally decide to take the plunge. Many entrepreneurs who have already successfully negotiated the bureaucracy say that, initially, advice from the DTI in London and the British Chamber of Commerce in Milan, proved invaluable.

Another starting point for those thinking of setting up business in Italy is the Italian Chamber of Commerce for Great Britain (296 Regent Street, London W1; tel 0171-637 3153; fax 0171-436 6037) which exists to promote two-way trade between Britain and Italy and to promote UK investment in Italy. They can supply a list of British firms operating in Italy and can also provide contact addresses in Italy and information on Italian government incentive schemes. The notorious inertia of the Italian Government in promoting Italy as an international business zone is only too evident in dealings with their representatives in Britain, so don't be put off. The most productive groundwork will undoubtedly be that carried out in Italy itself. Foreigners who have located their market pitch in Italy report that growth is usually meteoric, such is the buoyancy of the Italian market.

Euro Info Centres (EICs)

One of the first stops in the UK for information on doing business in Europe is the network of Euro Info Centres established in 1987 by the European Commission. There are now about 230 EICs in fifteen European countries. The Info Centres are linked directly to the European Commission's databases and are an up-to-date source of information on European standards, EU initiatives for small businesses, and new opportunities arising from the single market. By linking up with other Centres across Europe, information about national and local opportunities and regulations can be obtained. The cost of services is partly borne by the European Union and partly by the client.

Further details can be obtained from the British EIC's listed below.

UK Euro Info Centres

Belfast: EIC, Ledu House, Upper Galwally, Belfast BT8 4TB; tel 01232-491031; fax 01232-691432.

Birmingham: European Business Centre, 75 Harborne Road, Edgbaston B15 3DH; tel 0121-455 0268; fax 0121-455 8670.

Bradford: West Yorkshire Euro Info Centre, Mercury House, 2nd Floor, 4 Manchester Road, Bradford BD5 0QL; tel 01274-754262.

Bristol: EIC, Business Link West, 16 Clifton Park, Clifton, BS8 3BY; tel 01179-737373; fax 01179-745365.

Burgess Hill: EIC Sussex, Greenacre Court, Station Road, Burgess Hill RH15 9DS; tel 01444-259259; fax 01444-259190.

Cardiff: Wales Euro Info Building, UWCC Guest Building, P O Box 430, CF1 3XT; tel 01222-229525; fax 01222-229740.

Exeter: EIC Southwest, Exeter Enterprises Ltd. Reed Hall, University of Exeter EX4 4QR; tel 01392-214085; fax 01392-264375.

Glasgow: EIC Ltd., Franborough House, 123 Bothwell Street, G2 7JP; tel 0141-221 0999; fax 0141-221 6539.

EIC: Brynmor Jones Library, University of Hull, Cottingham Road, HU6 7RX; tel 01482-465940; fax 01482-466488.

Inverness: EIC North of Scotland, 20 Bridge Street, Inverness IV1 1QR; tel 01463-702560; fax 01463-715600.

Leicester: Leicester EIC, 10 York Road, Leicester LE1 5TS; tel 0116-2559944; fax 0116-2553470.

Liverpool: EIC North West, Liverpool Central Libraries, William Brown Street, Liverpool L3 8EW; tel 0151-298 1928; fax 0151-207 1342.

London I: EIC 33 Queen Street, London EC4R 1AP; tel 0171-4891992; fax 0171-489 0391.

London 2: EIC, Mitre House, 177 Regent Street, London W1R 8DJ; tel 0171-734
6406; fax 0171-734 0670.
Maidstone: Kent EIC, Springfield, Kent, ME14 2LL; tel 01622-694109.
Manchester: Manchester EIC, Churchgate House, 56 Oxford Street, Manchester
M60 7BL; tel 0161-237 4020; fax 0161-236 9945.
Newcastle-Upon-Tyne: EIC, Great North House, Sandyford Road, Newcastle-
upon-Tyne NE1 8ND; tel 0191-2610026; fax 0191-2221774.
Norwich: EIC East Anglia, 112 Barrack Street, Norwich NR3 1UB; tel 0345
023144; fax 01603-633032.
Nottingham: EIC, 309 Haydn Road, Nottingham NG5 1DG; tel 0115-9624624;
fax 0115-9856612.
Slough: Thames Valley Euro Centre, Commerce House 2-6 Bath Road, Berks,
SL1 3SB; tel 01753-577877; fax 01753-524644.
Southampton: Southern Area Euro Info Centre, Civic Centre, Southampton S014
7LW; tel 01703-832866; 01703-231714.
Staffordshire: Staffordshire European Business Centre, Commerce House,
Festival Park, Stafford ST1 5BE; tel 01782-202222; fax 01782-274394.
Telford: Shropshire and Staffordshire EIC: Trevithick House, Stafford Park 4,
Telford TF3 3BA; tel 01952-208213.

Useful Addresses

Italian Chamber of Commerce for Great Britain: 296 Regent Street, London W1;
tel 0171-637 3153; fax 0171-436 6037.
Direzione Generale della Producione Industriale: Via Molise 2, 00100 Rome,
Italy; tel 010-39 6 47051.
British Chamber of Commerce for Italy: Via Camperio 9, Milan. tel 02-
877798/8056094; fax 02-86461885; Internet: http://www.infosquare.it/bcci
(e-mail: bcci@bbs.infosquare.it)
Export Market Information Centre (EMIC): Kingsgate House, 66-74 Victoria
Street, London SW1E 6SW; tel 0171-215 5444/5; fax 0171-215 4231; e-mail:
(EMIC@xpd3.dti.gov.uk). Statistics, directories, market research reports, mail
order catalogues, country profiles etc.

Accountancy Firms: Anyone planning to start a business in Italy would be
advised to seek the advice of accountancy firms in Britain which have branches in
Italy. Price Waterhouse (32 London Bridge Street, London SE1; tel 0171-939
2117) publish a useful booklet *Doing Business in Italy* (1995) which comes with a
supplementary update. A list of international accountancy firms with offices in
Italy can be found in the list of *Major Employers* in the *Employment* chapter.

Chambers of Commerce in Italy

In the initial stages of setting up a business in Italy you will probably be dealing
with the Chamber of Commerce in Milan (tel 02-877798). The chamber can
provide you with contacts, make introductions and advise on offices if you need a
physical base in Italy.

In addition to all its other services the Chamber of Commerce for Italy
produces four publications:
Britaly: a monthly newsletter. Print run of about 1,000 copies.
Focus on Italy: a twice-yearly magazine (spring/summer and autumn/winter) of
facts, figures, articles contacts and information on doing business in Italy. Print
run about 4,000 copies.

Speak to the World: an annual brochure of the Chamber's English Language Consultancy Service. It has a print run of about 5,000 copies.

Trade Directory and Members' Handbook: bi-annual publication which lists all chamber members and is now on-line on the Internet. Print run of some 1,500 copies.

To advertise in any of the above you can phone (02-877798) or fax (02-86461885) or email (bcci@bbs.ifosquare.it).

The Chamber in Milan may refer you to a local chamber of commerce (*camera di commercio*) of which there are over 100 throughout Italy. During the 1990s the chambers of commerce have been reformed and given a totally independent status in their role of supporting and promoting business interests for their area. A partial list is given below (full list available from the Italian Chamber of Commerce in London).

Bologna: P Mercanzia 4, 40125 Bologna; tel 051-6093111; fax 051/6093451.

Bolzano: V.Perathoner 8b/10, 39100 Bolzano; tel 0471-945511; fax 0471-945620.

Catania: V Cappuccini 2, 95124 Catania; tel 095-321155; fax 095-321110.

Florence: P. dei Giudici 3, 50122 Florence; tel 055-27951; fax 055-2795259.

Genoa: Via Garibaldi 4, 16124 Genoa; tel 010-20941; fax 010-2094300.

Lucca: Corte Campana 10; 55100 Lucca; tel 0583-9765; fax 0583-976629.

Milano: Via Meravigli 9B, 20123 Milan; tel 02-85151; fax 02-85154232.

Naples: Piazza Bovio, 80133 Naples; tel 081-7607111; fax 081-5526940.

Perugia: Via Cacciatori delle Alpi 40, 06100 Perugia; tel 075-57481; 075-5748205.

Pisa: P.V. Emanuelle II 5, 56100 Pisa; tel 050-512111; fax 050-512250.

Rimini: Viale Vespucci 58, 47037 Rimini; tel 06-520821; fax 06-52082617.

Siena: P Matteotti 30, 53100 Siena; tel 0577/202511; fax 0577-288020.

Turin: v.S. Francesco da Paola 24, 10123 Turin; tel 011-57161; fax 011-571651-6.

Trieste: P. della Borsa 14, 34121 Trieste; tel 040-67011; fax 040-6701321.

Venice: V. XXII Marzo 2032, 30124 Venice; tel 041-786111; fax 041-786330.

Udine: via Morpurgo 4, 33100 Udine; tel 0432-2731; fax 0432-509469.

Choosing an Area

In addition to market research and preparing the ground, one also has to choose an area. As mentioned, northern Italy is the most dynamic business region of Italy (if not Europe). This does not mean however that the Mezzogiorno should be totally ignored. Generous incentives including a ten-year exemption from income tax have resulted in a rush of both foreign and Italian companies to the south. However, the deep south (Naples to Sicily) is traditionally the least-favoured region because of mafia activity and poor infrastructure.

The type of business envisaged will also have a bearing on the choice of area. Some foreigners find themselves partly or wholly dependent on other expatriates for clientele, while others will rely on Italian consumers and yet others on an international clientele. Medical and dental practitioners prefer the Milan area where there are an estimated 30,000 expatriates. For the Lombardy region as a whole the number is probably triple that. Those in the real estate business could find themselves based in the north, Rome, Tuscany or Umbria.

Useful Publications

Business Guide to Italy: published by Connect, with articles written by lawyers and executives on all aspects of doing business in Italy. Including forming a company, banking, auditing, from import/export guidelines to leasing an office, from contracts to registering a trademark and business etiquette. Section on the status of EU regulations implementation in Italy. Order tel +39 6 5809690; fax +39 6 5880851 or e-mail: business.italy@flashnet.it.

English Yellow Pages: These *Yellow Pages* are nothing to do with British Telecom. They are a source guide for the English-speaking foreign community in Rome, but with supplements for Florence and Milan. Available from international bookshops and news-stands in the above three cities.

The Informer: Buroservice SNC, Via Tigli 2, 20020 Milan; tel 02- 93581477; fax 02-93580280. A monthly news magazine aimed at expatriates in Italy. Provides regular updates on changes in the legislation regarding tax, businesses etc. plus the the best ways to tackle the bureaucracy. Subcription costs lire 40,000 (£18) per annum or lire 4,000 (£1.80) per issue. Subscriptions from overseas cost £36.

The Italian Business Review: Founded in 1967. Published monthly (except August) by The Italian Business Review Inc., European address: Suite 693 – 2 Old Brompton Road, London SW7 3DQ; tel 0171-413 9554; fax 0171-581 4445. Subcription US $510 annually. Comprehensive reporting of Italian business news and a good way to keep in touch with developments in Italy; includes forecasts and indicators and focus and analysis sections.

Opportunities for Investment and Joint Ventures in southern Italy: published by IASM (see below), Via Ariosto 24, Milano; tel 02-481 76 36.

Financial Times Surveys: From time to time the Financial Times produces surveys of business in different areas of Italy or on Italian industry as a whole. Further details from: the Readers' Enquiry Service, tel 0171-873 4211, open from 9.30am to 12pm and from 2pm to 4.45pm.

Wanted in Rome: Bi-monthly magazine aimed at the expatriate community. Has a large classified advertisement section. Edited by Mary Wilsey, Via dei Delfini 17, 00186 Rome; tel 06-6790190; fax 06-6783798.

Raising Finance

Those contemplating opening a business in Italy should note that UK banks in Britain will not be able to provide start-up loans in cases where the prospective proprietor intends to be resident abroad. As already mentioned Italian banks are unlikely to lend money to small businesses for start-ups, and in any case, the interest rates are prohibitive. The obvious way for prospective proprietors to raise money is by selling their UK home. If this proves insufficient then it should be possible to raise a mortgage on an Italian property. Abbey National and the Woolwich Building Society have opened offices in Milan (see *Mortgages* in the *Setting up Home* chapter).

Alternatively one could investigate the potential of the Italian government business incentive schemes (see below).

Investment Incentives

If raising finance is a problem, it may be worth investigating whether or not your proposed business could benefit from a government or EU incentive programme. Government schemes are heavily biased in favour of the Mezzogiorno (the provinces south of Rome, and Sicily and Sardinia), however certain small islands and specially designated zones in Tuscany, Umbria and the north of Italy also come with inducement packages, albeit less munificent ones. The government agency that handles new investment (ie. new businesses) in the Mezzogiorno is the Istituto Assistenza Sviluppo Mezzogiorno (Agency for the

Promotion and Development of Southern Italy) known as IASM, the head office of which is in Rome. There are also regional IASM offices in Brussels, Milan, Turin, Verona, Bologna and in the towns of southern Italy. The British Chamber of Commerce in Milan (tel 02-877798) can put you in touch with the nearest one.

Tax Incentives: Tax incentives take the form of freedom from income taxes (local and corporate) for ten years in the case of new companies incorporated in the Mezzogiorno, and 50% exemption for ten years for all other companies. In addition a 4% VAT rebate is granted on investment in new machinery and equipment. Employer's social security contributions are also refunded in the case of new investments.

Non-tax incentives: The governent also offers grants and low-interest loans up to the level of 70% to 75% of total investment. For joint ventures, regional and state agencies in the Mezzogiorno will put up half the share capital and then give the private partner the option to buy out the state's shares when the company is over the start-up period. Small and medium-sized businesses valued at not more than fifty million lire are entitled to loans at 10.3% interest (lower in the south). The maximum loan is 4,000 million lire.

Research and technological assistance: All businesses engaged in research projects 60% based in Italy are eligible for incentive grants subject to government approval.
Specific Activity Incentives: Companies engaged in certain types of business activities are eligible for grants throughout Italy:

Agriculture	Shipping yards and ship repairs
Cinema	Waste Disposal
Machine Tools	Publishing
Trading companies (retail and wholesale)	Mining
Aircraft	Energy Saving
Publishing	Hotel and Catering
Maritime Fishing	Handicrafts

European Community Incentives: Europeans carrying out business activities in Italy are entitled to grants and soft loans under aid programmes operated by the EU. The main programmes are:
The European Regional Development Fund: the ERDF exists to redress regional imbalances within the EU.
European Social Fund: aims to facilitate employment of workers through increasing their mobility.
European Agricultural Fund: aims to improve agricultural structures.
The New Union Instrument for Borrowing and Lending: The purpose of the NCIBL is to furnish loans for investment projects that contribute to the greater convergence and integration of the economic policies of the EU member states.
Other EU incentives are obtainable for the coal and steel industries and research and technology development.

Relocation Agencies and Business Services

Inspired by an increasing awareness of the business potential of Italy but deterred by the awfulness of the red tape, newcomers can turn to a relocation or business assistance agency. There is an expanding number of such agencies, particularly in the north and Rome, which can help aspiring business people not only with commercial contacts and guidance through the formidable procedures for setting up, but also the equally frustrating domestic problems of finding somewhere to live and arranging connections to the utilities, telephone, internet etc. In addition to the addresses provided below, a list of such agencies can be obtained from the British Chamber of Commerce for Italy (Via Camperio 9, 20123 Milan; tel 02-877798).

Useful Addresses

CORE (Cocchini Relocation S.r.L. Via Sirtori 13, 20129 Milan; tel +39 2 29512793; fax +39 2 29513075. Relocation services (securing of documents, school registration etc.) and location of homes and offices for individuals and businesses. Agents also in Rome, Florence, Turin, Genoa and Venice.

CSA snc: Via Pigna 14/A, 37121 Verona; tel 045-592482; fax 045-597629. CSA provides a full range of commercial services from set-up and relocation to providing essential contacts throughout northern Italy and is a member of the British Chamber of Commerce in Milan.

Imm. Montaldo SAS: Via Alberto Da Giussano 26, 20145 Milano; tel 02-4816742; fax 02-4816742.

International Transpack Group: Strada Principale, Pianbosco, 21040 Venegono (VA); tel 0331-866741; fax 0331-827180.

On the Spot Srl: Via Mandresca 50, 22044 Inverigo (CO); tel 031-609324; fax 031-609324. Contact Mrs Elisabeth Ann Ambler.

Property International: Via Correggio 55, 20149 Milan; tel 02-49 80 092; fax 02-48 19 41 70; also Rome office at Viale Aventino 79; tel 06 47 43 170; fax 06-57 43 182. Provides a wide range of services from rentals and sales of residential and commercial property to obtaining the necessary documentation for an expatriate to live and work in Italy.

Set Up: Via Conservatorio 22, 20122 Milan; tel 02-77291; fax 02-772940. Set up is run by Sarah Wood Pedrazzoli and organizes total relocation and setting up for individuals and business corporations.

Dr Roberto Gruttadauria: Corso Venezia 16, 20121 Milan; tel 02-76002157; fax 02-799334. Organizes setting up for companies and individuals.

Studio Papperini: 114 Via Ugo Ojetti, 00137 Roma; tel 06-86895810; fax 06-86896516. Comprehensive relocation service headed by Giovanni Papperini a solicitor specialising in immigration and nationality law. Based in Rome, but operates throughout Italy. Offers a pre-move service and cost effective, tailormade package to suit employer or employee.

Welcome Home: Via Barbarano Romano 15, 00189 Rome; tel +39-6 30366936; fax +39-6 30361706. A housing agency and complete expatriate relocation.

Companies Providing Business Services & Business Consultants:

Alfa Inter. Srl: Va Bocca di Leone 23, 00187 Rome; tel 06-6786529. Conference and interpreter services.

Cornell Rai – International Marketing and Foreign Trade Consultant: Via Polibio 45, 00136 Rome; tel 06-3454339. Market consultants (feasibility studies).

Executive Services Business Centres Srl: Via Vicenzo Monti 8, 20123 Milano; tel 02-467121; fax 02-48013233. Business Centres.

Georgina Gordon-Ham: Via Peccioli 58, 00139 Rome; tel 06-812834. Freelance interpreter/translator.

Mrs Olga Fernando: Via Olgiata 15, 00123 Rome; tel 06-3788371. Technical translator/simultaneous interpreter.

Reid Michael Francis: Via Palestro 11, 00185 Roma; tel 06-4822749. Independent financial advisor.

Regus Business Centre Srl: Via Torino 2, 20123 Milano; tel 02-725461; fax 02-72546400. Fully furnished offices.

Richmond-Hill Company Srl: Via Albalunga, 44/44a. 00183 Roma; tel 06-77203668; fax 06-7001815. Business consulting.

Secreto: Vittorio: Via Londinio 1, 20154 Milano; tel/fax 02-3318601. Financial and business development consultant.

Technical Services International Srl: Via Ludovisi 36, 00187 Rome; tel 06-485766; fax 06-485766.

Walter Hassimiani: Via di Villa Spada 167, 00199 Rome. tel 06-8120562. Freelance interpreter/translator.

Internet Services

Connect: Via Lorenzo Valla 40, 00152 Rome; tel 06-5809690; fax 06-5880851. E-mail: business.ital@flashnet.it. Internet site: (http://www.businesseurope.com). Connect provides American service (with free USA domain name research and registration) at American prices ($100 for the first megabyte for one year). Gets you on to the internet in two days and allows you access to your site to make changes yourself (as opposed to paying maintenance fees). You also get your own alias, your own directory with individual password, your domain name in plain view: 'www.yourname.com', web page design, visitor logs, guest books, online payment, shopping carts and strategic links for already existing or brand new sites.

Mondoweb Srl: Via de Amicis 4, 20044 Bernareggio, Milano; tel 0348-2210353 & 039-6093175; fax 039-6093175. www services and computer consultants.

Business Structures

In order to operate commercially in Italy, an individual or a company must have a recognized Italian business structure. The equivalent of a UK Limited Liability company is a *Societa per Azioni* or SpA. Individuals may prefer a simpler entity, the *Societa di responsibilita limitada* (SrL), or the simplest, *Societa in Accommodita Semplice* (SAS). The formalities of setting up a business structure are normally entrusted to a legal or fiscal advisor. Large international accountants such as Price Waterhouse, Arthur Anderson, KPMG, Ernst & Young etc. which have offices in Italy will sometimes recommend local consultants. Alternatively, the British Chamber of Commerce in Milan will be able to suggest ways of locating possible advisors.

The different business entities and the steps required to form them are as follows:

SpA. An SpA roughly corresponds to a UK Plc. To create an SpA specific information regarding the company, its shareholders and directors must be incorporated into a public deed. Before an SpA can be formed the entire capital (minimum 200,000,000 lire) must be underwritten by at least two of the shareholders and at least 60,000,000 lire of the capital must be deposited with the Banca d'Italia until the company is officially registered. After registration, the deposit will be refunded. Within 30 days of incorporating the company memorandum (*Atto Costitutivo*) and Articles of Association/Statutes (*Statuto*), they must be submitted by a notary to the clerk of the local tribunal court which is also the local business registry office. After ascertaining that the necessary legal requirements have been fulfilled, the court will enter the company in the business register. The company must also be registered with the local Chamber of

Commerce and publicly gazetted. Following incorporation, it is necessary to apply immediately for a VAT number (*numero di partita IVA*). You will also be given a company number (*numero REA*) and company register details (*registro imprese*).

In order to be quoted on the stock exchange an SpA must have a minimum capital of two hundred million lire. Stock exchange flotation is not however compulsory once this level of capital is reached. Once an SpA has gone public it is required to submit its accounts to outside auditors.

Formation procedures for an SpA are very costly: an SpA with capital of five hundred million lire will cost approximately thirty million lire.

Srl. An Srl is a private (limited liability) company. The procedures for an Srl are similar to an SpA. The minimum authorized capital is twenty million lire. Liability is limited to the paid-up company capital. The capital contribution of a participant in an Srl is referred to as a quota. Quotas may vary and can be as little as lire 1,000. Unlike SpAs, Srls are not required to appoint an outside auditor if their capital is less than one hundred million lire.

Partnerships. Partnerships of various kinds are suitable for the self-employed as the setting up procedures are less complicated and there are no minimum capital requirements as there are for companies and corporations. The main disadvantage of partnerships is that participants are personally liable for company debts. The types of partnership structures are:

Societa in nome collettivo (Snc): A general partnership with unlimited liability, (ie. all the partners are liable for the debts of the partnership).

Societa in accomandita semplice (Sas): A partnership in which the liability of individual participants is restricted by agreement to the amount of their capital input.

Societa in accomandita per Azioni (SapA): An incorporated partnership in which the main partners' liability is without limit.

All partnerships have to be incorporated in a deed which gives details of the partners including their duties and responsibilities, and the aims of the partnership. The registration procedure is the same as for an SpA.

There is a minimum limit of two partners, but no maximum. Companies, including Italian companies may be partners. Partnerships are required to keep a company journal and an inventory register, with invoices of all purchases and copies of all correspondence sent and received. There is no legal requirement for an audit.

Sole Proprietor: A sole proprietor has to register within 30 days with the business registry of the town where his or her business is located. Sole proprietorship is disadvantageous for tax reasons (see *Taxation* below).

Accountancy Addresses

Price Waterhouse: Corso Europa 2, 20122 Milan; tel 02-77851. fax 02-7785240.

Arthur Anderson Spa: Via della Moscova 3, 20121 Milano; tel 02-290371; fax 026572876.

Coopers & Lybrand: Via Vittor Pisani 20, 20124 Milano; tel 02-67831; fax 02-6704533.

Deloitte & Touche Spa: Palazzo Carducci, Via Olona 2, 20123 Milano; tel 02-88011; fax 02-433440.

Price Waterhouse: Corso Europa 2, 20122 Milan; tel 02-77851; fax 02-7785240.

Price Waterhouse: Via Giovanni Battista de Rossi 32/B, 00161 Rome; tel +39-6 441921; fax +39-6 44244890.

Ideas for New Businesses

Unlike Spain and Portugal where the majority of expatriates are concentrated in specific areas of the country, in Italy they are more widely dispersed. This makes it difficult to start up bars, restaurants, shops etc. that are largely dependent on expatriate patronage. As already mentioned, the Italians are avid, but very discerning consumers, so competition in the food and other retail businesses is likely to be keen, and in the case of fashion, unbeatable. It is for this reason that newcomers may feel happier taking over an established and profitable business through which new products can be gradually introduced on a trial-run basis. This can be a less risky way of creating a new business ie. by introducing new products with existing ones rather than starting from scratch.

Some ideas that have proved successful so far include: running a characterful, luxury guesthouse/hotel, offering cookery or painting courses in Tuscany, Umbria, Puglia and anywhere picturesque, also other types of holiday, horse-riding, cycling, walking etc., running an English book/video shop or one selling typically English products that the Italians will buy perhaps combined with an English tea shop or restaurant.

By European standards the majority of Italian businesses are on a small scale employing fewer than 100 staff; only 19% of the workforce are employed in companies with over 500 workers. This means there is no shortage of small commercial concerns available in the in the market place.

Doctors and Dentists

An area where foreigners are likely to succeed, sometimes beyond their wildest dreams is in the professions where the training, particularly in the medical and dental fields, is acknowledged to be vastly superior to those acquired by the vast majority of their Italian colleagues. Italians and expatriates alike prefer to trust their health and teeth to private practitioners, despite the enormous fees charged, rather than suffer the often abysmal public health and dental services. Under EU reciprocity regulations, doctors' and dentists' qualifications obtained in one EU country are recognized throughout the EU. There is therefore little difficulty for foreigners establishing a lucrative niche in private healthcare, once the initial, bureaucratic procedures have been dealt with.

Estate Agents

One professional that is in short supply in Italy is the estate agent. There are relatively few Italian estate agents and they deal mainly in city property. Although there are also a few British estate agents their clientele is almost exclusively British. There is definitely a gap in the market for estate agents to sell to Italians. Now that currency restrictions have been abolished in Italy, Italians are also beginning to buy up property in France, Spain, Portugal etc. and it would certainly be worth the while of estate agents with international contacts looking into this area of business.

Food

Health food is becoming an increasing fad in Italy and there is potential here for frozen and prepacked diet meals and other health foods.

The other food area that has become a craze amongst young Italians is *il fast food*. American hamburger joints are doing a roaring trade. For all their culinary skills, the Italians are not particulary good at fast food preparation and so at the moment, this is an outsiders' market.

Restaurants are another possibility although it will have to be something exotic to the Italians, for instance Indian or Thai restaurants and be in a big city where tastes are cosmopolitan.

The Garage Trade
There are no national chains of car repair centres in Italy and the trade is dominated by thousands of small, family-run businesses specializing in supplying services to the motorist: mechanical maintenance (*auto riparatori*), body shops (*carrozzieri*) and tyre supply and maintenance (*gommisti*). Such businesses are supplied by small local wholesalers who supply individual businesses with minimal quantities of parts.

Other
Other foreign professionals who have located a demand for their services in Italy, and who have set up successful businesses include lawyers qualified in international law, accountants, veterinarians, landscape gardeners and house restorers.

Agriculture

Wine Producer
It is the dream of some expatriates to be the proprietor of a vineyard but often they do not know where to begin and what it involves. In fact being the owner can be the easiest part and it is very common practice in Italy to sub-contract production (crop maintenance, harvesting, wine-making, bottling, labelling) in part or in full which is fine if all you want is to see your name on a wine label but not if you want to try to make a profit. Unless you are an experienced viticulturist, you will probably need some outside help while you learn more about the art of wine-growing, even if the house attached is going to be your main residence.

One company which specialises in properties with vineyards in the unspoilt Piedmont region is Piedmont Properties, the British trading agent for the Azienda Agricola Ute de Vargas. The eponymous Ute is a retired opera diva who has lived in Italy for 30 years and owned and run a successful vineyard in Piedmont since 1987. She has been marketing property, especially vineyards, in the region since 1989. The UK and USA marketing operations can be contacted online at http://www.smithgcb.demon.co.uk or telephone +44 (0) 1344-624096. Prices start at £49,000 for a small (1.5 hectare) vineyard on its own, and from £92,000 for a small vineyard with a period farmhouse.

See also *Appendix I, Personal Case Histories, John Matta.*

Exporters

The Italy Desk of the Overseas Trade Services of the Department of Trade and Industry (DTI) in London (Kingsgate House, 66-74 Victoria Street, London SW1E 6SW; 0171-215 5000; fax 0171-913 0397) and the regional Business Link offices (see below) provide help and information specifically for exporters in a number of ways. They are able to provide basic market information, commission status reports on specific companies and find suitable representatives for UK firms as well as giving current information on tariff rates and import procedures. Fees are charged for most of these services. Although this service will only be of use to those considering exporting to Italy, the DTI also publishes several booklets focused on Italy including *Italy Trade Brief* and *Italy, an Overseas Trade Supplement.* It can also advise small businesses thinking of venturing into Italy. All of these publications are available free of charge from the DTI by calling the above number and asking for the Italy Desk.

Additionally, the DTI's Export and Market Information Centre Library at (Room 150, First Floor, Ashdown House, 123 Victoria Street, London SW1; tel 0171-215 5444) is worth a visit for anyone researching into business opportunities in Italy. The library boasts a mine of statistical information and business and industry reports as well as an extensive supply of the Italian *Yellow Pages*. The library is open from 9.30am-5.30pm Monday to Friday, visitors may use the library at any time within these hours (you will have to sign in with a business address), although students are mysteriously required to make appointments in advance.

Areas of high demand for imports into Italy include high quality paper products and stationary, meat, electro-medical equipment (with technical support services) and security systems.

An alternative to the DTI's Italy Desk in London are the Business Link offices set up around the country as one-stop-shops for businesses. They can also advise on exporting to other countries including Italy. To find your nearest, look up Business Link in the telephone directory.

Running a Business

Employing Staff

Employer and employee relations in Italy are controlled by a mass of social and labour legislation, parts of which may vary according to the employer's principal industrial activity and the work status of the employee. The three main categories of staff are *dirigenti* (managers), *impiegati* (white-collar staff) and *operai* (workmen/women). Depending on their category, conditions of employment, including the level of employer/employee social security deductions, minimum salary, holiday allowance and minimum advance notice of dismissal, retirement and death benefits, will vary.

Successful small companies run by foreigners in Italy are unanimous in exhorting newcomers to take enormous care in the selection of staff. The Italian labour laws are significantly more protective towards employees than in other EU countries like Britain, and a small employer can be ruined by his or her virtual inability to dismiss inefficient staff.

Workers' rights. Italian workers' rights are guaranteed by Law number 300 of 20 May 1970. They are as follows:
1. Freedom of opinion.
2. The installation of audiovisual equipment is not permitted for checking workers' activities.
3. Employers are not permitted to check on a worker's fitness to work.
4. Personnel searches of unskilled workers may only be made by automatic selection systems and must respect the dignity and privacy of the worker.
5. Disciplinary action is only permitted under laid-down procedures.
6. Opinion surveys by employers are not permitted.
7. Employees may ascertain that safety regulations are being adhered to.
8. Employees may not be downgraded; no worker may be transferred from one unit to another, except for proven technical, organizational or production reasons.
9. Workers have the right to form and join unions and carry on union activities on work premises.

10. The courts may reinstate a worker judged to have been unfairly dismissed.
11. Companies may not suppress union activity.

Trade Unions: Apart from the major trade unions (see Chapter Six, *Employment*) which are unified into political rather than work-type categories, there are others which spring from a particular industry or sector of activity. Working hours lost through strikes have halved since 1984 thanks to Italy's economic boom which has brought prosperity to a large number of Italians. Nowadays, strikes are most likely to occur in the public sector and transportation industries. The continuing influence of Italy's trade union movement should not be underestimated at worker level although its powers have declined considerably since the 1970s. Workers are not obliged to belong to a union and an estimated 70% are non-unionized.

Employer Associations: Most of the employers' associations were set up in the aftermath of the First World War. The four main ones are: The General Confederation of Agriculture (Confagricoltura), The General Confederation of Commerce (Confcommercio) and The Confederation of Small Firms (Confabi). These Associations represent their members in discussions with the government; tax evasion is a regular subject on the agenda.

Categories of Underemployment There is no shortage of workers to employ in Italy where the unemployment figure topped three million in 1987 making it the highest in the EU, after Spain. Nearly all of the unemployment is in the south, especially amongst the young (under 24 years old) of whom an estimated 40% are unemployed, and female. Part-time work, which has caught on in Britain, especially amongst women wishing to supplement family income, is becoming an increasingly popular option.

Employee Training. There is no obligation for employers to provide employee training programmes but they may enhance the employer's activity. As an incentive to employers to engage young people, the 1986 Contract of Training and Work was passed. Under this, employees of less than 30 years of age can be engaged for a period of two years on normal salary rates but with minimal social security contributions. After two years the employer may confirm or terminate the contract with no further obligation.

Wages and Salaries. For each Italian industry there is a national minimum wage and salary scale. However most employers are obliged to pay way above the mininum, except in the most deprived regions. In common with many other European countries employees are entitled to an additional month's salary ('the thirteenth month'), payable in December. In commercial industries it is also customary to pay a further additional month's salary in June.

Social Security Contributions. The government social security system provides old age and disability pensions, sickness and unemployment benefits, healthcare and medical treatment. As the quality of public health service is extremely variable, most employees opt for private treatment. Nevertheless social security and welfare contributions are obligatory for employee and employer, the latter paying the major share of the employee contributions. For commercial concerns the employee's contribution is 8.54% and the employer's 42.81% (39.36% for dirigenti).

Paid Holidays: In addition to a statutory annual vacation, variable between five and six weeks according to the employer's activity, and the employee's category and length of service, staff are entitled to the ten statutory public holidays (see Chapter Four, *Daily Life*).

Women are entitled to five month's paid maternity leave beginning in the last two months of pregnancy.

Taxation

The scale of Italian tax evasion practised by businesses and individuals makes other Europeans look like amateurs and has already been dealt with in the *Daily Life* chapter. For the foreign business person the temptation to follow the Italian example is great, but probably not worth it, as the Italian tax authorities are likely to be far from lenient with foreign tax dodgers.

When contemplating setting up in business abroad some professionals consider opting for sole proprietor or freelance status. However, from a tax point of view this can be a handicap since you are taxed at source, usually at an excessive rate, which obliges you to claim rebate from the tax authorities; a process which can take several years by which time bankruptcy may well have occurred.

Once a business structure has been registered in Italy, the company becomes liable for Italian taxes. Unlike the UK, the fiscal year for companies can begin or end on any date in a period not exceeding twelve months. However since it is easy to overlook the dates when tax instalments fall due and thus become liable for a 15% surcharge plus 9% interest charges per annum, it may be advisable to stick to the calendar year ie. 1 January to 31 December which is easily remembered.

Each corporation must file an annual tax return on Form 760, giving company results. The tax return must be accompanied by a balance sheet, a report from the statutory auditors (*sindaci*) and the directors' reports and resolutions approving the accompanying financial statements.

The tax return covers both Corporate Income Tax and Local Income Tax (see below). The main company taxes are:

Imposta sul Reddito delle Personne Giuridiche (IRPEG). IRPEG, or Corporation Income Tax, is levied on corporations at the fixed rate of 37%. Note that the Mezzogiorno is a tax-free zone for newly established companies. Other company tax-free zones abut on Livigno, Trieste and Gorizia.

Partnerships will either pay IRPEG, or in some cases personal (IRPEF) income tax.

IRAP IRAP replaced ILOR (a local income tax payable by businesses as well as individuals) in January 1998. It is levied at the base rate of 4.25% and has other local taxes appended to it.

Imposta sul Valore Aggiunto (IVA). The Italian equivalent of VAT is charged at the standard rate of 20%. Other rates 4% and 10%. The area of VAT exemptions can cause complications for businesses. Certain types of supply, principally services, are VAT exempt. As far as companies are concerned this means means that no VAT is charged on output; correspondingly no input deductions may be made. The main categories of exemption are sales and leasing of both land and buildings (except newly constructed buildings and leasing of buildings used as fixed assets by a business), insurance, banking and financial services, certain health services and education.

The payment and collection of VAT is separate from other taxation. Traders are required to produce monthly computations of the VAT payable and the VAT receivable. If the balance is in favour of the payable this must be paid to the tax authority by the twentieth day of the following month. If the balance is in favour of the trader, the amount is carried foward to be offset against future payable amounts. If, at the end of the calendar year, the balance still shows in the trader's favour the amount may be reclaimed from the authorities.

For small businesses with a turnover of less than three hundred and sixty million lire there is a simpler administrative procedure.

Imposta Comunale sull'Incremento di Valore Degli Immobili (INVIM): Capital Gains Tax. Corporations are liable to pay for capital gains on the sale of property, machinery etc. under business and local income taxes. However, it is permissable to defer payment by declaring the gain in equal installments for a maximum period of five years.

Tassa di Concessione Governativa. This is a company registration tax introduced in 1988, payable on June 30th and every year thereafter. The tax varies according to the capital and legal entity of the company.

Accountancy Advice

Owing to the complexity of the Italian tax system it is essential to have expert fiscal advice. There are a number of international accountancy firms with offices in Italy, including Price Waterhouse, Ernst & Young and Arthur Anderson (see the list of *Major Employers* at the end of the *Employment Chapter*. The first two produce free booklets on doing business in Italy, obtainable from their London offices (see below).

Useful Addresses

Price Waterhouse Publications Department: 32 London Bridge Street, London SE1 9SY; tel 0171-939 3000.

Appendix 1

Personal Case Histories

Georgina Gordon-Ham (Jinks)

Georgina has an Italian-French mother and an English father and so, apart from being trilingual from an early age she has always had familial links with Italy, and some of her schooling took place there. After finishing a PhD in Languages at the University of Rome in 1975 she did a Postgraduate course in translating and interpreting at the University of Westminster. For six years she was the permanent staff translator/interpretor for the ENI Group (Italy's National Petroleum Board). She is a Member of the Institute of Translating and Interpreting and the Institute of Journalists, London and has been a freelance translator/interpretor/journalist since 1982.

She has lived in Italy for about 20 years and her husband who is English, is in the IT business.
We asked her?

How do you find the Italian red-tape?
It is very irritating. For instance the *Permesso di soggiorno* has to be renewed every five years even if you have lived in Italy for 20 years. However belonging to the European Union has caused some improvements. Things do move a bit faster.

I suppose you had a head-start setting up in business with your connections?
Well yes, but you still have to work very hard at it, especially the international marketing aspect. To be taken seriously you should also become a member of the Chamber of Commerce and belong to a recognised professional body.

What about your work?
Being an interpretor/translator is an ongoing process as you have to maintain contact with all your languages, which in my case are English, Italian and French. Interpretors charge fees on a per day basis. Translations are generally charged by the page in Italy although sometimes by words which works out at about £65-70 per 1,000 words.

What is the social life like?
Here in Rome there are clubs for the British, Canadian and Americans. Actually

they tend to be mixed nationality as there are a lot of Italian husbands. It's not so easy for a newcomer to socialise with Italians who although open and welcoming are reserved. Playing sports is another good way to socialise. Also, there are two types of foreign communities, those *en passage* who are here for two or three years and those who live here permanently.

Is it pleasant living in Rome?
Yes, apart from July and August when it is very humid, the climate is very pleasant and mild, especially in winter. The area around, particularly the hills are beautiful and in winter you can go skiing for the day at Terminillo and Campo Felice about one and half hour's drive away. The sea is also close and there are some lovely resorts such as Sperlonga, Circeo, Friggene, Santa Marinella.

Have you any advice for those thinking of going to work in Italy?
I would advise that you don't have too many romantic ideas about Italy, coming here to work is not like coming here on holiday when you are free from all cares. You need to have a pragmatic approach. If you don't already know the country and the language very well then I would recommend that you start by working here on a full-time basis because then the company posting you, or the employer recruiting you does all the paperwork and sometimes fixes up your accommodation as well. This way you get to know your way around the procedures so that it is all familiar when you come to do it for yourself and you feel less like an outsider.

Maria Makepeace

Maria Makepeace, a freelance artist and teacher, moved from the UK to Siena in 1988. In 1997 she moved to Florence. She is a qualified teacher of art, English and geography and has over 20 years' teaching experience. Despite being half Italian she did not learn to speak Italian properly until she arrived in Italy and has now made contact with the Italian side of her family who live in Tuscany. She has had over 30 exhibitions of her work in Italy. Her 'bread and butter' work is Tuscan landscapes and she paints to commission including animal portraits (tel 055-223819). She also writes poetry based on the history, traditions and/or culture of Tuscany. Her exhibitions have been very successful with a large part of her work going to clients abroad including the United States.
We asked her:

Is it difficult to survive on painting alone?
It would be, but I do some teaching as well. For instance I have given private English lessons, and taught art in *elementari* and *scuola media* schools in extra-curricular classes paid for by the parents. I also taught at the *Università Populare* (a kind of Italian WEA) in Siena. Also, I have just recently done my first simultaneous translation.

How do you find the Italian bureaucracy
It is very irritating. For instance when I have to send one of my paintings to a client abroad there are forms to be filled out in triplicate and I have to take an actual painting (and they can be very big) to the Belle Arti inspector in the main national gallery for checking that I am not illegally exporting anything. The other thing you have to do is register for tax. Freelances have to register for *partita EVA*

(VAT), but I am not generally earning enough for this. I am now also registered with the British Chamber of Commerce in Milan.

Another small niggle concerns publicity. Posters have to be stamped by the *comune* and each stamp costs money. I have been known to make myself a T-shirt instead of a poster and walk around Siena for a few days before an exhibition – wearing my publicity!

Permits from the *Vigili Urbani* (Traffic Wardens) to transport exhibitions into central pedestrian areas are yet another bureaucratic nightmare – unless you know someone who knows the chief traffic warden.

How do you find social life and the Italians

In Siena, I was living just outside the town in the countryside and met a lot of Italian country people. In Florence I tend to meet only English people. I am not a club person at all and the nature of my work is such that I need to be alone quite a lot of the time. I go to lectures at the British Institute here in Florence and use their wonderful library. I am also going to life-drawing evenings occasionally to keep my drawing 'in form'.

How do you find a place to exhibit?

You usually have to ask the *Comune* (town hall). Sometimes they will rent you space and sometimes it will be provided free. Another possibility is to 'pay with a picture', for example in hotels.

Have you any advice for anyone, particularly artists thinking of setting up in Italy?

Firstly, don't come to Florence thinking it is the art centre of the world. In one sense it is – for art from the past, but definitely not for modern art.

Another tip is about exporting. If you sell to foreigners make sure that you charge enough so as not to make a loss on the carriage abroad which can be very expensive if you go to *spedizionari* (specialised freight companies), especially if they have the local monopoly. You have to have special wooden crates for packing. You need a friendly carpenter to make the crates at a fraction of the price and then take them to the freight company's office yourself, having been to Belle Arti yourself with the picture first, so that it is ready packed.

You can save a lot of money by doing your own framing and publicity (see above). You need adaptability, imagination, staying power....and a knowledge of several languages, not just Italian, is useful; as is an interest in the history and cultural heritage of Italy.

John Matta

John Matta, originally from London had an Italian-British father who ran a wine importing business (F.S. Matta Ltd) in the UK. In the 1960s his father bought into a Chianti vineyard and John began to shuttle back and forth between London and Italy which meant he could spend a total of four to five months a year there. He did a three year course in oenology at the Istituto Tecnico Agrario Umberto Primo, (a state-run college that specialises in oenology) located in Alba in Piemonte. He now runs the family vineyard, Castello Vicchiomaggio (75 acres) and produces, a Chianti Classico DOCG. As well as being a wine producer, he also exports worldwide, lets holiday apartments and owns a restaurant. He has been permanently resident in Italy since 1980.

We asked him:

Obviously you had a head start, but how difficult is it to set up a business in Italy?
Setting up a business in Italy is definitely not as easy as the UK where you can buy an off the peg company one day and be trading the next. Here, you have to allow at least four months for all the processes to be completed. It is a big mistake to think you can do it all on your own. You should start by using one of the specialist companies that make their living from company start-ups. They charge a fee yes, but in the end it will save you a lot of time and be worth it. Also, unless you can communicate freely in Italian you cannot expect to make a success of business here.

What about foreigners in the wine business. Are there any British-run vineyards here?
I don't believe so, though there are a couple of Swiss and Germans and one American that I know of. Also, the big American company Kendall-Jackson from Napa Valley have taken over the vineyard of San Leonino which is a Chianti Classico.

What would your advice be to prospective wine-growers?
You need at least fifteen hectares (about 45 acres) if you want to bottle and market your own label. Less than 15 hectares would be a 'hobby vineyard' and you could sell your grapes to the local wine cooperative. If one person wanted to grow, harvest and sell the grapes themselves then four hectares is manageable if you wanted to do the picking yourself (though there is always local help willing to come and pick for you).

Any final words of advice?
You must realise from the outset that Italy is a different country and that things are done quite differently here in a more time consuming way and there are procedures for everything. The UK is different from most European countries in this respect and it stems partly from the fact that Britain was never invaded. Napoleon invaded Italy and imposed the Code Napoleon which affects the laws and systems here. So if you are planning to come here and earn your living then think very carefully about it and the cultural adaptation it involves.

If you want to come here as a retiree, then things are quite different and it's much less of a big decision that coming here to start a business. Italians are so friendly and helpful and you can get by with conversational Italian.

Roger Warwick

Roger Warwick who is is his late forties has been based in Italy for about twenty years. He settled in Italy, after a period of taking 'extended holidays' there, because he knew it better than other countries. He grew to like northern Italy and he prefered the climate to that of Britain. He was at one time manager of the duty-free facilities at Heathrow Airport and during his trips to Italy in the 1970s he taught English at private schools. In 1978 he and his Italian wife set up a business offering financial investigative services, which includes everthing from assessing companies prior to merger or acquisition, to advising on counter industrial espionage tactics. Roger is also the regional secretary of the local Chamber of

Commerce for Bologna and Emilia Romagna. He lives just outside Bologna on a modern development. We asked him:

Was it difficult to set up a business?
Yes it was. We are the only British-run organization offering investigative services that has a licence from the local *prefetto* (magistrate). It is extremely difficult to obtain such a licence.

How do you find living and doing business in Italy compared with the UK?
Obviously I prefer it in Italy, or I wouldn't be here. Northern Italy is fine because it is efficient and things work well. I'm talking about the private sector; the public sector and the bureaucracy are Kafkaesque. I'm lucky enough to have found a niche and doing business here amongst normal people (ie. not bureaucrats) is enjoyable, partly because a high standard of education is more widespread than in the UK. Italians are very good at pulling something out of the hat. When you ask an Italian engineer to produce something unusual or new he can do it. In Britain, it would be damned on the drawing board. On the other hand Italians are extremely bad at marketing their products whereas the British, French, Germans etc. are very good marketers. I think this is partly due to the poor image the Italians have abroad. English promoters use Englishness and French promoters Frenchness and the world recognizes these as something chic. There is no similar regard for Italianness; in fact you'd be hard put to think of anything except *The Godfather* and stilletto murders.

There is definitely scope for British experts in marketing techniques to promote Italian products in the UK.

The cost of living in Italy is greater than in the UK. In Bologna it is particularly high – the highest in Italy I believe, because there is no umemployment in this region and so there is no need to lower the prices. Bolgogna is one of the most pleasant towns in Italy. It is small enough to be human and big enough to be a city.

How do you find the social life and the Italians? I live on a modern development of fifteen houses and all the couples there are Italian and of a similar age to us; much of our social life revolves around them. I speak fluent Italian which is essential. I know foreigners who have lived in Italy for twenty years and can only mumble a few words in Italian which severely limits the possibilities of making friends with Italians as hardly any of them speak English well enough to have an interesting conversation. The other part of my social life revolves around the events organized by the local Chamber of Commerce.

Have you any advice for those thinking of taking the plunge?
Forget your preconceptions about all Italians being gangsters and come to the north of Italy.

Realize you are going to be up against a bureaucracy like something out of Kafka's *The Trial*.

Learn to speak Italian.

Appendix 2

Reading List

Buongiorno Italia!, BBC Books, (£9.99): a beginners' course in Italian comprising 20 lessons; comes with three cassettes of exercises.

A Concise History of Italy, Peter Gunn, Thames and Hudson 1971: An illustrated history from the dissolution of the Roman Empire in the fifth and sixth centuries to 1948. Outlines the main events and characters that shaped the regions' history. 244 pages.

Excellent Cadavers: Alexander Stille, Vintage (£8.99). The story of the mafia.

Getting it Right in Italy, William Ward, Bloomsbury 1990 (£9.99): a combination of insight into and practical advice on, all aspects of Italian life including money, family life, sex, politics and the economy, by a journalist and broadcaster who has made Italy his home for over ten years. Full of fascinating facts and figures in an easy access format. 390 pages.

A History of Contemporary Italy: Society and Politics 1943-1988, Paul Ginsborg, Penguin 1990 (£7.99): Ginsborg's book charts the success of Italy's transformation from a war-torn country to the success story of the late 1980s and also traces the failed and repeated attempts at much-needed political reform. 425 pages.

The Honoured Society, Norman Lewis, Collins 1985 (£6.99): the journalist Norman Lewis writes absorbingly and authoritatively about the the development of the Mafia's power and influence in Italy. 266 pages.

Italian Labyrinth, John Haycroft, Penguin, 1985: a wide-ranging portrait of contemporary Italy exposed through a series of revealing interviews on topics as diverse as economics, education and the arts to family life, the Mafia, bureaucracy and small businesses. 303 pages.

The Italians: Luigi Barzini, Penguin 1964 (£8.99).

Italy Today – Social Picture and Trends: Censis £20. Published annually in February). A wealth of data on processes in education, welfare, work, economic factors etc. supported by analytical text. Available from Fondazione Censis in Rome (fax +39 6-86211367).

The New Italians: Charles Richards, Penguin 1994 (£7.99).

A Traveller's Wine Guide to Italy: Aurum Press 1997 (£9.99): a wealth of practical information on Italian wine, some reflections on cultural and gastronomic points of interest in Italy, and some suggested itineraries for visiting wineries. 144 pages.

Touring in Wine Country: Northwest Italy: Maureen Ashley, Mitchell Beazley 1997 (£12.99): an exploration of Northest Italy, the source of some of the country's finest wines, unveiling the secrets behind its esteemed winemaking traditions. 152 pages.

The above books can be obtained through the Italian Book Shop (7 Cecil Court, London WC2N 4EZ; tel 0171-240 1634). Nearest tube Leicester Square.

Vacation Work publish:

	Paperback	Hardback
The Directory of Summer Jobs Abroad	£8.99	£14.99
The Directory of Summer Jobs in Britain	£8.99	£14.99
Adventure Holidays	£7.99	£12.99
Work Your Way Around the World	£12.95	£16.99
Working in Tourism – The UK, Europe & Beyond	£10.99	£15.99
Kibbutz Volunteer	£8.99	£12.99
Working on Cruise Ships	£8.99	£12.99
Teaching English Abroad	£10.99	£15.99
The Au Pair & Nanny's Guide to Working Abroad	£9.99	£14.99
Working in Ski Resorts – Europe & North America	£10.99	–
Accounting Jobs Worldwide	£11.95	£16.95
Working with the Environment	£9.99	£15.99
Health Professionals Abroad	£9.99	£15.99
The Directory of Jobs & Careers Abroad	£11.95	£16.99
The International Directory of Voluntary Work	£9.99	£15.99
The Directory of Work & Study in Developing Countries	£8.99	£14.99
Live & Work in Russia & Eastern Europe	£10.99	£15.95
Live & Work in France	£10.99	£15.95
Live & Work in Australia & New Zealand	£10.99	£14.95
Live & Work in the USA & Canada	£10.99	£14.95
Live & Work in Germany	£10.99	£15.95
Live & Work in Belgium, The Netherlands & Luxembourg	£10.99	£15.95
Live & Work in Spain & Portugal	£10.99	£15.95
Live & Work in Italy	£10.99	£15.95
Live & Work in Scandinavia	£8.95	£14.95
Travellers Survival Kit: Lebanon	£9.99	–
Travellers Survival Kit: South Africa	£9.99	–
Travellers Survival Kit: India	£9.99	–
Travellers Survival Kit: Russia & the Republics	£9.95	–
Travellers Survival Kit: Western Europe	£8.95	–
Travellers Survival Kit: Eastern Europe	£9.95	–
Travellers Survival Kit: South America	£15.95	–
Travellers Survival Kit: Central America	£8.95	–
Travellers Survival Kit: Cuba	£10.99	–
Travellers Survival Kit: USA & Canada	£10.99	–
Travellers Survival Kit: Australia & New Zealand	£9.99	–
Hitch–hikers' Manual Britain	£3.95	–
Europe – a Manual for Hitch-hikers	£4.95	–

Distributors of:

Summer Jobs USA	£12.95	–
Internships (On-the-Job Training Opportunities in the USA)	£16.95	–
Sports Scholarships in the USA	£12.95	–
Making It in Japan	£8.95	–
Green Volunteers	£9.99	–

Vacation Work Publications, 9 Park End Street, Oxford OX1 1HJ
(Tel 01865–241978. Fax 01865–790885)
Web site http://www.vacationwork.co.uk